Financial Milestones

Englisch für Bank- und Versicherungsberufe

Rosemary Annandale

Dr. Richard Hooton

Michaela Prüfer

Herbert Stummer

Frank Treichel

Barbara Ware-Thürwächter

Ernst Klett Verlag
Stuttgart · Leipzig

Financial Milestones
Englisch für Bank- und Versicherungsberufe

Autoren: Rosemary Annandale; Dr. Richard Hooton; Michaela Prüfer; Herbert Stummer;
Frank Treichel; Barbara Ware-Thürwächter

Beraterin: Andrea Otto

Werkübersicht:
Schülerbuch, 978-3-12-808221-9
Lehrerhandbuch, mit Lehrer-Service-CD-ROM und 2 Audio-CDs 978-3-12-808222-6
Lehr-/Arbeitsbuch Banking, 978-3-12-808223-3
Lehr-/Arbeitsbuch Insurance, 978-3-12-808224-0
Online-Ergänzung unter www.klett.de/online

1. Auflage

1 5 4 3 2 1 | 13 12 11 10 09

Alle Drucke dieser Auflage sind unverändert und können im Unterricht nebeneinander verwendet werden.
Die letzte Zahl bezeichnet das Jahr des Druckes.

Redaktion: Volker Wendland
Herstellung: Angelika Lindner

Satz und Gestaltung: Beckers Büro, Claudia Becker, Stuttgart
Umschlaggestaltung: B2 Büro für Gestaltung, Andreas Staiger, Stuttgart
Reproduktion: Meyle + Müller Medien-Management, Pforzheim
Druck: Himmer AG, Augsburg

Printed in Germany
ISBN 978-3-12-808221-9

Mit der ständig wachsenden Globalisierung und Dynamisierung der Finanzwelt und mit dem Zusammenwachsen von Unternehmen und der Erschließung neuer Märkte sind auch die Anforderungen an die Finanzunternehmen in Deutschland gestiegen.

Im Zuge dieser Entwicklungen gewinnt auch die im Europäischen Referenzrahmen geforderte Vermittlung von Kompetenzen immer mehr an Bedeutung. Mit dem Basis-band (Schülerbuch) **Financial Milestones** werden deshalb in berufsbezogenen Situatio-nen zunächst die Grundkompetenzen in der Fremdsprache vermittelt, die bei einer Tätig-keit im internationalen Banken- und Versicherungswesen häufig vorausgesetzt werden.

In den beiden Workbooks **Financial Milestones: Banking** und **Financial Milestones: Insurance** werden dann in praxisnaher Form die entsprechenden fachbezogenen Inhalte behandelt, wobei die Workbooks durch Verweise mit dem Schülerbuch verknüpft sind. Die Units im Schülerbuch sind wie folgt aufgebaut:
* Jede Unit beginnt mit einem Starter in Form von Fotos, die als einfacher Sprechanlass dienen und in das Thema der Unit einführen.
* Alle Units sind in mehrere Topics (A, B, C …) unterteilt, wobei einzelne anspruchs-vollere Texte und Aufgaben auch eine Binnendifferenzierung ermöglichen.
* Jede Unit endet mit umfassenden – nach beruflichen Situationen strukturierten – Redewendungen (Phrases) zu den jeweiligen Schwerpunkten der Unit.

Strukturelemente der Units:
* Communicating across cultures: Infos und Hinweise zur Förderung der interkultu-rellen Kompetenz.
* Language and grammar: Hier werden ausgewählte sprachliche oder gramma-tikalische Inhalte angesprochen, die den Lernenden oft Schwierigkeiten bereiten (z. B. False friends; Conditional clauses).
* Role cards / Flowcharts: Rollenspiele mit Rollenkarten oder gelenkte Rollenspiele mit deutschen oder englischen „prompts".
* **Financial Milestones** ist in den Berufsschulklassen der Bank- und Versicherungskauf-leute auf der Stufe B1 / B2 des Gemeinsamen Europäischen Referenzrahmens ein-setzbar. Das Lehrwerk eignet sich zudem für die Vorbereitung auf die KMK-Zertifikate Englisch für Wirtschaft und Verwaltung. Darüber hinaus ist das Lehrwerk aber auch nach der Ausbildung für alle Angestellten in der Finanzdienstleistungs- und Ver-sicherungsbranche interessant.

Ihre Autoren, Berater und Redaktion

Symbole:	
R	Rezeption
M	Mediation
I	Interaktion
P	Produktion
⊙ 1	Audiomaterial mit Tracknummer
☞	Verweise (z. B. auf Phrases)
www	Internetaufgaben
KMK	Aufgaben zur Vorbereitung auf die KMK-Prüfung
CD 01	Kopiervorlagen auf der Service-CD-ROM

Unit 1
Introducing yourself and your place of work

In the banking and insurance business you will be dealing with all kinds of people, such as colleagues, superiors, visitors and clients. Some of them will be older, some of them younger and some your own age. Some will be strangers. You may have to describe a product or service, discuss your work, exchange information or make small
5 talk. On some occasions you may have to use English because they don't speak your language. People in other countries and cultures have different expectations of what sounds friendly and polite and what sounds rude or unfriendly. So the situation you are in and the relationship you have with a person determines the language you use to communicate and to introduce yourself. Remember that first impressions count.
10 Your body language, gestures and your facial expression tell people a lot more than you may realise.

R **Exercise**
Match the following phrases with the pictures above.

"Have a seat, please.
Mrs Becker will be with you in a minute."

"Good morning. I'm Sabrina Weber, your customer service assistant."

"How can I help you?"

"Did you have a nice flight?"

A Talking about yourself

Students on their first day at a vocational school in Germany are asked to introduce themselves to an Irish teaching assistant who is going to spend the next half year at their school.

Ⅰ Exercise 1
Take the roles of the assistant and the students and read the text.

Tyra:	Hi, I'm Tyra Reilly. I'm from Cork in Ireland and I'll be your teaching assistant for the next six months. It would be nice if you could all introduce yourselves so I can get to know you. Perhaps you could tell me briefly what company you are with, what you're training for and what your interests are.
Stefanie:	Hello, I'm Stefanie Kriel, but please call me Steffi. I'm from Waiblingen but I was born in Dresden. I'll be 18 next month. I'm doing an apprenticeship at S-Bank AG in Stuttgart to become a bank clerk. I'm interested in politics. I do quite a lot of sports, including cycling and skiing.
Tyra:	Thank you Steffi. I'll make sure to remember your birthday! Let's go on with your classmate. What's your name?
Thomas:	Hi. My name's Thomas Huber. I'm from Böblingen and I'm 19 years old. I'm doing an apprenticeship to become an insurance clerk. I'm a big Borussia Dortmund fan! I work out regularly at a local gym. I like music, especially "Indie" music.
Tyra:	Thank you, Thomas. I prefer music from the 80s. Let's hear from the young lady next to you.
Christine:	My name is Christine Arnoldt. Like Steffi, I'm with the S-Bank AG and I'm training to be a bank clerk, too. I was born in Metzingen in 1990, but my family originally comes from Hungary. I'm interested in languages, and I love Italian food. I also do kick boxing.
Tyra:	Wow. Kickboxing sounds dangerous and it's quite unusual for a girl. We'll go on with our introductions later.

R **Exercise 2**

Say whether the following statements in the text are true or false and correct them if necessary.

1. Steffi was born in Dessau.
2. She is training to become an office administration clerk.
3. She is interested in computers.
4. Thomas is the oldest of the students.
5. He supports a football club from North Rhine-Westphalia.
6. He likes music from the '80s.
7. Christine is at the same bank as Thomas Huber.
8. One of her hobbies is cooking Italian food.

R **Exercise 3**

Complete the following introduction using the prepositions from the box.

> for (2 x) • from • in (2 x) • near • to • on

I was born 1 Böblingen 2 23 March 1964. Böblingen is a small town 3 Stuttgart in Germany. My family comes 4 Berlin. I work 5 a regional bank and I'm taking part 6 a training programme for investment banking. I regularly go 7 a gym 8 a work-out.

R **Exercise 4**

Read the text on page 6 again and answer the following questions.

1. Who will you be in contact with at your place of work?
2. Why could you find yourself in situations where you have to speak English?
3. Why is the language, whether German or English, and the style of the language you use so important?
4. How do others form an impression of you?
5. How do you form an impression of someone you meet for the first time?

Communicating across cultures: Greeting people

Introductions are usually less formal in English speaking countries than in Germany. A simple "Hi, I'm Wendy" is quite often enough. In a slightly more formal situation, you introduce yourself using your first and last name, "Hi, I'm Henry Adams"; you never just use your last name as is customary in Germany.

A greeting that is very formal and rarely used these days is "How do you do?" One should only reply with "How do you do?", adding "Pleased to meet you".

Most people greet each other by saying "How are you?". The most common reply to such a question is "Fine, thanks". This can be followed by "And you?".

After being introduced for the first time to someone it is polite to say "Nice to meet you". This is usually followed by a "Nice to meet you too".

Among friends a simple "Hi" or "Hello Jim, how are you doing?" is common.

M Exercise 5

Below is a personal file card. Find the English equivalent to the German file card by matching the numbers (1.–15.) with the letters (a.–o.).

Persönliches Datenblatt	(Personal File Card)
1. Familienname:	a. marital status
2. Vorname(n):	b. mobile phone
3. Geburtsort:	c. male
4. Geburtsdatum:	d. occupation
5. Ort	e. town/city
6. Postleitzahl:	f. surname
7. Handy:	g. first name:
8. Beruf:	h. sex
9. Geschlecht:	i. female
10. weiblich	j. single
11. männlich	k. divorced
12. Familienstand:	l. date of birth
13. alleinstehend	m. post code
14. verheiratet	n. place of birth
15. geschieden	o. married

P Exercise 6

Now use the file card above as a guideline to introduce yourself to the class. Keep in mind that you are still in training as an apprentice. The following job titles may help you to explain what you are being trained in:

| bank clerk | insurance clerk | insurance agent | insurance broker |

| investment consultant | customer service officer | loan advisor |

Language and grammar: Introducing yourself	
Im Englischen wird das Geburtsjahr mit *simple past* angegeben.	• I was born in Metzingen. *(Ich bin in Metzingen geboren.)*
Außerdem wird im Englischen erst der Ort und dann der Zeitpunkt genannt.	• I was born in Munich in 1992. *(Ich bin 1992 in München geboren.)*
Im Englischen steht vor dem Beruf der unbestimmte Artikel.	• I'm training to become an insurance agent. *(Ich mache eine Ausbildung als Versicherungskaufmann/-frau.)*

B Talking about your work

P **Exercise 1**

Describe what work activities the people in the pictures are performing.

R **Exercise 2**

Here are some typical office duties. Match the actions on the left with suitable expressions on the right. *Example:*

9. processing	h. claims

1. filling in	a. customers
2. advising	b. an account
3. taking care of	c. application forms
4. checking	d. a meeting
5. assessing	e. loan applications
6. scheduling or postponing	f. deadlines
7. meeting	g. records and accounts
8. opening	*h. claims*
9. processing	i. visitors and customers

R **Exercise 3**

◎ 1 You have invited Tyra Reilly, your Irish teaching assistant, for a visit to your bank. She is very interested in your work and is trying to find out as much as possible about the German banking and insurance system. You are giving her a tour of the regional branch office of the S-Bank AG.

Listen to the CD and complete the table below (on a separate sheet of paper) with information about the different departments.

Department	Activities
customer service	paying out money

P **Exercise 4**

Which departments were not described in detail? What are the main activities in these departments?

P **Exercise 5**

Now use words and expressions from the exercises above to talk about the department you work in and the work you are doing.

Language and grammar: Simple past and present perfect	
Wird ein Zeitraum genannt, der bis in die Vergangenheit reicht, steht **simple past.**	• Our bank was founded in 1893. • The Baden Bank went public at the Berlin Stock Exchange.
Wenn ein Zeitraum genannt wird, der bis in die Gegenwart reicht, steht das **present perfect.**	• For decades our bank has offered the full range of customer services in all branches. • Since the beginning in Berlin in 1894 we have acquired several smaller retail banks. • I have been with this company for four months now.
"since" and "for"	
Since bezieht sich auf den Anfang eines Zeitraums (Zeitpunkt).	• Since Christmas / Since last year / Since my last meeting
For bezieht sich auf den Zeitraum selbst (Zeitraum).	• For three weeks / For several days / For a couple of years
Merke: Im Deutschen wird „seit" mit der Gegenwart verwendet, **since** und **for,** in der Bedeutung von „seit", stehen im Englischen mit dem **present perfect.**	• Ich bin seit drei Monaten Bank-Azubi bei der Baden-Bank. **I have been a banking apprentice / trainee with the Baden-Bank for three months.** • Seit Januar bin ich in der Darlehensabteilung. **Since January I have been working in the loan / credit department.**

Exercise 6

◉ 2+3 **Listen to Milly and Jack describing a typical day at work and answer the questions below.**

1. Who starts work at 8:00 am?
2. Who starts work at 9:00 am?
3. Who needs the computer at the office all day?
4. Who needs to check their e-mails every day?
5. Who doesn't receive much mail?
6. Who has meetings with clients outside the company?
7. Who spends all day dealing with clients at the service counter?

Exercise 7

It is often quite difficult to find the correct English translation for many German occupations, especially those offered within the German system of dual education. There are different translations for "Kaufmann/-frau" and quite often you have to paraphrase the occupation because you cannot find just one word to get the correct meaning in English.

Match the German occupations (1.–9.) with their English equivalents (a.–i.).

1. Versicherungskaufmann/-frau	a. real estate assistant/agent
2. Bankkaufmann/-frau	b. corporate business advisor
3. Versicherungsmakler/-in	c. personal loan advisor
4. Anlageberater/-in	d. customer service officer/advisor/ clerk/assistant
5. Kassierer/-in	e. insurance clerk
6. Immobilienkaufmann/-frau	f. insurance broker
7. Darlehensberater/-in	g. cashier/teller
8. Kundenberater/-in	h. asset/investment (management) consultant/assistant
9. Firmenberater/-in	i. bank clerk

Exercise 8

Use the words from the box to complete the text.

debit card • exchange rate • foreign currency • bank clerk • insurance policies • real estate • cash dispenser • branch office

As a customer service advisor I usually work in a **1** . I am basically a **2** who helps customers if they have problems with the **3** or with their **4** Foreigners come to my counter and ask about the **5** and to exchange **6** . I usually do not handle **7** or sell **8** .

M **Exercise 9**
Translate the following statements into English.

1. Ich mache eine Ausbildung als Bankkauffrau bei der … Bank.
2. Ich mache eine Ausbildung zum Versicherungskaufmann bei der … Versicherung.
3. In der Immobilienabteilung lernt man auch, wie Baudarlehen zu handhaben sind.
4. Ich möchte später gern in der Personalabteilung tätig sein.
5. Wer am Kundenschalter arbeitet, ist auch für den Geldautomaten zuständig.
6. Als Bankkaufmann und als Versicherungskaufmann hat man jede Menge Ablage zu machen.
7. Die letzten drei Wochen habe ich Kunden über unsere Telefonhotline beraten.
8. Ich helfe unseren Kunden mit Problemen am Geldautomaten und mit der Bank/EC-karte.
9. Die Arbeit in der Schadensabteilung ist sehr interessant, aber ich muss viele Unterlagen überprüfen.
10. Die Arbeit mit den Kunden macht Spaß, da sie nie langweilig ist.

I **Exercise 10** ☞ Phrases
Role play: Act out the following conversation using the prompts.

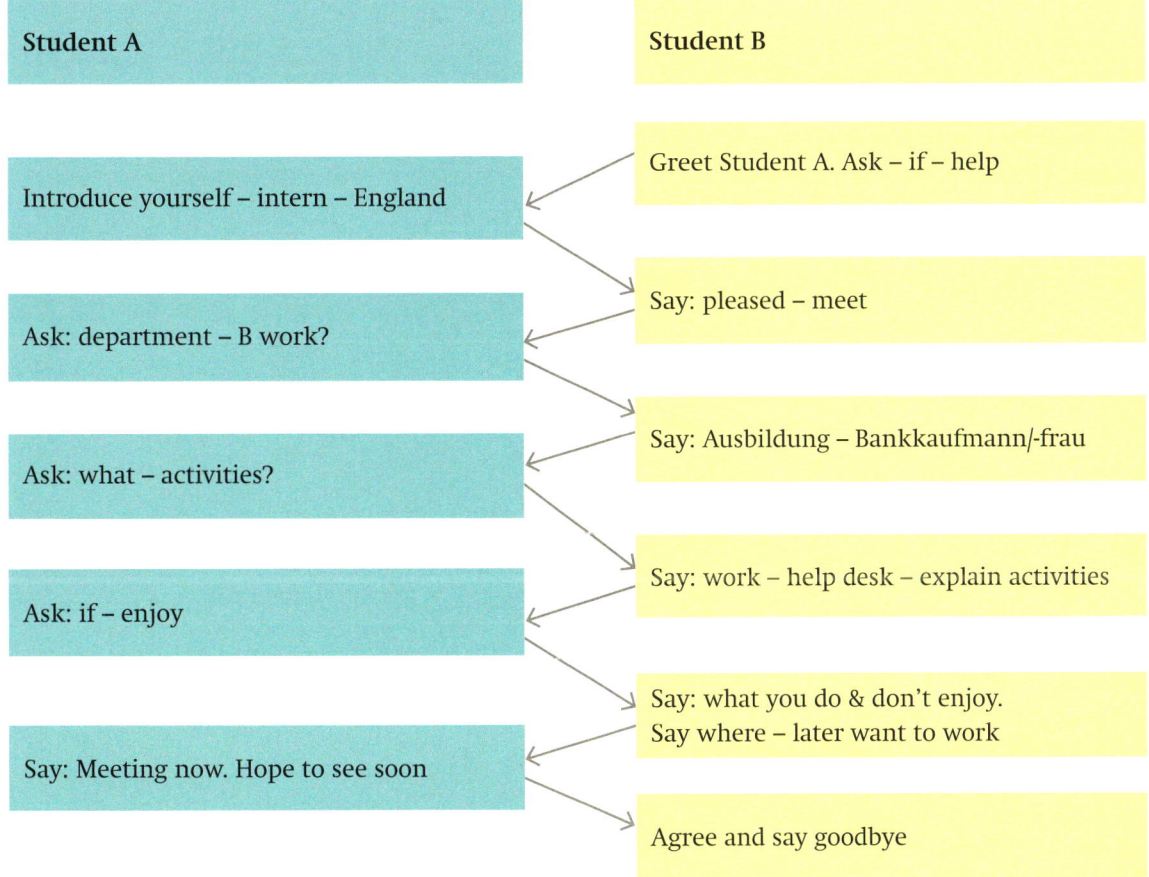

Student A	Student B
	Greet Student A. Ask – if – help
Introduce yourself – intern – England	
	Say: pleased – meet
Ask: department – B work?	
	Say: Ausbildung – Bankkaufmann/-frau
Ask: what – activities?	
	Say: work – help desk – explain activities
Ask: if – enjoy	
	Say: what you do & don't enjoy. Say where – later want to work
Say: Meeting now. Hope to see soon	
	Agree and say goodbye

C Helping foreign customers

Stefan Angerer works at the counter of a bank in the centre of a big German city. He often helps new customers who have just moved to Germany and are not familiar with German banking. They need assistance opening an account, making payments and using the cash dispenser and statement printer. Clara Bailey has just entered the German bank branch where Stefan is at the customer service counter.

Stefan:	Guten Morgen, was kann ich für Sie tun?
Clara:	Hi. Do you speak English?
Stefan:	Yes, sure. What I can do for you?
Clara:	I need to open an account.
Stefan:	No problem. What account would you like to open?
Clara:	Well, in England we call it a current account. It's for my wages and for paying my bills while I am here in Germany.
Stefan:	I see. So You've got a job here in Germany.
Clara:	I've got a job as a language trainer with one of the major German car companies.
Stefan:	Then you'll need a current account so that your employer can transfer your salary into it.
Clara:	That's it. And I can get cash when I need to?
Stefan:	Yes, you'll get an EC-card to make withdrawals at the ATM or at the cash dispenser in the lobby of our bank.
Clara:	Is that a credit card?
Stefan:	Oh no. It's just a debit card. You can use it to pay in shops as well.
Clara:	And what about paying my bills, like the rent or my phone bill? Will I get a cheque book so I can write out cheques to pay them?
Stefan:	I could give you cheques, but you don't really need any, because in Germany most people don't use cheques anymore to pay bills. They make transfers, use standing orders, pay by direct debit authorisation depending on the bill.
Clara:	That sounds fine.
Stefan:	By the way, you get your statements at the statement printer in the lobby of our bank. I'll show you how to use it after you've gotten your bank card.
Clara:	Can we open the account right now? I've got my passport with me.
Stefan:	Of course. Let's go over here to my desk. Then I can fill in the application form on the computer and enter all the necessary information … Would you come this way please … Take a seat, please.

R Exercise 1

4 Read / Listen to the dialogue on page 14 and find out about the following:

1. What is Clara doing in Germany?
2. Why does she need a current account?
3. What does Stefan tell her about making withdrawals?
4. What does Stefan tell Clara about paying bills in Germany?
5. Which services can Clara use in the lobby of the bank?

R Exercise 2

Fill in the missing prepositions.

1. Clara's employer can transfer her salary ? her account.
2. She can withdraw cash ? the ATM.
3. She can pay her bills ? direct debit.
4. She can get her statements ? the statement printer.
5. Stefan fills ? the application form ? the computer.

I Exercise 3

KMK Role play: Act out the part of the customer and the part of the bank customer service assistant.

Student A: Sie arbeiten am Schalter der XY-Bank; Student B kommt auf Sie zu.

Student B: Sie kommen aus Kanada, arbeiten als Praktikant bei einer deutschen Versicherung.

Begrüßen Sie den Kunden, sagen Sie, dass Sie sich bemühen Englisch zu sprechen und fragen Sie was Sie für ihn/sie tun können.

Sprechen Sie den Bankangestellten an und fragen Sie, ob er/sie Englisch spricht.

Sagen Sie, dass Sie ein Girokonto eröffnen wollen.

Teilen Sie dem Kunden mit, dass das kein Problem sei, es sei nur ein Antrag auszufüllen und Sie bräuchten einen Ausweis oder Reisepass.

Entgegnen Sie, dass Sie den Antrag gerne ausfüllen würden, aber keinen Ausweis/Reisepass dabei hätten.

Teilen Sie dem Kunden mit, dass Sie ihm/ihr dabei helfen, das Formular auszufüllen und es aufbewahren, bis er/sie mit dem Ausweis oder Reisepass in Ihre Zweigstelle kommt.
– beide füllen nun das Formular aus –

– beide füllen nun das Formular aus –
Bedanken Sie sich für die Hilfe und sagen Sie, dass Sie morgen Nachmittag kommen, um sich auszuweisen *(to prove your identity)*!

Geben Sie dem Kunden zu verstehen, dass es Ihnen ein Vergnügen war, ihm/ihr zu helfen und wünschen Sie ihm/ihr einen schönen Tag.

Verabschieden Sie sich bis morgen.

Exercise 4

Read the German text below and present the essential information in
English. The following graph will help you to visualise the information for
your audience. Use a dictionary if necessary.

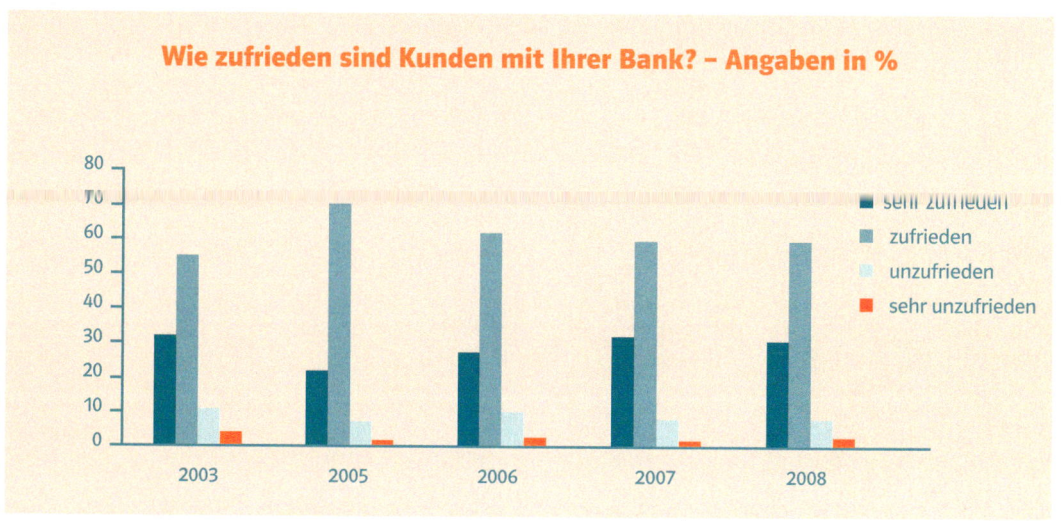

Banken und Kundenzufriedenheit

Die schwierige Lage auf den internationalen Finanz-
märkten hat die Beziehung der deutschen Kunden
zu ihrer Bank nach Erkenntnissen des Bankenver-
bandes nicht ernsthaft beeinträchtigt. Zwar hätten
5 die vom amerikanischen Hypothekenmarkt ausge-
henden Finanzmarktturbulenzen sicherlich nicht
dazu beigetragen, das Ansehen der Bankenbranche
insgesamt zu verbessern. Unabhängig davon sei
jedoch das Vertrauen der Kunden zu ihrer Bank
10 hierzulande nach wie vor unverändert hoch. So
waren nach einer repräsentativen Umfrage im April
fast neun von zehn Bürgern von den Leistungen
ihrer Bank überzeugt: 59 % zeigten sich zufrieden,
30 % sogar sehr zufrieden. (…)

15 Die Zufriedenheit der Kunden mit der Beratung in
ihrer Bank ist ebenfalls hoch und wächst weiter.

Sieben von zehn Befragten lassen sich bei Geldan-
lagen von Ihrer Bank beraten. (…)

Trotz der zunehmenden Beliebtheit des Online
Banking steht die Bankfiliale für das persönliche Gespräch mit dem Berater weiterhin bei den 20
Kunden hoch im Kurs: Für acht von zehn Deutschen ist die persönliche Beratung bei der Bank
wichtig (39 %) oder sogar sehr wichtig (42 %).
Das drückt sich auch bei den Angaben zur Häu-
figkeit der Filialbesuche aus: fast drei Viertel der 25
Befragten (73 %) besuchen ihre Bank mindestens
einmal im Monat – Tendenz allerdings fallend.

Exercise 5

www **Check the web for information concerning customer satisfaction today.
Compare the results and describe the development.**

D Taking care of foreign visitors

Sometimes it is difficult enough to make small talk in your own language. In a foreign language it can be a real challenge! Remember that native English speakers are always happy to help you.

I **Exercise 1**

Which of the following topics are suitable for small talk and which are not? Why? Discuss in class.

| religion | travel | politics | family | hobbies | sports |

| working hours | forms of entertainment | income | health |

I/P **Exercise 2**

Work in groups of four to six students and draw a mind map of useful topics for small talk. Compare your results with the other groups in your class.

Example:

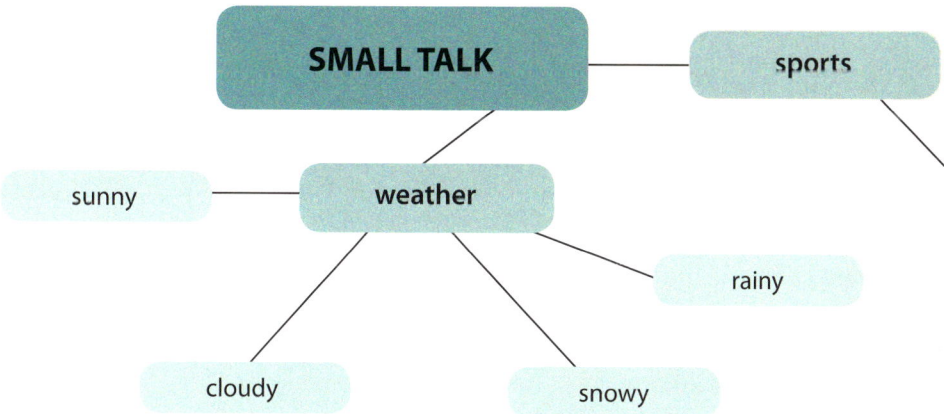

R **Exercise 3**

Claudia Kirsch, a tax accountant at HBR Versicherungen, is meeting Chris Stewart, a colleague from the New York partner office, at the airport in Munich.

Put the jumbled dialogue between Claudia and Chris into the right order.

1. Claudia:	Fine, my car is right over there in the car park. It's not too far.
2. Chris:	That's right. Nice to meet you Ms Kirsch, and thank you for picking me up.
3. Claudia:	Would like to go by your hotel first? It's on our way to the office.
4. Claudia:	My pleasure. I'm glad you made it. Did you have a good flight?
5. Chris:	Yes, it was very smooth and we were on time.
6. Chris:	I would love that. I could drop my luggage there before going to the meeting
7. Claudia:	Are you Mr Stewart? I'm Ms Kirsch from the Munich office of HBR.

P **Exercise 4**

What would you say in the following situations?

1. The customer service assistant Tony Meyer, doesn't know Linda Pratt, the new trainee from England.
2. Your boss says to you, "This is Linda Pratt. She's from England."
3. You are in an office full of strangers. Someone comes up to you and asks if they can help you.
4. A visitor arrives after travelling a long distance to see you.
5. You want your visitor to feel comfortable in your office.

P **Exercise 5**

Have you ever welcomed a foreign visitor in your office, at the station or at the airport? Tell your story to the class. What were the biggest problems?

M **Exercise 6**

Tell a colleague in German how to get to Mr Cole's office.
Use the following English directions:

1. Turn left and walk along the main street
2. Go to the third building on the left.
3. Go up the steps and enter the building
4. Walk across the main lobby.
5. Take the elevator to the third floor.
6. On the third floor, walk along the corridor to the end.
7. Mr Cole's office is the sixth door on the right.

Communicating across cultures: Floors (GB / USA)

There is quite a difference between the USA and Great Britain when talking about the different floors of a building.

In Great Britain "ground floor" stands for your German "Erdgeschoss" whereas in the USA this is already called "first floor" and the German "1. Stockwerk" is called "second floor" etc.

In Great Britain the German "Aufzug" is called "lift" and in the USA it is called "elevator".

R **Exercise 7** ☞ CD / Online-Link

◎ 5 **Listen to the CD and study the floorplan below. Find out what the numbers in the plan stand for. Match the numbers with the letters in the box.**

A. Ladies' room • B. Human resources department • C. Private loans department • D. Conference room • E. Reception • F. Gents' room • G. Investment department • H. canteen

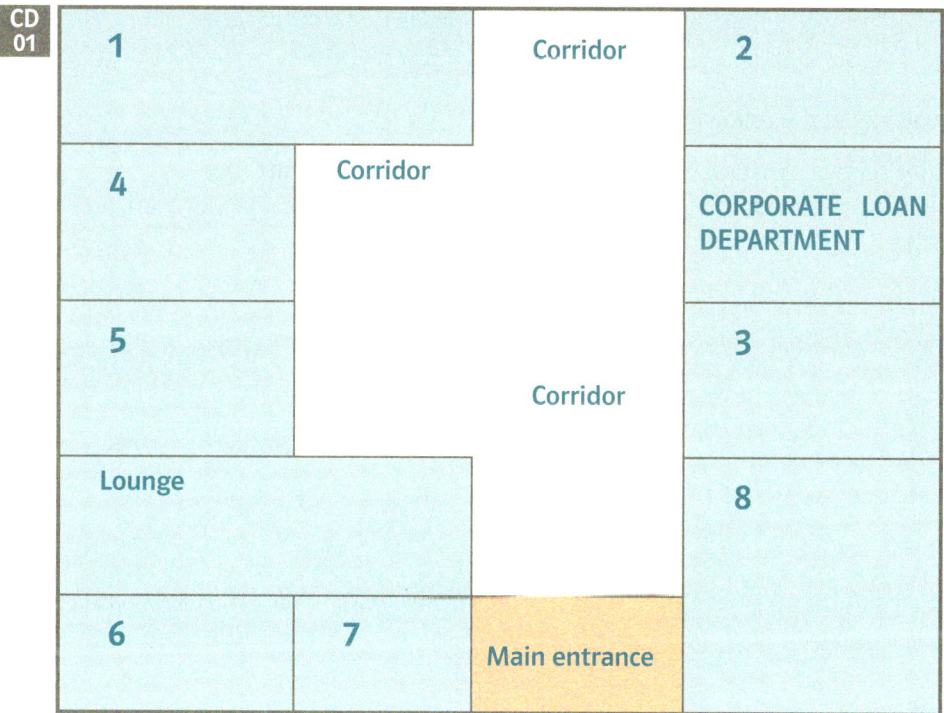

I/P **Exercise 8** ☞ Phrases

Work with a partner. You work as an investment consultant assistant. Use the floorplan above and describe to your partner how to get to your office. Then it's your partner's turn to choose an office and give you directions. Start from the main entrance.

Phrases: Introducing yourself and others

I'm Peter./My name is Alex Myers.	Ich heiße Peter./Ich heiße Alex Myers.
Please call me David.	Nennen Sie mich doch David.
My surname is Mc Dermot, my first name is Tom.	Mein Familienname ist Mc Dermot, mein Vorname Tom.
How are you today? (How are you doing?)	Wie geht es Ihnen/Dir? (informelle Begrüßung)
I'm from Stuttgart, and I'm 20 years old.	Ich stamme aus Stuttgart und bin 20 Jahre alt.
I'm English/Welsh/Scottish/Irish/American.	Ich bin Engländer/-in/Waliser/-in/Schotte/Schottin/Ire/Irin/Amerikaner/-in.
I was born in Saskatchewan (Canada) on 15 October 1981.	Ich bin am 15. Oktober 1981 in Saskatchewan (Kanada) geboren.
Have you met Ms Banks?	Kennen Sie Frau Banks?
May I introduce Dr. Fisher to you?	Darf ich Ihnen Herrn Dr. Fisher vorstellen?
Let me introduce you to …	Ich möchte Ihnen gerne … vorstellen.
Pleased/Nice to meet you.	Ich freue mich, Sie kennen zu lernen.
And how are you?	Und (wie geht es) Ihnen?
Fine thanks, and you?	Danke, gut und Ihnen?
Please take/have a seat.	Nehmen Sie doch bitte Platz.
Would you mind waiting for a moment/second?	Würde es Ihnen etwas ausmachen kurz zu warten?

Talking about your hobbies and interests

I'm interested in computers.	Ich interessiere mich für Computer.
I love travelling more than anything else.	Ich reise schrecklich gern.
I like to go clubbing.	Ich gehe gern in die Disko.
I'm into skiing and snowboarding.	Ich fahre gern Ski und Snowboard.
I do a lot of text messaging.	Ich schreibe viele SMS.
I spend a lot of time chatting with friends around the world.	Ich chatte gerne mit Freunden und Bekannten weltweit.

Talking about your training or your work

I'm doing an apprenticeship as a bank clerk.	Ich mache eine Ausbildung zum/zur Bankkaufmann/Bankkauffrau.
I'm training to become …	Ich mache eine Ausbildung zum/zur …
an insurance clerk/ insurance management assistant.	Versicherungskaufmann/-frau.

I'm taking part in a further education programme.	Ich nehme gerade an einem Fortbildungsprogramm teil.
I'm in the loan department.	Ich bin in der Darlehensabteilung.
I work at/for Süd-Bank Ltd.	Ich arbeite bei der Süd-Bank Ltd.
I attend vocational school.	Ich besuche die Berufsschule.
What do you do (job-wise), Nina?	Nina, was machst du beruflich?
What are you training to be, Timo?	Was machst du für eine Ausbildung, Timo?
What do you like about your job?	Was gefällt dir an deiner Arbeit?
What branch office do you work in?	In welcher Zweigstelle arbeitest du?
My job involves the following tasks …	Meine Arbeit beinhaltet die folgenden Aufgaben …
I am responsible for …	Ich bin verantwortlich für …
I am in charge of …	Ich bin zuständig für/betreue/leite …
The loan department deals with …	Die Kreditabteilung befasst sich mit …

Conversation with visitors

Good afternoon, welcome to …	Guten Tag! Willkommen bei …
May I offer you tea, coffee, …?	Darf ich Ihnen Tee, Kaffee, … anbieten?
Mr. Kerner will be with you in a few minutes.	Herr Kerner wird in ein paar Minuten hier sein.
Ms. Müller is ready for you now.	Frau Müller erwartet Sie jetzt.
How was your flight?	Wie war Ihr Flug?
Have you been to Munich before?	Waren Sie zuvor schon einmal in München?
What was the weather like when you left …	Wie war das Wetter, als Sie … verließen?

Giving directions

Go straight on/ahead!	Gehen/Fahren Sie geradeaus.
Go down until you get to …	Gehen/Fahren Sie bis Sie zu(m) … kommen.
Turn right/left at the …	Biegen Sie rechts/links ab an …
Just follow the main street.	Folgen Sie einfach nur der Hauptstraße.

Guiding visitors through the company

Our main departments are …	Unsere wichtigsten Abteilungen sind …
If you go through this door you are in the …	Wenn Sie durch diese Tür gehen, betreten Sie …
I'd like to show you around the company.	Ich würde Ihnen gerne unsere Firma zeigen.
The car park is behind the company building.	Der Parkplatz ist hinter dem Gebäude.

Unit 2
Telephoning

The telephone, always an important business and banking tool, has now been revolutionised by modern mobile telephony. Financial institutions encourage the use of the telephone (along with online banking) to cut costs and reduce the pressure on branches and, at the same time, to improve access to banking services. Some savings
5 and deposit accounts are operated entirely online or by telephone and offer a higher rate of interest thanks to the lower costs involved. Banks and insurance companies also use the telephone for marketing purposes. Finally, m-banking provides access to financial services especially in countries with a poor network of landlines and unreliable internet access where mobile phones are the fastest growing medium
10 of communication. These new technologies have not made a suitable "telephone manner" any less important.

P **Exercise 1**
Describe the telephone situations shown in the pictures above.

R **Exercise 2**
Read the text above and answer the following questions.

1. Why do banks encourage customers to use telephone banking?
2. Why do online accounts offer better rates of interest?

A Telephoning in English

R **Exercise 1**
Read the text below and answer the following questions in writing.

1. Why do people often prefer to send e-mails to their business partners in other countries rather than call them on the phone?
2. What are people often afraid of when they have to make telephone calls abroad on business?
3. What aspects of communication are missing when speaking on the phone?

Info: Telephoning in a foreign language

Telephoning in a foreign language can be rather frightening. No wonder people often prefer to send an e-mail where they can plan what they want to say and need not fear immediate comeback. However, a telephone call is sometimes unavoidable and one wonders: Will I understand what they are saying? What do I say if I can't? Can I just hang up in embarrassment? Will I be able to express what I want to say? Will they laugh if I make some awful mistake? We all know these kinds of fears when we have to ring someone abroad. And, to some extent, the fears are justified. The non-verbal side of communication is missing. We can't see the person's face, their lips and gestures. They can't see our gestures and the look of despair on our faces! It's best to remain calm and ask them to speak slowly and repeat anything that is not clear.

M **Exercise 2**
Match the following German telephone terms with their English equivalents.

1. Durchwahl	a. receiver
2. Handy	b. area code
3. Festnetzanschluss	c. extension
4. Anrufbeantworter	d. country code
5. Freisprechanlage	e. settings
6. Landesvorwahl	f. answering machine
7. SMS-Nachricht	g. hands-free telephone
8. Vorwahl	h. text message
9. Kopfhörer	i. local call
10. Telefonhörer	j. land line/fixed line
11. Einstellungen	k. headset
12. Ortsgespräch	l. mobile/mobile phone/cell phone

6 **When telephoning in a foreign language it makes life a lot easier if you have the necessary standard phrases at your fingertips. Read / Listen to the following dialogue. Then match the German sentences given on page 25 with their English equivalents.**

X:	Guten Morgen, Flexibüros GmbH, Schmidt.
GB:	Good morning, Ms Schmidt. I'm afraid I don't speak German. My name is Giulia Belfiore. I'm ringing from Milan, Italy. Could I speak to Dr. Claudia Friedrichs, please?
X:	I'm afraid there's no-one of that name in this company. You must have got a wrong number.
GB:	I didn't quite catch what you said. The line is bad. Could you please repeat it?
X:	You must have got a wrong number. There is no-one of that name here.
GB:	Oh, I see. I'm terribly sorry. I'll try again. (re-dials) Good morning. Is that the XYZ Bank?
PH:	Yes it is. My name's Peter Hansen. How can I help you?
GB:	My name's Giulia Belfiore from Costruzzione Milano. Could I speak to Dr Claudia Friedrichs, please?
PH:	Certainly. I'll put you through to her extension … I'm afraid she's not answering now. Apparently she has just left for an appointment.
GB:	I didn't quite catch that. Could you repeat it more slowly, please?
PH:	Certainly. It seems she has just left for an appointment.
GB:	Oh dear. I must get in touch with her urgently. I need an appointment with her to finalise a major redevelopment loan. Are you in the picture?
PH:	I'm afraid not. Could you give me your telephone number and I'll ask her to get back to you. Would you like to leave a message?
GB:	Not really. Just that I need an appointment with her in Munich as soon as possible. My landline is 0039–02 3 76 83 41. In Italy the zero at the beginning of the area code is not omitted. My mobile number is 0039–333 4 49 26 22. Could you also give me

	Dr Friedrich's mobile and extension? I assume she won't mind me ringing her on her mobile.
PH:	Her extension is 3551 and her mobile is 0178–7 84 71 34. I'm sure she won't mind, though she may switch her phone off if she's in conference. But I will still try to contact her. May I just ask you to give me your name again? I'm not sure I got it right.
GB:	Certainly. My name is Giulia Belfiore.
PH:	Could you possibly spell it for me?
GB:	G – i – u – l – i – a B – e – l – f – i – o – r – e
	If I don't manage to catch her now, when is the best time to get hold of her?
PH:	She usually works late at the office – often till about 7 pm and she comes to the office in the morning at about 8.15. If all else fails, you might get her this evening.
GB:	Thank you very much for your help. Goodbye.
PH:	Goodbye, Ms Belfiore.

Now find equivalents for the following German sentences:

1. Sie müssen sich wohl verwählt haben.
2. Ich werde sie bitten Sie zurückzurufen.
3. Hier gibt es niemanden, der so heißt.
4. Könnten Sie das bitte buchstabieren?
5. Möchten Sie eine Nachricht hinterlassen?
6. Das habe ich nicht (ganz) mitbekommen/verstanden.
7. Ich stelle Sie durch/verbinde Sie.
8. Die Verbindung ist schlecht.
9. Können Sie mir bitte ihre Durchwahl/Handy-Nr. geben?
10. Könnten Sie das bitte langsamer wiederholen?
11. Wann kann ich sie am besten erreichen?
12. Sie antwortet im Moment nicht.

Communicating across cultures: Politeness on the phone

It is important to use suitable, polite phrases when ringing people in English-speaking countries. If you know the person you are ringing it is usual to ask how they are getting on, etc. before you get down to business (e. g.: "How are you doing? I haven't spoken to you for a long time."),

If you are about to mention a problem or difficulty, you should begin with: "I'm afraid …". A request often begins with: "Could you possibly …?" ("Could you possibly repeat the address?") or "I would be grateful if you would/could …".

When someone does you a service, it is usual to say something like: "Excellent", or "Brilliant!". When someone thanks you for your help you can say: "You're welcome", or "Not at all".

Don't just say "yes" or "no". Say: "Yes, I think so"; "No, I'm afraid not". The problem for German speakers is that short answers (like ja and nein), which are *not* impolite in German, come across in English as unfriendly or impolite.

B Receiving and redirecting calls

R Exercise 1
Match the pairs.

1. I'd like to speak to Mr Peppiat, please.	a. Certainly. Would next Tuesday at 3 pm be convenient? The appointment is with Samantha Atkins.
2. My name is Peter Krause from Flexiburos GmbH. I'm phoning about your letter of 10 May.	b. I'm afraid she is no longer with the company. What was your name again?
3. My name is Daniel Schreiber. Could I have an appointment with one of your personal loan advisors, please?	c. Just a second please. I'll have a look at the file on my monitor.
4. I called yesterday and left a message for Patricia Dowling asking her to ring back but I'm afraid she hasn't so far.	d. I am sorry about this, but she is still away on business. Can I be of assistance?
5. You promised I would get the report today but I'm afraid it hasn't arrived yet.	e. I am very sorry to hear that but my secretary did mail it yesterday morning
6. Good morning. My name is Jonathan Spencer. I'd like to speak to Mary Jones in accounts.	f. I'll see whether he's available … I'm sorry but he's not in the office at the moment.

R Exercise 2
Complete the following sentences using words and expressions from the box.

on behalf of • head of accounting • unacceptable • agree to • completed •
postpone • proposal • cancelled • chaired by • with regard to • extension •
interference • matter • deadline

1. Unfortunately, the international conference in Dublin has had to be **1** due to bad weather conditions over the Atlantic.
2. If we have to consider all the recent developments in our presentation we will have to **2** the meeting by at least a week.
3. We regret to say that your latest **3** is **4** to us.
4. I believe we can **5** your terms.
5. Please put me through to **6** 288.
6. I am calling **7** my client Mr Green.
7. **8** your request we would like to inform you that we need more information about the **9** first.
8. The conference will be **10** Ms Brown who is our **11**.
9. The report has to be **12** by the end of the week. Friday is the **13**.
10. Could you repeat that please? There's slight **14** on the line.

Exercise 3 ☞ Phrases
KMK Roleplay this telephone conversation with a partner.

Far Eastern Shipping Co., Shanghai, People´s Republic of China

Vereinigte Versicherungen, Hamburg, Germany

Nennen Sie Ihren Namen und den Namen der Firma. Sie möchten Herrn Berger sprechen.

Nehmen Sie den Anruf entgegen. Sagen Sie dem Anrufer, dass die Verbindung leider sehr schlecht ist und bitten Sie um Wiederholung des Namens.

Wiederholen Sie Ihren Namen und ihr Anliegen.

Antworten Sie, dass Herr Berger noch bis Ende der Woche geschäftlich in Tokio ist. Fragen Sie, worum es geht und ob Sie weiter helfen können.

Sagen Sie, dass es um eine Transportversicherung für eine Lieferung von Flachbildschirmen geht, die auf dem Seeweg von Schanghai nach Hamburg transportiert werden. Herr Berger ist mit dem Vorgang vertraut.

Informieren Sie den Anrufer, dass Frau Schönig Herrn Berger vertritt. Leider wird Frau Schönig erst morgen wieder im Büro sein. Drücken Sie Ihr Bedauern aus. Fragen Sie, ob der Anrufer dann noch einmal anrufen kann. Oder kann Frau Schönig morgen zurückrufen?

Es ist einfacher wegen der Zeitverschiebung, wenn Sie morgen um neun Uhr vormittags deutscher Zeit noch einmal anrufen. Fragen Sie nach der Durchwahl von Frau Schönig.

Die Durchwahl ist 2883. Sie werden Frau Schönig Bescheid sagen.

Bedanken Sie sich und verabschieden Sie sich.

Wünschen Sie dem Anrufer einen schönen Tag und verabschieden Sie sich ebenfalls.

C Taking messages

M **Exercise 1**

Übertragen Sie den folgenden Text ins Deutsche.

> **Info: How to take a message**
>
> When taking messages it is important to make sure that you take down all the relevant details. You should first make sure that you take down the name of the caller. It is usually necessary to ask him/her to spell names and addresses. Be sure to get the postcode.
>
> It is essential to note down telephone numbers accurately. Failure to do so will lead to a lot of problems. Read back telephone numbers to check that you have got them right. Telephone numbers are often read differently in different countries. In Britain numbers are simply given in the order they occur, eg: 0044–020 363 2991 = "oh oh four four – oh two oh – three six three – two nine nine one".
>
> Instead of "oh" Americans usually say "zero". People often say: "double oh" or: "two double nine one". If necessary, ask the caller to repeat the number more slowly.

R **Exercise 2**

7 **There are different international telephone alphabets but people very often make up their own as they go along. Spell the following names and addresses using the international telephone alphabet below. Then listen and check.**

> Sally MacLennane • Gottlieb Bleibtreu • Direct Insurance plc • Sauchihall Street • Pembroke Lane • Fitzwilliam Square • Herbert Rinzinger • Papenburg • Wladiwostok • Sean Dillon • Köln-Mühlheim • Yeoville • Leipzig • Ian Winterbottom • Clearflow Data Ltd • Münchener Straße

A for Alpha
G for Golf
A for …
R … …
W … …
A … …
L … …

I/P Exercise 3

Work in pairs. Sit back to back and spell your name and the name and address of your company using the international telephone alphabet. Then change roles and check the results.

I/P Exercise 4

Work in groups. Dictate the following telephone numbers and e-mail and website addresses to your group. Compare the results.

info@terstegen.com	www.rbos.co.uk	universalbox@aol.com	info@sykescottages.com
p.ruehman@t-online.de	enquiries@elliotsconstruction.co.uk		languagematters@vodafone.net
+44 1234 68 77 91	dieter.wilhelmsen@abconsulting.de		www.mittelpunkt.de / abo
witch_fashions@yahoo.co.uk	www.subscribeonline.co.uk / gardensillustrated		(051) 27 81 13
(0203) 4 67 09 76	www.tate.org.uk	man-with-a-vanremovals@aol.com	0171 25 33 39 80

I/P Exercise 5

Work with a partner. Dictate telephone numbers and e-mail and website addresses (e.g. taken from the Internet) to your partner. Use the examples above and the information in the box below. Then change roles and check the results.

Symbol:	Name:	Example:
'	apostrophe	O'Neil
@	at	info@
A/a	capital letters / small letters	VfB Stuttgart
-	hyphen / dash / minus	HSV-Hamburg
Ö	o-umlaut / oe / o with 2 dots	Öhringen
:	colon	http:
/	slash / stroke	http://
\	backslash	\docs.nt\
.	dot	.com
_	understroke	banking_insurance

Codes / numbers

+49	(0)40	76 88 66 88	12
country code	area code	office number	extension

20354	Hamburg
post code (BE) zip code (AE)	city

R Exercise 6 ☞ CD / Online-Link

◉ 8+9 **There are two recorded messages on your answering machine in the office. Copy the grids below and fill them in while listening. You will hear each message two times.**

Message 1   Message 2

CD 02

Name:					
Loan number:					
Mobile number:					
Office number:					
Call back when?					

Name:					
Contract number:					
E-mail address:					
Mobile number:					
Call back when?					

M Exercise 7 ☞ CD / Online-Link

KMK Sie arbeiten bei einer britischen Investmentbank in Frankfurt. Wenn Sie von Ihrer Mittagspause zurückkommen, finden Sie folgende Nachrichten für Ihre Vorgesetzten Sarah Smart und Alan Clark vor. Kopieren Sie den Vorduck und tragen Sie die Nachrichten auf Englisch ein (Datum usw. nach Wahl).

CD 03

Message for _____   Date _____   Time _____

While you were out you were called by

Name:
Company:
Phone:
Message:

1.
1:52 pm
Guten Tag, mein Name ist Ulrich Davidis von Flexibüros GmbH in Berlin. Frau Smart möchte bitte dringend zurückrufen. Der Termin auf der Messe in Frankfurt Mitte nächsten Monats muss leider um einige Tage verschoben werden.
Meine Handynummer ist 0175–6 16 74 30.

2.
2:05 pm
Hallo, mein Name ist Marcel König von der Provita-Versicherung in Köln. Ich bin nächste Woche am Dienstag und Mittwoch in Frankfurt und möchte für Mittwoch einen Termin mit Herrn Clark vereinbaren. Vielleicht können wir uns zum Mittagessen treffen. Bitte rufen Sie mich unter meiner Büronummer zurück. Sie lautet 0221–3 66 32 78.

3.
2:25 pm
Hier spricht Elmar Hensel von der Wettiner Bank in Dresden. Herr Clark möchte mich bitte umgehend zurückrufen, damit wir die weiteren Schritte im Fall Hibernia Building Society diskutieren können. Meine Büronummer lautet: 0351–6 99 32 21-Durchwahl 723.

R Exercise 8

Match the expressions on the left with the explanations on the right.

1. personnel	a. to send the products to the buyer
2. to dispatch the goods	b. the process of returning a phone call
3. to have a certain item in stock	c. to be in a position to deliver a product right away
4. form	d. the department in a company responsible for recruiting people.
5. call back	e. a pre-printed sheet containing questions and spaces for answers

I/R Exercise 9

Work in pairs and make up telephone messages. Copy the English (page 30) and the German (see below) forms for telephone messages. Sit back to back. Partner A "rings" partner B and leaves a short message. Partner B takes down the message, either in German or in English – depending on the recipient. Then change roles.

Example:

Partner A: This is Sam Houston speaking. I've got a message for Herr Braun, your personnel manager. Please tell him that the required forms are in stock again and that I could dispatch them tomorrow morning. Ask Herr Braun to ring me as soon as possible please.

Partner B takes down the message on a form:

Telefonnotiz

Nachricht für: Herrn Braun, Personalabteilung

aufgenommen von: (Ihr Name)   am:

Anrufer: Sam Houston

Betreff: Benötigte Formulare wieder vorrätig.

Herr Houston könnte die Formulare morgen früh schicken.
Bittet möglichst bald um Rückruf.

Language and grammar: will-Future

Die „will"-Zukunftsform wird im Englischen u.a. bei spontanen Entscheidungen (z.B. am Telefon) benutzt und entspricht dem Präsens im Deutschen.

- I'll put you through to Ms Keller.
- I'll ring you back tomorrow morning.
- I'll tell Mr Meyer you called.

D Making telephone calls

R Exercise 1
Match the expressions on the left (1.–12.) with the explanations on the right (a.–l.).

1. provisional	a. a list of topics to be discussed at a meeting
2. accommodation	b. an employee taking part at a conference in the name of his company
3. financial district	c. the person heading a meeting
4. agenda	d. a list of people who regularly receive mail/e-mails
5. premises	e. the part of a city where all the banks are located
6. representative	f. provided for the moment only and to be updated later
7. chairman of the conference	g. rooms/space/office for commercial use
8. mailing list	h. a condition to be fulfilled
9. reply	i. an organisation promoting the interests of a certain branch of industry
10. speaker	j. available hotel rooms
11. requirement	k. someone who makes a formal speech at a conference
12. association	l. answer

I Exercise 2 ☞ Phrases
KMK Your boss asks you to call the Banking and Insurance Association in order to obtain some information. Roleplay the telephone conversation with a partner using the vocabulary introduced in Exercise 1.

Sie (eigener Name) möchten wissen:

Fergus O'Leary of the Irish Banking and Insurance Association answers:

… wann die Konferenz über internationales Bank- und Versicherungsmarketing in Dublin stattfindet und welcher Tagungsort vorgesehen ist.

Am Freitag, den 28. Juni in den Räumlichkeiten der Irish Stock Exchange.

… ob noch gesonderte Einladungen verschickt werden und wie viele Vertreter ihres Institutes maximal teilnehmen können.

Einladungen werden am Anfang des nächsten Monats verschickt.
Maximal zwei Vertreter je Institut.
Rückmeldung innerhalb von zwei Wochen.

… ob Sie schon Details über die Tagesordnung und die Referenten erfahren können.

Die endgültige Tagesordnung liegt noch nicht vor, da bisher nicht alle Referenten ihre Teilnahme bestätigt haben; eine vorläufige Tagesordnung kann per E-Mail zugeschickt werden; Leiter der Konferenz wird Conor O'Brien vom irischen Banken und Versicherungsverband sein.

… welche Unterbringungsmöglichkeiten in der Nähe vom Tagungsort zur Verfügung stehen.

Große Auswahl an Hotels steht zur Verfügung und eine Aufstellung kann gerne zugeschickt werden.

… ob aktuelle Informationen vom Banken- und Versicherungsverband zukünftig automatisch erhalten werden können.

Das ist problemlos möglich, wenn Sie sich in unseren E-Mail-Verteiler aufnehmen lassen *(put on mailing list)*.

… ob … (jetzt sind Sie gefragt, d.h. was möchten Sie noch wissen?)

Individuelle Antwort

Sie bedanken sich für die Auskünfte und verabschieden sich.

Sie verabschieden sich ebenfalls.

R **Exercise 3 (preparatory task for Exercise 4)**
Nowadays banking and insurance are closely linked, which means nearly all banks offer insurance products at their branches. However, some of the insurance-related vocabulary may be new to you. Match the following words and expressions on the left (1.–10.) with the definitions on the right (a.–j.).

1.	term (life) assurance	a. period of time
2.	to take out an insurance	b. contract which covers a risk
3.	insurance cover	c. the sum of money stipulated in the insurance policy
4.	to secure a loan	d. assets or life insurance to cover a loan
5.	security	e. if someone dies unexpectedly
6.	beneficiary	f. a life insurance policy for a specific period of time
7.	premature death	g. to sign an insurance contract
8.	duration	h. person or bank receiving the sum insured in the event of death
9.	sum insured	i. the monthly or annual payment for insurance
10.	premium	j. to accept other assets, e.g. real estate, shares, etc. to cover the loan in the case of default.

I Exercise 4 ☞ Phrases

KMK Imagine you work at a bank and receive a call from an English speaking customer who wants to take out a life insurance policy.
Work in pairs, where one person takes the role of a bank clerk and the other the role of a customer, and act out the following situation based on the information in the flow chart.

Clerk	Customer
Melden Sie sich am Telefon.	Melden Sie sich, nennen Sie Ihren Namen und sagen Sie, dass Sie Kunde bei der Bank sind und eine Frage haben.
Bitten Sie den Kunden seinen Namen zu buchstabieren.	Buchstabieren Sie Ihren Namen.
Erkundigen Sie sich, um was es geht.	Erklären Sie, dass Sie dabei sind eine Wohnung zu kaufen und dass Sie das Darlehen absichern möchten, um Ihre Familie zu schützen.
Bieten Sie eine Risikolebensversicherung an als Sicherheit für das Darlehen im Falle eines vorzeitigen Todes.	Melden Sie Interesse am Abschließen eines solchen Versicherungsschutzes an.
Fragen Sie nach der Höhe der Versicherungssumme.	Nennen Sie 100.000,– €, da dies die Höhe des Darlehens ist.
Sie haben die Summe nicht verstanden und bitten um Wiederholung.	Nennen Sie die Summe noch einmal.
Fragen Sie nach der Laufzeit des Darlehens.	15 Jahre
Bitten Sie den Kunden zu einem Termin in die Bank, um Details wie Prämienzahlungen und Begünstigte zu besprechen und um den Vertrag zu unterschreiben.	Schlagen Sie einen Termin vor drücken Sie Freude über das bevorstehende Treffen aus.
Verabschieden Sie sich.	Verabschieden Sie sich ebenfalls.

E   Leaving messages on an answering machine

> **Info: A message on an answering machine**
>
> 1. Begin by saying "Good morning" etc. Do not say your name first as the first few words may get "lost".
> 2. Pronounce your name very clearly, give your company's name as well and mention the place / country you are calling from, if necessary.
> 3. Be as clear and concise as possible when leaving the message.
> 4. Be polite and friendly.
> 5. Repeat figures and spell names, if necessary.
> 6. At the end repeat your name and telephone number.
> 7. Dictate the telephone number slowly, pausing between each number.

R/M **Exercise 1** ☞ **CD / Online-Link**
KMK **Kopieren Sie den Vordruck, hören Sie die Nachricht ab und fassen Sie sie auf**
◎ 10 **Deutsch in einer Telefonnotiz zusammen.**

CD 04	**Telefonnotiz**

Telefonnotiz

Nachricht für:

aufgenommen von: am:

Anrufer:

Betreff:

P **Exercise 2**
Work with a partner. Write out a message to be left on an answering machine. Use the following details:

Arrival Dublin • 28 November • 10 am • Dublin airport • Ryanair flight from Hahn • staying at The Shelbourne • urgently request appointment with Mr O'Flanagan 28 or 29 November at the latest • to negotiate joint financing of project "Go Eire 2010" • required capital about 15 m € • decision to be made by end of the year • suggest early meeting • contact at hotel or on mobile 0049 (0)1577 281 333 • suggest place to meet • possibly at the Stock Exchange or at Mr O'Flanagan's downtown office • Regards

"If you wish to be put on hold, press one … hear a recording, press two … get rudely disconnected, press three …"

35

Phrases: Telephoning

To make friendly remarks at the beginning of a telephone conversation

Good morning, Ms Black. Nice to hear from you. How are things over there?	Guten Morgen, Frau Black. Schön, von Ihnen zu hören. Wie läuft es denn so?
Good afternoon Mr Ahern. What's the weather in Ireland like?	Guten Tag, Herr Ahern. Wie ist das Wetter in Irland?

Reactions

Fine, thank you. And how are you?	Gut, vielen Dank. Und wie geht es Ihnen?
We've had an awful lot of rain recently, I'm afraid. What's it like in Germany?	Es hat in der letzten Zeit leider schrecklich viel geregnet. Wie ist das Wetter in Deutschland?

To ask the caller to speak more slowly, to spell sth., to repeat sth., etc.

Sorry, I didn't quite catch that. Could you repeat it more slowly, please?	Es tut mir Leid, das habe ich nicht verstanden. Könnten Sie es etwas langsamer wiederholen?
Could you speak up a bit?	Könnten Sie etwas lauter sprechen?
Could you spell that? Is that the name of the town or the street?	Könnten Sie das buchstabieren? Ist das der Name der Stadt oder der Straße?
I'm afraid I didn't get the phone number. Could you repeat it, please?	Leider habe ich die Telefonnummer nicht mitbekommen. Würden Sie sie bitte wiederholen?
Could you possibly spell your boss's name?	Könnten Sie mir den Namen Ihres Chefs vielleicht buchstabieren?
The connection is rather poor. I can hardly understand you.	Die Verbindung ist ziemlich schlecht. Ich kann Sie kaum verstehen.
We were cut off.	Wir wurden getrennt.

To ask for somebody

Could I speak to Ms Johnson, please?	Könnte ich bitte Frau Johnson sprechen?
Could you put me through to Mr Clark?	Könnten Sie mich mit Herrn Clark verbinden?
Could you give me his/her extension, please?	Könnten Sie mir bitte seine/ihre Durchwahl geben?

To say that someone is not available

I'm afraid Claudia Friedrichs is not in the office at the moment.	Claudia Friedrichs ist z. Zt. leider nicht in ihrem Büro.
… is in a meeting.	… ist in einer Besprechung.

To offer to ring back or take a message

Would you prefer to hold or shall I get/ask Mr O'Leary to ring back?	Möchten Sie lieber warten oder soll ich Mr O'Leary bitten, Sie zurückzurufen?
Would you like to leave a message?	Möchten Sie eine Nachricht hinterlassen?
Can I give him/her a message?	Kann ich ihm/ihr etwas ausrichten?

To apologise

I'm afraid there's been a mix up/ misunderstanding.	Leider ist da etwas durcheinandergeraten/ Leider liegt ein Missverständnis vor.
I'm extremely sorry.	Es tut mir sehr Leid.
Thank you for being so understanding.	Vielen Dank für Ihr Verständnis.
I'm terribly sorry but I'm afraid we simply cannot help you.	Es tut mir sehr Leid, aber wir können Ihnen beim besten Willen nicht helfen.

To insist that something is done by a certain date

We need the credit report by Wednesday at the latest.	Wir brauchen die Kreditauskunft bis spätestens Mittwoch.
Can we rely on that?	Können wir uns darauf verlassen?

To refuse something

I'm afraid we can't agree to your proposal.	Leider können wir uns mit Ihrem Vorschlag nicht einverstanden erklären.
We find this level of service quite unacceptable.	Für uns ist diese Art von Kundendienst absolut inakzeptabel.
This is unfortunately not what we had in mind.	Leider hatten wir uns das nicht so vorgestellt.
That is a pity.	Das ist wirklich schade.
That is most regrettable.	Das ist überaus bedauerlich.
There must have been a misunderstanding.	Hier muss ein Missverständnis vorliegen.

To end the conversation

Goodbye Mrs Sears. Thank you for calling.	Auf Wiederhören, Frau Sears. Vielen Dank für Ihren Anruf.
Thank you for the information. You're welcome.	Vielen Dank für die Information. Gerngeschehen.
Thank you. Goodbye. Have a nice weekend! You too. I look forward to meeting you in Frankfurt.	Danke schön. Auf Wiederhören. Schönes Wochenende! Gleichfalls! Ich freue mich darauf, Sie in Frankfurt zu treffen.

Unit 3
Presentations

You may be required to present your company and its services or products – either informally or on a more formal level. This may range from the introduction of a specific service or product to presenting the company as a whole. Although many may feel a bit scared of standing up in front of an audience, the ability to make good oral presentations is a key skill, and one that can be acquired and improved by practice. The essential elements of a good presentation are careful preparation and, of course, knowledge of your subject.

P **Exercise**
Look at the pictures above and give a brief description of the situations they illustrate.

A   What makes a good presentation?

I **Exercise 1**
Look carefully at pictures 1 and 4 above. How do you interpret the body language of the different participants in these presentations? How important is body language? Discuss in small groups and be prepared to present your conclusions to the class.

P **Exercise 2**

What do the following signals often communicate?

1. crossed arms
2. foot and finger tapping
3. sitting on the edge of the chair
4. not directly facing a speaker

R **Exercise 3**

Read the following text and answer the questions below.

© Mike Baldwin / Cornered

"Which brings us to my next point."

Making a Presentation – Good Practice

- Know your subject. The audience is there to learn from you.
- Know your aims. This is essential when deciding on the exact content. Are you trying to "sell" to the audience or to inform them? If the aims are not clear to you, they will not be clear to your audience.
- Know your audience. Ask yourself the questions "Who are they?" and "What do they expect from me?". You will need to find out in advance how much your audience knows about the subject of your presentation, so that you neither bore them nor make any technical content too complicated.
- Plan the stages. There must be a structure – a beginning, a middle and a conclusion.
- Know what you want to say. Know it so well that you do not need to read a text – which may send your audience to sleep. Instead, refer to numbered prompt cards with key information written on them.
- Use visual aids. They will make your presentation look more professional and hold the interest of your audience.
- Practice your delivery. Not just once, but many times. The style and manner of your presentation is as important as the content. Like athletes, dancers and actors, you need to rehearse your "performance".

1. Can you think of any other points or details?
2. Think of a presentation – or a speech – that you have attended. Did you think it was good? Or were there points that could have been improved?
3. How did the presenter hold your attention? Write down the points that you found good and those that could have been better.

Good	Could have been better
It wasn't too long.	The presenter kept turning his back to us.

I/P **Exercise 4**

In small groups, discuss your lists and decide what factors help to make an excellent presentation. Agree on a list of the most important factors. Make a master list with the rest of the class.

P **Exercise 5**

www Type *cross-cultural presentations* into an English language browser. Find an interesting cultural fact that could be helpful in a presentation and report this to the class.

M **Exercise 6**

Ein Kollege muss eine Präsentation halten und hat Sie um Rat gebeten. Beziehen Sie sich auf den Text auf Seite 39 und schreiben Sie ihm eine E-Mail auf Deutsch mit Hinweisen für eine Präsentation.

P **Exercise 7**

At the end of this unit, you are going to prepare your own 5 – 8 minute presentation and deliver it to the class. Choose one of the following topics with the help of your teacher. Keep your presentation in mind as you work through the unit.

1. The apprenticeship system in your sponsoring company and a) your proposed changes to this system or b) the reasons why you wouldn't make any changes.
2. A product or service offered by your sponsoring company.
3. Why knowledge of other cultures can be essential for the success of a presentation.
4. Why your local town or city would be a perfect place for the location of the German HQ of a major insurance company from Britain.
5. The Bank of England

B Preparing a presentation

1 Selecting the content

When you know what your topic and your objective is, the next step is to gather your ideas.

P **Exercise 1**

Imagine you are going to give a presentation about the history of your company, its current status and future plans. Brainstorm your ideas.

P Exercise 2

Now prioritise and organise your ideas for the main part of the company presentation. One way of doing this is as a mind map. Try this, using the following diagram as an example. The bold lines represent major categories of the presentation; the other lines represent sub-categories.

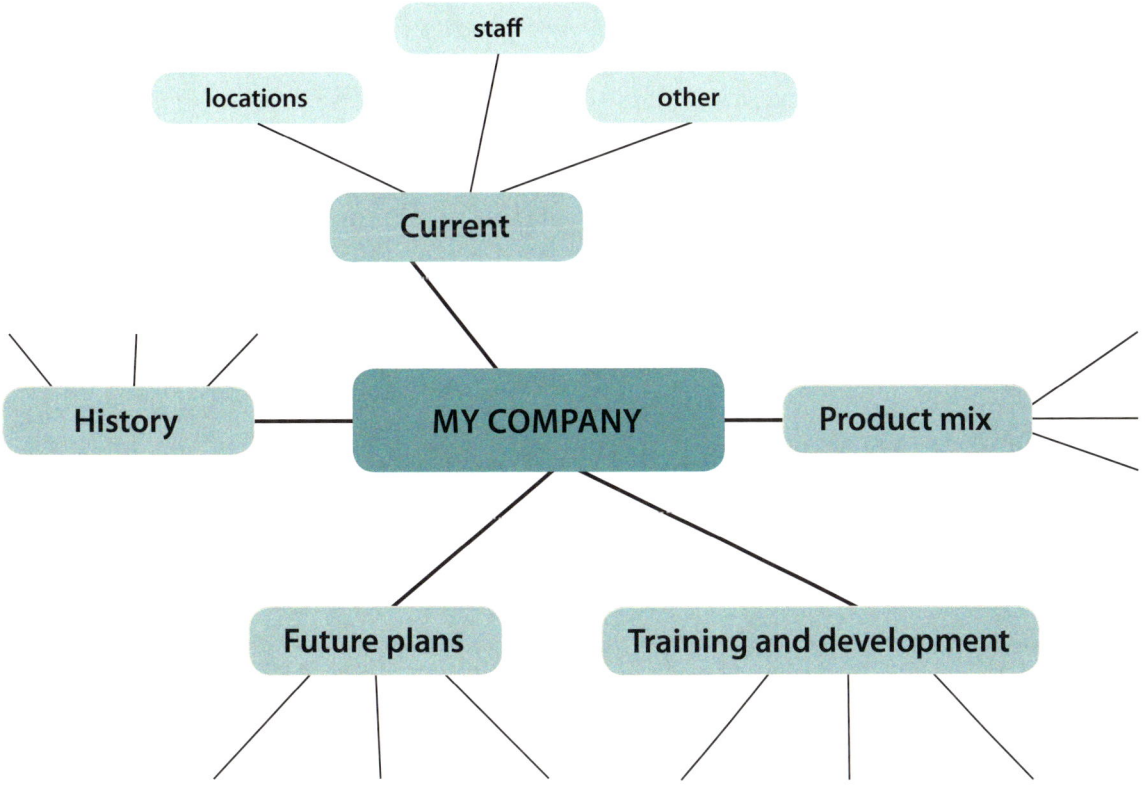

2   Structuring the content

A presentation should be structured into three major, clearly defined stages: a beginning, a middle – or body – and a conclusion – or summary. All three parts of your presentation are vital. The functions of these stages are popularly described as being:

1. Tell them what you're going to tell them.
2. Tell them.
3. Tell them what you told them.

I Exercise 1

Why are the openings and closings of a presentation so important?
Discuss this in the class and draw up a list of reasons.

Exercise 2

⊚ 11 **Hören Sie der Eröffnung einer Präsentation zunächst aufmerksam zu und entscheiden Sie, ob die folgenden Aussagen richtig oder falsch sind.**

Aussagen:

1. Susanne Mienert ist Versicherungsmaklerin.
2. Sie arbeitet in der Konzernzentrale der Safe Hands Versicherungsfirma.
3. Der Zweck ihrer Präsentation ist es zu zeigen, wie sich die Umsätze im Laufe der letzten drei Jahre entwickelt haben.
4. Sie möchte, dass ihre Zuhörer sich während der Präsentation Notizen machen.
5. Sie ist damit einverstanden, dass die Zuhörer die Präsentation unterbrechen, falls sie etwas nicht verstanden haben.

Exercise 3

Working with a partner, answer the following question and give your reasons:

Is Susanne Mienert's audience well briefed about the purpose and structure of the presentation and what the audience itself is expected to do?

Exercise 4

You should give the audience a signal when you are about to move on to another stage of your presentation or show them a visual. This helps them to refocus. Sort the following signalling phrases under the headings given.

| In conclusion … | | I am here to … | | Turning to … | | And finally … |

| I'd like to show you … | | This leads me to my next point … | | *To start with …* |

| To sum up … | | I'd like to begin by … | | That brings me to the end … |

| Firstly, I'd like to … | | As you can see … | | The central issue is … |

| Moving on now … | | Take a look at this … | | To summarise the main points … |

Example:

Opening phase	Main phase	Visuals	Conclusion
To start with			

Exercise 5

Translate the following passage into English.

Der Schluss

Der Schluss rundet eine Präsentation ab. Ein guter Schluss erfüllt eine dreifache Rolle:

- die Hauptpunkte zusammenzufassen und den Kernpunkt, den Sie bei der Einführung bereits erwähnt haben, zu unterstreichen.
- die Hörer letztendlich zu überzeugen, Ihren Standpunkt anzunehmen.
- die Hörer zu der von Ihnen geforderten Handlung zu bewegen.

3 Visual aids

Most presentations are enhanced by the use of visual aids. Visual aids help you to explain complicated ideas more easily, arouse and hold the interest of your audience and make your presentation more professional. Printed out they can double as a handout. They can take the form of overhead transparencies or computer files showing graphs, pictures, flowcharts, brief statements / cues (e.g. the key words from your prompt cards).

> **In the case of text, it is important to:**
>
> ➢ Limit the text to six lines.
> ➢ Use maximum six words per line.
> ➢ Print the text in large letters.
> ➢ Use upper and lower case letters.
> ➢ Use dark colours.
> ➢ Centre the text on the page.

M/P **Exercise 1**

Fassen Sie den obigen Text über die Vorteile von Anschauungsmaterial unter Beantwortung folgender Fragen auf Deutsch zusammen.

1. Welche Vorteile bietet Anschauungsmaterial?
2. Welche Arten von Anschauungsmaterialien gibt es?
3. Wie müssen Folien aussehen, damit sie wirken?

P **Exercise 2**

Some pieces of information, e.g. statistics, are easier to understand / more interesting if presented in the form of a graph or diagram. Identify the following diagrams using the names from the box below.

> pie chart • bar chart • line graph • organigram • data table

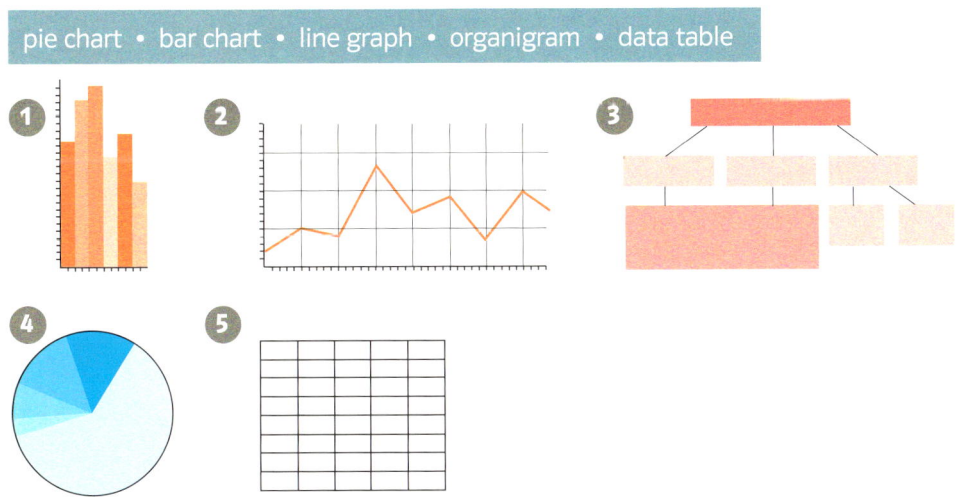

Exercise 3

Match each graphic with its best use.

1. pie chart	a. Used to show a sequence of events.
2. organigram	b. Used to show comparisons and rankings.
3. line graph	c. Used to show company structure or hierarchy.
4. plan	d. Used to show data without interpretation.
5. bar chart	e. Used to show one or more parts in relation to the whole.
6. flow chart	f. Used to show development over time.
7. data table	g. Used to show locations.

4 Equipment

Exercise

To use your visual aids, you will need equipment. What kinds of equipment can you think of?

Type *presentations equipment* into an English language browser. Make a list of different kinds of equipment that are used in presentations and imagine their advantages and disadvantages.

Example:

Overhead projector and transparencies
Can be prepared in advance and look professional

Info: The most important piece of equipment
The most important piece of equipment is YOU! Make sure you are in good working order, well prepared, well rested and professionally dressed. Your confidence will be transmitted to the audience.

5 Prompt cards

You should *not* read out a prepared text. You do not want to bore your audience. When you know what you are going to say, the order in which you are going to say it, and you have decided on your visual aids, it is time to prepare the prompt cards. These are postcard size cards for your own use which should contain all the essential information and facts that you need for your presentation. They should be written on one side only, in writing large enough to read easily, and should be numbered in case you get them mixed up.

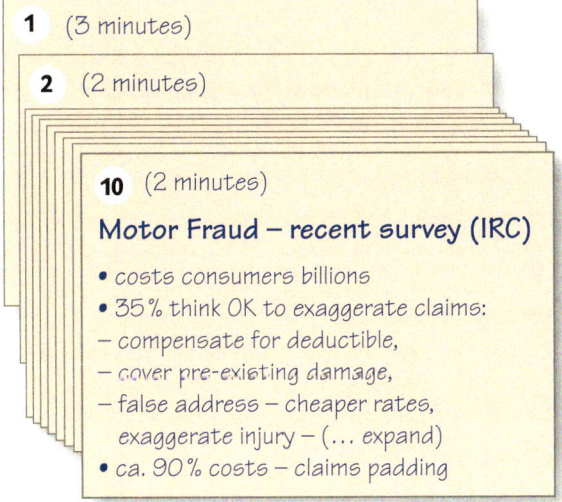

1 (3 minutes)

2 (2 minutes)

10 (2 minutes)

Motor Fraud – recent survey (IRC)

- costs consumers billions
- 35 % think OK to exaggerate claims:
- – compensate for deductible,
- – cover pre-existing damage,
- – false address – cheaper rates,
  exaggerate injury – (… expand)
- ca. 90 % costs – claims padding

Example:
What you intend to say:

Last year we achieved pre-tax profits of €295 million. This represented a massive reduction compared to the profits of €1.3 billion the previous year. Only two months ago we were still estimating a profit of €755 million, but this had to be dramatically revised downwards in order to compensate for the losses arising from unfortunate investments in US real estate. But now we've learnt our lessons and, turning to the coming year I am pleased to announce that our forecast …

Prompt card

3 (1 minute)

Last year

- profits €295 m.
- massive reduction – 1.3 b. prev. year
- 2 months ago estimate 755 m.
- downward revision – US real estate investments.
- learnt lessons! forecast coming year …

P **Exercise**

This is what you intend to say. Now reduce your script to the important facts and write your prompt card.

Personal accident and sickness insurance

This type of policy pays a regular cash benefit to a person unable to work as a result of an accident or sickness. This is especially valuable if you are self-employed and would have no income if disabled or sick. Personal accident policies are arranged for one year and are renewable at the option of the insurer. If you are sick or injured, regular payments are usually made on a weekly basis up to a maximum number of weeks (usually 52 or 104). There will normally be a deferred period (such as 7 days) before payments start. A lump sum may also be payable on death or in case of specified disabilities such as loss of a limb or eye.

C The language of presentations

R **Exercise 1**

🎧 11 **The same things can be said in many different ways. Listen to the opening phase of a presentation (Exercise 2, page 42) again and match these phrases with similar phrases from Susanne Mienert's presentation.**

1. Good morning everyone.
2. Thank you all for coming …
3. Let me introduce myself. My name is …
4. The purpose of my talk today is to …
5. And finally, I'll show you how …
6. I'll deal with questions …

R **Exercise 2**

When describing trends and developments, you will need to be as precise as possible. There are many words and word combinations which help you with this. Sort the following verbs under their correct heading. If you can think of any others, add them as well.

> rise • peak • decline • increase • bottom out • fall • fluctuate •
> reach a high • decrease • climb • drop • rocket • reach a low • remain
> stable • go up • slump • stabilise • plummet • level off

Example:

up	down	up (very fast)	down (very fast)	constant	move backwards and forwards	top	bottom
rise							

P **Exercise 3**

Trends and developments can also be described in more detail by modifying a verb with an adverb or with an adjective. Using verbs from the boxes "up" and "down" and adverbs or adjectives from this diagram, make sentences describing the changes shown on the line graph below.

Example: Demand for securities fell sharply from January to February.

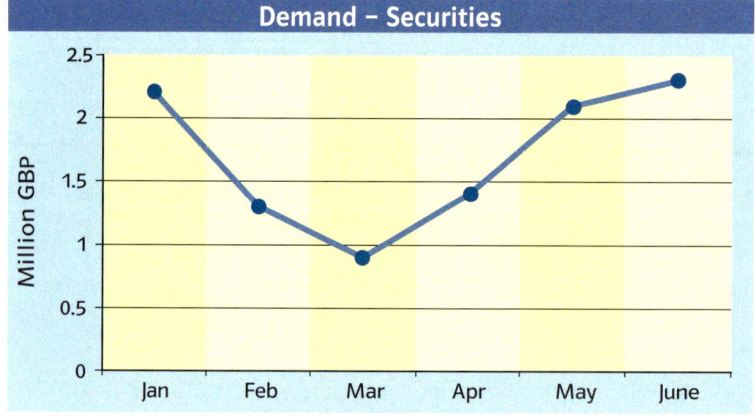

slight(ly)
slow(ly)
moderate(ly)
gradual(ly)
steady/steadily
significant(ly)
dramatic(ally)
sharp(ly)

46

R Exercise 4
Match the following graphs and statements.

1. The number of new policyholders fluctuated slightly.	a.
2. The number of new policyholders plummeted.	b.
3. There was a peak in numbers of new policyholders.	c.
4. Numbers of new policyholders fell steadily.	d.
5. There was a steep rise in numbers of new policyholders.	e.
6. Numbers of new policyholders remained stable.	f.

P/R Exercise 5
◎ 12 **Listen to the CD and draw a line graph following the instructions. Describe your graphs in writing as accurately as possible using words you have learnt in this unit. Now compare your graphs and descriptions.**

I Exercise 6
With a partner, take turns describing the chart below. Use these expressions:

- to be higher / lower / bigger / smaller / more / less expensive than …
- to be as high / low / expensive as …
- to be the biggest / lowest / most expensive of …
- to be / come first / second / last with
- to be / follow in first / fifth / last place
- to be followed by …
- to be at the bottom / top / of the list / table

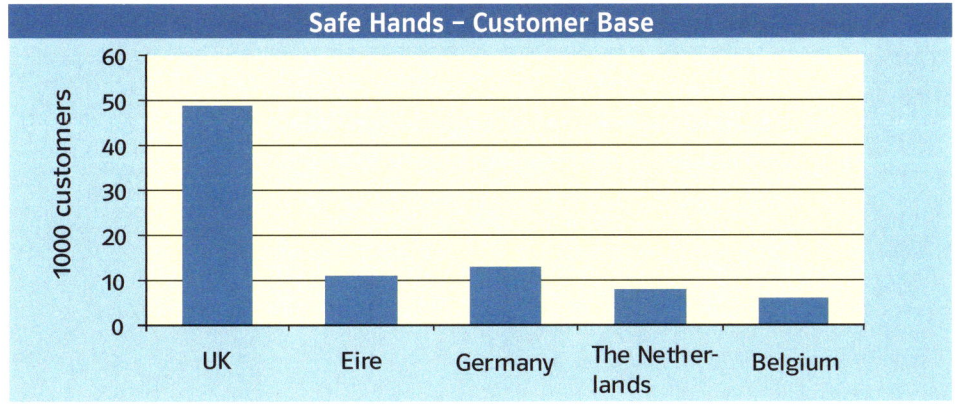

Safe Hands – Customer Base

P **Exercise 7**

Describe the pie chart using the phrases in the box above.

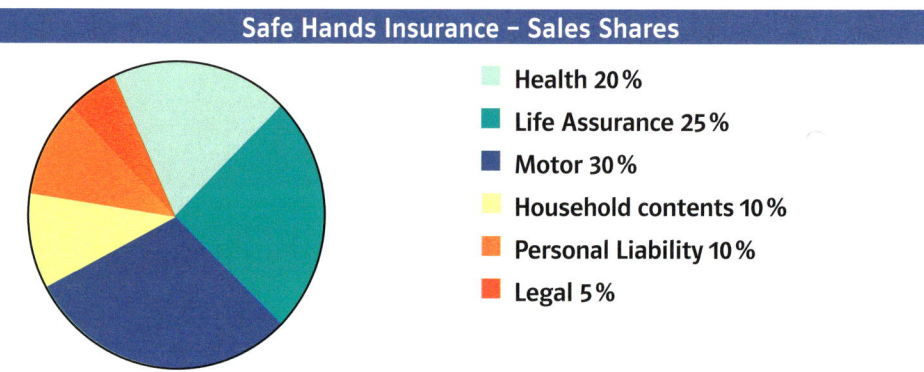

Safe Hands Insurance – Sales Shares

- Health 20%
- Life Assurance 25%
- Motor 30%
- Household contents 10%
- Personal Liability 10%
- Legal 5%

I/P **Exercise 8**

Draw up a pie chart of your or another company's products, using real or fictional figures. Give a partner a list of the products but do not let him/her see the original chart. Give him/her one piece of information, e.g. "Legal insurance has the smallest share." After that, you are only allowed to answer "True" or "False". Your partner has to keep making statements until he/she can draw the pie chart accurately. Then swap roles.

Example:

If legal insurance has the smallest share, then health must make up the largest.	False
I think health insurance accounts for a larger share than household contents.	True

I/P **Exercise 9**

In small groups, brainstorm possible ways of dealing with the following situations during question time at the end of your presentation and make a list of useful phrases.

1. You don't understand a question.
2. You still don't understand the question, even when it has been repeated.
3. You don't know the answer to the question.
4. You think that the question is aggressive.
5. You don't want to give an answer to the question.
6. You want to disagree tactfully.

D Delivering the presentation

At one of the internal meetings held at regular intervals to update senior staff on activities in other arms of the company, Bryson Spears of Eastern Tide Capital, the investment banking arm of Britain's bank Eastern Tide, is giving a brief presentation on their expansion into China.

P/R Exercise 1

🔊 13 **Listen to this shortened example of a presentation and answer the following questions in German.**

1. Does the speaker state his objective? What is it?
2. Why doesn't the audience have to take notes?
3. Does he give a summary? What is it?
4. What kind of visual aids do you think he is using?

I Exercise 2

Before you start preparing your own presentation (see Exercise 7 on page 40), discuss the answers to the following questions in class.

1. Do you think the seating arrangement for the audience is particularly important?
2. Should you wait for everybody to arrive before starting the presentation?
3. Do you think it is as important to be well dressed as it is to be well prepared and good at your subject?
4. Should you give out the handouts before the presentation so that the audience can refer to them while you are speaking?
5. Is it the responsibility of the technical department to make sure that the equipment is working correctly?
6. Which is better, to stand or to sit when giving a presentation?
7. Should you give as much information to your audience as possible, bearing in mind that this will be your only chance?
8. Why do you think it is important to signal to your audience that you are about to conclude the presentation?
9. If questions do not come immediately, should you finish the presentation?
10. When you are answering a question, do you reply to the individual who asked it or to the audience?

I/P Exercise 3 ☞ Phrases

Make a checklist for preparing presentations, using information from this unit. Prepare your presentation to the final detail, working carefully through the checklist. Write out your text, reduce it onto prompt cards and practise it with a partner who has chosen a different topic. Look at the evaluation sheet below to see the criteria your audience is going to use when they evaluate your performance.

I Exercise 4 ☞ CD / Online-Link

Give your presentation to your fellow students. The other students listen carefully, ask any questions and then assess the presentation according to the following evaluation scheme. The audience should award points out of ten under each heading.
If you could only give one suggestion to the presenter for his / her next presentation, what would it be?

CD 05

Presentation Evaluation Sheet

Area	Details to watch for	Points
Preparation	evidence of careful preparation	
Structure	introduction, statement of objective(s), main body – clear emphasis on small number of main points – conclusion	
Content	relevance, well substantiated with facts and figures	
Visual aids	appropriate use of simple, easy-to-understand visual aids	
Delivery	not too fast, eye contact, appropriate body language, confident, relaxed, spoke from prompts, not monotonous, not repetitive	
Language	no jargon, good use of signalling expressions like "I should like to begin / conclude by …"	
Timing	different parts in proportion, total length just right	
Unplanned parts	dealt well with questions, unexpected issues	
Overall impression	lively, humorous, easy to follow, informative	

I/P Exercise 5

Listen to your fellow students' feedback.
Now look back at your list from Exercise 4 on page 39 and evaluate your own presentation. What are you particularly pleased about? What are you unhappy about? What was difficult to prepare? What will you do differently next time? How will you do it? Discuss this in small groups.

E Public speaking strategies

Do you get terrified if you are asked to speak in public? Don't worry – you're not alone. One survey found that more than 40% of respondents said their top fear was not death, or loneliness, or getting into debt, but speaking in front of a group of people. By following the advice you have received in this unit, you can
5 be sure that you have prepared a solid, professional presentation, well-tailored to your audience. In order to deliver this presentation confidently, you have been advised to rehearse it, if possible in front of supportive friends, family members or colleagues who will give you useful feedback and advice. Additionally, there are various exercises and techniques that you can practise to help you become
10 confident in delivering your presentations.

- Check your pronunciation. Use a good dictionary, or ask a native speaker.
- Practise turning the key notes from your prompt cards into connected sentences. This can be difficult at first, but the more you practise, the more fluent you will be. You can write connecting words at the bottom of your
15 prompt cards to help you with this.
- Practise speaking in front of a mirror. Check for gestures, twitches, etc.
- Record your presentation. Is your voice too soft, too hesitant, too boring, too jerky? Try again – and again. Aim for a smooth and confident delivery.
- Practise your intonation. Do you want to emphasise a point? Do you want to
20 sound definite? Or questioning?
- Silence is often as important as speaking. Make use of pauses. Pause before an important point. Pause before moving on to the next part of the presentation. Do not gallop along – there will be no prizes for finishing early!

I Exercise
Try the following activities, which are designed to help with fluency and confidence.

Activity A:
Get together in small groups. Choose a group leader, who will need a stop watch. The group leader gives one of the group members a topic. He/she then has to speak on this topic for 60 seconds. If there is hesitation or repetition the next person has to carry on until the 60 seconds are up or until he or she hesitates and so on. After the 60 seconds, a new topic is given to the next person in line. Do not choose deliberately difficult topics – the idea is to speak without hesitating, not to catch out the speaker!

Activity B:
Think of a subject that you can speak on confidently for 2–3 minutes. Tell the other members of your group what your topic is going to be. Each person then writes down a key word which is relevant to your topic on a piece of paper. You do not see these words. Begin giving your speech. The members of the group take turns holding up their key word and you have to incorporate the word or idea coherently into your speech.

Phrases: Presentations

The opening

Let me introduce myself. My name is …	Darf ich mich kurz vorstellen. Mein Name ist …
At present I am responsible for …	Im Moment bin ich verantwortlich für …
I am very happy to see you here.	Es freut mich sehr, dass Sie hier sind.
I'd like to start by telling you something about my company/organisation.	Zunächst möchte ich Ihnen etwas über meine Firma/mein Unternehmen sagen.
First, I'd like to introduce my bank/company briefly.	Als Erstes möchte ich Ihnen meine Bank/mein Unternehmen kurz vorstellen.
My presentation will deal with …	Meine Präsentation behandelt …
I am going to tell you about …	Ich werde Sie heute über … informieren.
I am here to give you an update on …	Ich bin hier, um Sie auf den neuesten Stand bezüglich … zu bringen.
I intend to keep my presentation as brief as possible.	Ich möchte meine Präsentation so kurz wie möglich halten.
I would like to focus on the following points/areas/products/services:	Ich möchte mich auf folgende Punkte/Gebiete/Produkte/Dienstleistungen konzentrieren:
I would welcome any questions at the end of my presentation.	Ich wäre gern bereit, etwaige Fragen am Ende meiner Präsentation zu beantworten.
As time is a little tight, I'd be grateful if you could keep any questions to the end.	Da die Zeit etwas knapp bemessen ist, wäre ich Ihnen dankbar, wenn Sie etwaige Fragen erst am Ende stellen.
We will have 15 minutes at the end of the presentation to answer any questions.	Wir haben 15 Minuten Zeit am Ende der Präsentation, um Fragen Ihrerseits zu klären.
At the end of the presentation you will receive a handout which summarises the main points and gives an overview of the relevant figures and statistics.	Am Ende der Präsentation bekommen Sie einen Handzettel, der die Hauptpunkte enthält und einen Überblick über die entsprechenden Zahlen und Statistiken gibt.
Has everyone received a copy of the handout?	Haben alle den Handzettel bekommen?

Structuring the main message

Now my second point is …	Ich komme nun zu Punkt 2 …
Thirdly, let me give you some basic statistics.	Drittens darf ich Ihnen ein paar grundlegende Statistiken zeigen.
That leads/brings me to my next point …	Damit komme ich zum nächsten Punkt …
The gist of the matter/central issue is …	Der Kernpunkt/die zentrale Frage ist …

I would now like to move on to the next topic.	Ich möchte nun gern zum nächsten Thema kommen.
Furthermore, it's important …	Darüber hinaus ist es wichtig …
An excellent example of this is …	Ein hervorragendes Beispiel dafür ist …
I'd like to give you an example to illustrate this point.	Ich möchte diesen Punkt mit einem Beispiel erläutern.
Let me show you …	Lassen Sie mich Ihnen zeigen …
This graph shows …	Dieses Schaubild zeigt …
With the help of a graph, I would like to show you …	Anhand eines Schaubildes möchte ich Ihnen … verdeutlichen.
A distinct trend emerges from the figures.	Aus den Zahlen geht ein deutlicher Trend hervor.
In this connection it is worth mentioning …	In diesem Zusammenhang sollte man erwähnen …
Turning to the future …	Den Blick in die Zukunft wendend …
As you can see, there is a trend towards …	Wie Sie sehen können, gibt es einen Trend zu …

The conclusion

To sum up/Summing up, we can say that …	Zusammenfassend kann man sagen, dass …
I'd like to sum up.	Ich darf zusammenfassen./Ich fasse zusammen.
I have reached the end …	Ich komme zum Schluss …
I'd like to conclude by saying …	Lassen Sie mich am Schluss anmerken, dass …
I'd like to thank you very much for your attention.	Ich möchte mich ganz herzlich für Ihre Aufmerksamkeit bedanken.
Now I shall be pleased to answer any questions.	Wenn Sie Fragen haben, werde ich Ihnen diese jetzt natürlich gerne beantworten.
We have about 10 minutes for questions.	Uns stehen noch rund 10 Minuten für Fragen zur Verfügung.
I hope that you enjoyed this short presentation.	Ich hoffe, dieser kleine Vortrag hat Ihnen gefallen.
If you don't have any further questions, I'll end at this point.	Wenn Sie keine weiteren Fragen haben, möchte ich jetzt meinen Vortrag beenden.
I should like to finish by saying/thanking the organisers/pointing out …	Ich möchte schließen mit den Bemerkungen/dem Dank an die Organisatoren/dem Hinweis …

Unit 4
Meetings and negotiations

Meetings are essential to share information, achieve objectives and establish a personal contact. Despite all the advantages of modern communication media, which make it possible to hold conferences over large distances, it is often easier to work with people you have met face to face. It is an important part of the job of banking
5 and insurance staff to organise both internal and external meetings and conferences. It is important for meetings to be carefully organised and given a clear structure and a reasonable time limit so that participants are under some pressure to express themselves succinctly and arrive at decisions. Depending on the purpose of the meeting, a vote may be taken to add weight to a decision taken by the participants.

10 Negotiations range from informal situations in private life to much more formal situations in business contexts. You may be required to organise meetings or be involved in negotiations with customers. Finally, it should be noted that there are many cultural differences as to what is regarded as appropriate behaviour.

I/P **Exercise**
Discuss the following questions with a partner and present your ideas to the class.

1. Why is it often easier to work with people you've met face to face?
2. What kind of meetings do you think are most/least worthwhile?
3. What kind of meetings have you experienced?

A Making an appointment

Alexandra Schmalenbach is a PA at the head office of the XYZ Bank in Düsseldorf. Her boss Claudia Meyer asks her to arrange a meeting with Peter Davidson at the bank's London office. She plans to arrive about 13.00 local time and return on the evening flight. She suggests a working lunch at a restaurant of Peter's choice. She asks Alexandra to book a return flight from Düsseldorf to Gatwick online.

Alexandra has Ms Meyer's diary in front of her and rings Peter Davidson's secretary, Janet Pope. They try to decide on what day it would be possible for them to meet. Claudia would prefer mid week. (Remember: one hour earlier in UK due to time difference).

I **Exercise 1** ☞ **Phrases**

Work with a partner and act out the dialogue between Alexandra and Janet in which they arrange an appointment for a working lunch in London.

| Role card: Student A – Claudia Meyer's diary | (see role card Student B on page 150) |

Montag	8:30	Gespräch Herr Ellman – Geschäftskundenabteilung
	10:00	Rückmeldung der Quartalszahlen an die Geschäftsführung
Dienstag	9:00 – 16:00	München – Tagung der Investmentberater –
	14:00	Vortrag zu Änderungen im Steuergesetz im laufenden Jahr
Mittwoch	9:00	Termin für Check-up bei Zahnarzt Dr. Rottenwallner
Donnerstag	11:30	Geschäftsessen mit Chris Stewart
Freitag	11:00	Mitarbeiterbesprechung
	14:00	Besprechung mit Fr. Neuländer, Privatkundenabteilung

Language and grammar: Present continuous

Die Verlaufsform in der Gegenwart beschreibt
1. eine gerade vor sich gehende Handlung.
2. eine vorübergehende, zeitlich begrenzte Handlung / Situation.
3. eine Handlung, die für die Zukunft fest geplant ist.

- Alexandra is talking to her boss.

- Peter is working in the investment department this week.
- Claudia Meyer is meeting Peter Davidson next week.

P **Exercise 2**

Take the role of Alexandra Schmalenbach. Consult with Claudia Meyer and then write an e-mail to Janet Pope (jp.xyzbanklondon@aol.com) confirming time and date (any appropriate date) of the appointment. Ask Janet to confirm for Peter Davidson asap.

Trains: There are no supplementary charges for faster trains in Britain (the Eurostar to Brussels and Paris is more expensive!). How often and where trains stop is given on the indicator and timetables. It is very important to make sure that the train stops where you want to get off! Do not assume that all trains will stop at the same station on your return journey. Each train may stop at a different selection of stations. 5

Pubs: Pubs are an important institution in Britain and are a popular venue at lunchtime for an informal meal. 10 Many provide food at lunchtime, less often in the evening. As a rule there is no waiter service. You go to the bar to buy drinks, where turn-taking is observed although there is no visible queue. If the pub is crowded it may be a good idea to discreetly wave a 10 15 pound note to let the barman/barmaid know you are waiting. Often English people buy rounds, saying things like "What's yours?" or "What are you having?". Everybody is in principle expected to buy a round. If you don't, there may be an embarrassed silence. Food 20 is also ordered and paid for at the bar and is brought to the table where you are sitting. All drinks and food are paid for straight away.

Tipping (taxis and restaurants): In Germany you frequently tip by rounding up the amount of the bill. If the taxi fare is Euro 8.10 you might say Euro 8.50 or 25 Euro 9.00. In Britain a taxi driver would not know what you meant. If the fare is £ 5.30 you could give the driver a £ 10 pound note and say "Please give me change for £ 6". In restaurants the bill is generally brought on a little tray. You put enough money on the tray to pay 30 the bill. The waiter returns, takes the tray away and comes back again with your change on the tray. You then decide what to put on the tray as a tip. It does not have to be a percentage of the bill.

I/P Exercise 3
Discuss in groups the cultural differences you have observed when visiting other countries. Present your results to the class.

B Preparing agendas, meetings and conferences

M Exercise 1

Match the following expressions with their German equivalents.

1.	implement a decision	a. ein Meeting absagen
2.	take a vote	b. einen Vorschlag zur Diskussion stellen
3.	put forward a suggestion	c. ein Meeting abschließen
4.	draw up an agenda	d. eine Entscheidung umsetzen
5.	call off a meeting	e. abstimmen
6.	conclude a meeting	f. eine Tagesordnung erstellen

R Exercise 2

Complete the sentences using words from the box.

> take the minutes • conclude • agenda • approve • non-attendance •
> welcoming • chairing • miscellaneous • monopolise • any other business •
> chair / chairman / chairperson • circulated

When organising a meeting or conference it is first necessary to draw up an **1** .
This should be **2** well in advance so that all the participants are familiar with
it. It is also important for someone to be appointed to **3** . Usually it is necessary
to **4** the minutes of the previous meeting. **5** those present is usually the
first point on the agenda. Apologies from participants for **6** should also be
noted. An important part of the role of the person **7** the meeting is to make
sure that everyone has his/her say and no individual is allowed to **8** the
proceedings. The heading **9** or **10** is useful for discussing matters that
could not be discussed under the other headings. Finally, to **11** the meeting,
the **12** sums up the main results/decisions particularly if action is to be taken
by specific people.

Exercise 3

The XYZ bank is organising a conference in Germany on Thursday 16 and Friday 17 March for young bankers at the head office in Düsseldorf with participants from the offices in Düsseldorf, Frankfurt, London, Amsterdam, Stockholm, Riga, Prague, Bratislava and Milan. The conference language is English. Alexandra Schmalenbach has received the draft agenda for the conference in German and has been asked to produce an English version.

Take her role and write an English version of the agenda.

Tagesordnung

1. Tag

9:00 – 9:30	Begrüßung der Teilnehmer
9:30 – 11:00	Vortrag: Veränderung der Bankenlandschaft in der Bundesrepublik Deutschland *(Dr. Vanessa Gerlach, Frankfurt)*
Pause	
11:45 – 13:00	Diskussion und Workshop
13:00 – 14:00	Mittagessen
14:00 – 15:30	Vortrag: Realisierung eines einheitlichen Marktes im Bankensektor in der EU – unterschiedliche Bankenkultur und Traditionen *(Joachim Müller-Jena, Düsseldorf)*
Pause	
15:45 – 17:00	Diskussion und Workshop
18:30	Abendessen in einem Düsseldorfer Traditionslokal

2. Tag

9:00 – 10:30	Vortrag: Neue Investmentprodukte im Privatkundengeschäft der XYZ-Bank. *(Dr. Thomas Winckelmann, Frankfurt)*
Pause	
10:45 – 12:00	Diskussion und Workshop
12:00 – 13:00	Mittagessen
13:00 – 14:00	Neue Wege bei der Betreuung von Geschäftskunden *(Angelika Schmidt-Gerlach)*
14:00 – 15:00	Zusammenfassung der Ergebnisse und Verabschiedung der Teilnehmer

M/P Exercise 4

KMK Take the role of Alexandra Schmalenbach and write the text of an e-mail in English to the heads of personnel at the various offices covering the following points (for Claudia Meyer's approval – to be sent later):

- Einladung zur Konferenz
- Teilnehmer: maximal 2 junge Nachwuchsbanker pro Institut
- Bitte Teilnehmer möglichst umgehend anmelden
- Tagungsort: Konferenzräume in der Hauptverwaltung, 40245 Düsseldorf, Barabarossa Allee 27–29
- Unterkunft im 3-Sterne Hotel Grafen von Berg in Düsseldorf
- Ankunft am Abend vor der Konferenz möglichst vor 20:00 Uhr – sonst bitte Hotel informieren (Tel +49 211–5 92 73 82)
- Die Konferenz endet am Freitag, den 17. März um 15:30 Uhr
- Das Hotel bietet Teilnehmern, die das Wochenende in Dusseldorf verbringen möchten, eine Übernachtung am Freitag und am Samstag zu einem Sonderpreis an von insgesamt € 100,– einschließlich Frühstück.
- Sonderwünsche der Teilnehmer – etwa vegetarisches Essen – bitte angeben
- Anhang: Tagesordnung auf Englisch / Stadtplan mit Standort des Hotels

I Exercise 5 ☞ Phrases Unit 2
Roleplay the following conversation with a partner.

Student A **XYZ Investment Bank London**	**Student B** **XYZ Bank, Düsseldorf**
Nennen Sie Ihren Namen. Sie möchten Frau Alexandra Schmalenbach sprechen.	
	Nehmen Sie den Anruf entgegen. Frau Schmalenbach ist leider noch in Urlaub und kommt erst Ende nächster Woche wieder. Bieten Sie Ihre Hilfe an.
Es geht um die Konferenz im nächsten Monat. Ein Kollege, der leider verhindert ist, fragt an, ob Sie das Material in irgendeiner Form für ihn mit zurückbringen können. Sie fragen, ob das möglich wäre.	
	Das Material kann entweder als Ausdruck oder in digitaler Form zur Verfügung gestellt werden. Das dürfte kein Problem sein. Sie machen eine Notiz für Frau Schmalenbach. Sie werden sie bitten, das Material für den Kollegen zusammenzustellen. Sie bitten den Anrufer seinen Namen zu buchstabieren.
Sie buchstabieren Ihren Namen.	
	Sie bedanken sich.
Sie bedanken sich ganz herzlich und freuen sich auf Ihren Besuch in Düsseldorf.	
	Sie bedanken sich ebenfalls für den Anruf.

Exercise 6

As PA to Claudia Meyer it is part of Alexandra Schmalenbach's job to help organise the conference. This involves supervising the preparation of the room and making sure that there is an adequate supply of beverages and snacks available. Any equipment required such as a computer projector, whiteboard or flip chart with a supply of board markers must be available and in working order. Her boss may require files, additional information, or she may need to make telephone calls, etc. Alexandra must be on hand to provide any assistance necessary. Some of the German executives' English leaves much to be desired and so she may be asked to interpret or mediate.

Read the definitions of equipment and refreshments required at a meeting below and rearrange the following scrambled letters accordingly. Use the text above for help.

> c. feocef • plif rhcat • hiwet bdroa • ofst kdrnis • ramrek • rmenila rteaw • mtourcpe rporoejtc

Definitions:

1. The Germans call it "Beamer"
2. A pen that is used to highlight parts of a text
3. The most popular drink in Germany
4. Non-alcoholic drinks
5. A board that is the opposite of black
6. A drink with zero calories
7. A number of large sheets of paper attached to an upright frame

C Taking the minutes

It is important for an accurate written record of the transactions of a meeting or conference to be kept. It is essential for those involved to be able to refer back to the minutes and see what was said and, in particular, what was agreed. The minutes are evidence in law of the proceedings of the meeting.

5 The names of those present and any apologies for non-attendance must be recorded. In this case there are the German bankers from Düsseldorf and Frankfurt, the young

bankers from other EU offices, and the senior executives giving the lectures. Claudia Meyer acts as chairperson or chair, assisted by Alexandra Schmalenbach.

Especially in a discussion it is difficult to keep a word for word account of what is being said. The person taking the minutes may be able to note down only the most important points. It is particularly important that any figures or dates should be recorded accurately.

The minutes have to be presented to those present at a later date for approval or corrections.

Alexandra Schmalenbach has also been asked to take the minutes. As the topics on the agenda are presentations which will be available in written form, her minute-taking will be largely restricted to the questions and answers following the presentations.

M **Excrcise 1**

Summarise the above text on "Taking the minutes" in German covering the following points:

- importance of accurate and detailed minutes
- details of those present
- other important details
- approving the minutes of the previous meeting

R **Exercise 2**

A meeting was called to make the final arrangement for an important staff meeting. Your job was to take the minutes. Unfortunately, your notes got mixed up. Put the following points in the correct order.

1. Minutes of the last meeting were read and approved.
2. Final arrangements were agreed on.
3. Next staff meeting on May 7th 15:30 – 17:00.
4. Second, input on flexitime for this year's agenda – Mr. Brisle.
5. Absent: Ms. Mirren, Investments.; Mrs. Noles, Mortgages.
6. Participants: Mr. Kranch, Customer Services; Mr. Endrich, Personal Loans; Ms. McHalen, Corporate Business; Ms. Van Norton, Personnel.
7. First, report by Ms. Van Norton on training programs this year and changes in working hours / flexitime.
8. Duties assigned: Ms. Van Norton team leader; Ms. McHalen contact trade union representatives.

M/P **Exercise 3**

KMK **Your boss has asked you to write an e-mail in English to the participants of the last conference and to include the following points:**

- sich für die Teilnahme bedanken
- Tagung sehr erfolgreich / einige wichtige Entscheidungen getroffen
- Protokoll der Tagung beigefügt / Änderungswünsche oder Berichtigungen bitte umgehend per E-Mail zusenden
- Einladung zur nächsten Tagung / Vorschläge für die Tagesordnung erbeten / Teilnahme bitte auf beigefügtem Formular bis 15. Februar bestätigen

D Negotiations

I **Exercise 1**

Discuss the following with a partner and present the results to the class:

1. Where do you have to negotiate in your private life or in your job?
2. What skills and qualities does a good negotiator need?

R **Exercise 2**

Match the words on the left (1.–12.) with the explanations on the right (a.–l.).

1. benchmarking	a. be different
2. bottom line	b. negotiating position
3. bargaining position	c. something you give up to get something in return
4. scope	d. way you view something
5. concede	e. person you are negotiating with
6. empathise	f. changing your position in order to achieve an agreement
7. infringe	g. measuring things according to a defined standard
8. opposite number	h. to give way on a point
9. perception	i. not to respect
10. trade off	j. freedom of action
11. differ	k. understand the other person's feelings and thinking
12. compromise	l. minimum you want to achieve

`I/R` **Exercise 3**
Now read through the following tips and discuss the questions below with a partner. Present your answers to the class.

Negotiations: Dos and don'ts

1. You should make thorough preparations and go through different scenarios ("What do I do/say if …?")
2. Expect the unexpected. Have all the relevant information at your fingertips.
3. Benchmarking – i. e. knowing the strengths and weaknesses of your competitors' products or services – is also important.
4. Work out your strategy beforehand. Have a fall-back position or bottom line that you are not prepared to go beyond.
5. Do not define your bargaining position at the beginning of the negotiations as this reduces your scope for flexibility. However, avoid conceding too much too quickly.
6. Empathise with the other side. Try and find out what he/she expects/wants/needs. Listen carefully to what he/she says. Where possible create a feeling that you are partners rather than opponents.
7. However, avoid direct questions that might seem impertinent or infringe privacy. There are cultural differences regarding what is perceived as the private sphere.
8. Do not underestimate your opposite number/client/customer. He/She will most probably have also done his homework.
9. Watch out for possible compromises or trade-offs – i. e conceding something in order to get something important in return.
10. Finalise the agreement. Summarize verbally or follow up with a written summary. Make sure everyone involved has the same perspective on what has been agreed (it is often surprising how much perceptions of the same situation can differ).

Questions:
1. What should you do when preparing for negotiations?
2. Why is it important to define a bottom line for yourself?
3. Which of the above points refer to the flexibility of the negotiator?
4. What does empathy involve?
5. Why should you be careful when asking direct questions?
6. Why is it a good idea to have a written summary of what was agreed.
7. Why is it important to be familiar with the strengths and weaknesses of your competitors' products?
8. Why is it often necessary to compromise or make concessions?

KMK **Sie sind Angestellte(r) der Schuster Privatbank in Nürnberg. Die Bank hat eine**
◎ 14 **Niederlassung in Cork, Irland. Der Geschäftsführer Ihrer Bank bittet Sie, als**
Protokollführer/in bei einem Geschäftstreffen in Nürnberg teilzunehmen und
die wichtigsten Punkte schriftlich festzuhalten. Hören Sie gut zu und machen Sie
sich Notizen, indem Sie das Formular auf Deutsch ausfüllen bzw. Zutreffendes
ankreuzen. Sie hören das Gespräch zweimal.

CD 06

Kurzprotokoll

Datum:

Teilnehmer: Hr. Pfeiffer (Geschäftsführer)
Mr John Smith ( )
Ms Kelly Taylor ( )
(jeweilige Funktion im Unternehmen)

letztes Gespräch/ Datum: _____

Hauptthema: _____

Erste Produktgruppe: _____
gestiegen um _____%
gefallen um _____%
gleich geblieben ☐ ja ☐ nein

Zweite Produktgruppe: _____
gestiegen um _____%
gefallen um _____%
gleich geblieben ☐ ja ☐ nein

Inhalt des heutigen Gesprächs:
Tagesordnungspunkt 1:_____

Tagesordnungspunkt 2:
betrifft Verbesserungen im folgenden Verkaufsgebiet:
_____

1. Verbesserungsvorschlag:
☐ die Werbeausgaben beträchtlich erhöhen
☐ die Werbung speziell auf dieses Gebiet anpassen
☐ die Vorteile des Versandhandels herausstellen

2. Ergänzung durch Herrn Pfeiffer und Kelly Taylor
Verkaufsbereich
☐ die Verkaufsmitarbeiter besser schulen
☐ die Verkaufsniederlassungen vor Ort ausbauen
☐ den Verkaufsmitarbeitern umfassende Kundeninformationen bieten
☐ telefonische Kontakte ausbauen
Kundendienst
Zusätzliche Mitarbeiter im Bereich einstellen, weil ...
_____
_____

Aufgabenverteilung:
Kelly stellt Kundendaten zusammen bis: _____ (Datum)
Termin des nächsten Treffens: _____ (Datum)

2 Tage vor _____ (Anlass)

Unterschrift _____
(Protokollführer/-in)

Communicating across cultures: Cross-cultural negotiations

Negotiating, like any other form of communication, is profoundly influenced by culture. It is culture that dictates what is felt to be appropriate behaviour.

Successful negotiating in a cross-cultural context involves looking at all the factors that may influence the outcome. Does eye contact convey confidence and sincerity or is it considered impolite or obtrusive? Is it essential to establish a friendly and trusting relationship before the negotiation or are negotiations seen as being purely functional? How much small talk is expected (probably more in the UK than Germany) and what topics are appropriate? 5

The physical distance between two speakers instinctively felt to be right also varies from culture to culture, as does the amount of "touching". In Germany or Britain this would be restricted to a handshake during introductions. Giving your opposite number a hearty slap on the back or a hug probably wouldn't go down too well. 10

How should people be addressed? In English-speaking countries first names are generally used. When introducing yourself it is important to give both first name and surname. Academic titles are not used in business contexts. 15

Regarding the level of language, research shows that British speakers prefer less direct strategies to express disagreement or reluctance than their German counterparts , who tend to go for greater directness. Thus, "I agree with you up to a point, but …" may signal quite definite disagreement, while "Do you really think so?" may mean "That cannot possibly be true" and "I'm not entirely happy about this proposal" may indicate rejection. The danger is that a German speaker, who is used to greater directness, may underestimate the communicative force of these expressions. 20

Finally, punctuality is also an important intercultural issue. In some cultures (southern Europe, South America) being on time in a business context is not considered quite so essential as in Germany, the UK and the US, for example. As very few people are really familiar with a culture other than their own, it is absolutely essential to adopt an investigative approach, i.e to observe the other's behaviour carefully without passing value judgments. 25 30

KMK Use the phrases at the end of the unit to roleplay the following dialogue in English with a partner.

Situation: eine mittelständische Firma (medium-sized company) möchte expandieren und braucht eine Kreditlinie (credit line) von der Bank.

Bankberater Joachim Paulsen	Vertreter der Firma

Bankberater Joachim Paulsen

Guten Tag, meine Herren. Was kann ich für Sie tun?

Vertreter der Firma

Guten Tag, Herr Paulsen. Wir möchten unsere Expansionspläne mit Ihnen besprechen.

Sehr gut. Könnten Sie das bitte etwas näher erläutern?

Was wir erreichen möchten, ist eine Erhöhung unserer Kapazität um 10 %.

Ist das eine gute Idee? Die wirtschaftlichen Aussichten sind zur Zeit nicht sehr positiv und …

Darf ich Sie unterbrechen? Unsere Auftragsbücher (order books) sind voll.

Dennoch ist es riskant, im Moment zu investieren.

Ja. Wir stimmen Ihnen bis zu einem gewissen Grad zu, aber unsere Situation ist vollkommen anders. Wir haben langfristige Verträge (long-term contracts) mit unseren Kunden.

Wenn ich Sie richtig verstanden habe, wollen Sie einen Kredit aufnehmen, um Ihre Expansion zu finanzieren.

Ja. Was wir eigentlich sagen wollen, ist, dass wir investieren müssen, um unsere vertraglichen Verpflichtungen zu erfüllen (meet contractual obligations).

An welchen Betrag denken Sie?

Wir möchten € 5.000.000 leihen.

Wie sieht es aus mit Sicherheiten (collateral) und einer Versicherung zur Abdeckung (coverage) des Kreditrisikos?

Wir können entsprechende Sicherheiten bieten. Eine Versicherung würde die Kosten des Darlehens beträchtlich erhöhen.

Gut, da stimme ich Ihnen zu. Allerdings kann ich das selbst nicht entscheiden. Ich werde Ihnen aber innerhalb der nächsten Tage Bescheid geben.

OK. Vielen Dank. Wir freuen uns, von Ihnen zu hören.

Vielen Dank für Ihren Besuch.

Phrases: Meetings and negotiations

To book flights or trains

Please reserve a window/aisle seat on the 8.30 am flight to Munich.	Bitte reservieren Sie einen Platz am Fenster/Gang für den Flug um 8:30 Uhr nach München.
Are you travelling economy or business class?	Fliegen Sie Economy- oder Business-Class?
I'd like to reserve a window seat in an open-plan coach on the 9.15 ICE train to Hamburg.	Ich möchte einen Fensterplatz in einem Großraumwagen des ICE um 9:15 Uhr nach Hamburg reservieren lassen.
Is that first or second class, one way or return?	Erster oder zweiter Klasse? Einfach oder hin und zurück?
Is there a supplementary charge for the InterCity to Edinburgh?	Muss für den Intercity nach Edinburgh ein Zuschlag bezahlt werden?
There is no supplementary charge.	Es wird kein Zuschlag erhoben.
You are booked on flight no ZY 652 on 23 March, departing London Gatwick at 7.30 am, arriving Munich 10.15 am.	Sie sind am 23. März für Flug Nr. ZY 652 gebucht, Abflug London Gatwick um 7:30 Uhr, Ankunft München 10:15 Uhr.
You should check in two hours before departure to allow for the security check.	Sie sollten wegen der Sicherheitsüberprüfung zwei Stunden vor Abflug einchecken.

To book hotel or conference rooms

We require a single/double room with ensuite bathroom.	Wir benötigen ein Einzel-/Doppelzimmer mit Bad.
I'd like to book an executive suite with Internet access for three nights from 3 to 6 March.	Ich möchte eine Präsidentensuite mit Internetzugang für drei Nächte vom 3. bis 6. März buchen.
We require a conference room to seat 25–30 people.	Wir brauchen ein Besprechungszimmer für 25–30 Personen.
We would be grateful if you could confirm the booking in writing/by e-mail/by fax.	Wir wären für eine Bestätigung der Buchung per Brief/E-Mail/Fax dankbar.
Is it possible to order a buffet lunch?	Besteht die Möglichkeit ein Lunch-Buffet zu bestellen?
We regret that we have to cancel the reservation. We realise that it is very short notice.	Wir bedauern, diese Reservierung stornieren zu müssen. Wir sind uns dessen bewusst, dass dies sehr kurzfristig geschieht.
For our recruitment interviews we require a reception room with Internet access and a computer projector.	Für unsere Einstellungsgespräche benötigen wir einen Empfangsraum mit Internetzugang und Beamer.

To make appointments

I'm afraid I'm busy all day on Wednesday.	Leider bin ich am Mittwoch den ganzen Tag beschäftigt.
Friday would suit me fine.	Freitag würde mir gut passen.
I'd prefer Thursday morning.	Donnerstagmorgen wäre mir lieber.
It's Monday at 11, then.	Also bleibt es bei Montag um 11:00 Uhr.
Could we meet on Monday 17 at 10 am?	Könnten wir uns am Montag, den 17. um 10:00 Uhr vormittags treffen?
– Certainly. Monday at 10 am is fine.	– Ja, sicher. Montag 10:00 Uhr ist o.k.
Would Tuesday suit you?	Würde Ihnen Dienstag passen?
– It's not so good. My diary's full, I'm afraid. Wednesday would be better.	– Eigentlich nicht. Mein Terminkalender ist leider voll. Mittwoch wäre besser.
I'm free all day Wednesday.	Am Mittwoch geht es den ganzen Tag.

To prepare the agenda

A draft agenda has already been drawn up.	Ein Entwurf für die Tagesordnung ist bereits erstellt worden.
Notification of any additions or changes is requested within a week.	Es wird gebeten, eventuelle Zusätze oder Änderungen innerhalb einer Woche anzugeben.

To prepare and assist at a meeting

He/She is chairing the meeting.	Er/Sie leitet die Sitzung.
He is the chairman. He/She is the chairperson.	Er ist der Vorsitzende. Er/Sie ist der/die Vorsitzende.
The following are unable to take part:	Folgende Personen sind verhindert:
Perhaps you could each introduce yourself briefly indicating your role in the company.	Vielleicht könnten Sie sich kurz vorstellen und dabei auf Ihre Stellung in der Firma eingehen.
Has everyone got a copy of the agenda?	Haben alle eine Kopie der Tagesordnung bekommen?
We'll be adjourning for lunch at …	Um … unterbrechen wir für das Mittagessen.
Lunch will be provided by our own caterers.	Unser eigener Versorgungsbetrieb wird das Mittagessen liefern.
Are there any further comments?	Gibt es noch Wortmeldungen?
Shall we take a vote?	Sollen wir nun abstimmen?
The proposal is accepted.	Damit ist der Vorschlag angenommen.

To state your position and make suggestions

What we're looking for is …	Was wir erreichen möchten, ist …
How about …	Wie wäre es, wenn …
Don't you think we should …?	Meinen Sie nicht, dass wir … sollten?

To ask for more information

Could you give me more details, please?	Könnten Sie mir bitte mehr Einzelheiten geben?
Could you explain this in a little more detail?	Könnten Sie das bitte näher erläutern?

To interrupt

Sorry to interrupt you, but …	Darf ich Sie unterbrechen?
I'm afraid I've got to stop you there, because …	An dieser Stelle muss ich Sie leider unterbrechen, weil …

To ask for clarification

What is the reason for that?	Was ist der Grund dafür?
What do you have in mind?	Woran denken Sie?
What do you mean when you say …?	Was meinen Sie, wenn Sie sagen, …?

To rephrase a point

What I'm trying to say is …	Was ich eigentlich sagen will, ist …
Let me put it another way.	Lassen Sie mich es anders formulieren.

To ask for a reaction

What do you think about this?	Was halten Sie davon?
How do you feel about …?	Was halten Sie von …?

To correct misunderstandings

No, I'm sorry. That's not what I said.	Nein, es tut mir Leid. Das habe ich nicht gesagt.
I'm afraid you've misunderstood me.	Sie haben mich leider missverstanden.

To express partial agreement / disagreement

I take your point, but …	Da gebe ich Ihnen Recht, aber …
I agree in principle, but …	Ich stimme prinzipiell zu, aber …

To disagree / to reject a proposal

Do you really think so?	Glauben Sie das wirklich?
I'm afraid I can't go along with it.	Da kann ich leider nicht zustimmen.

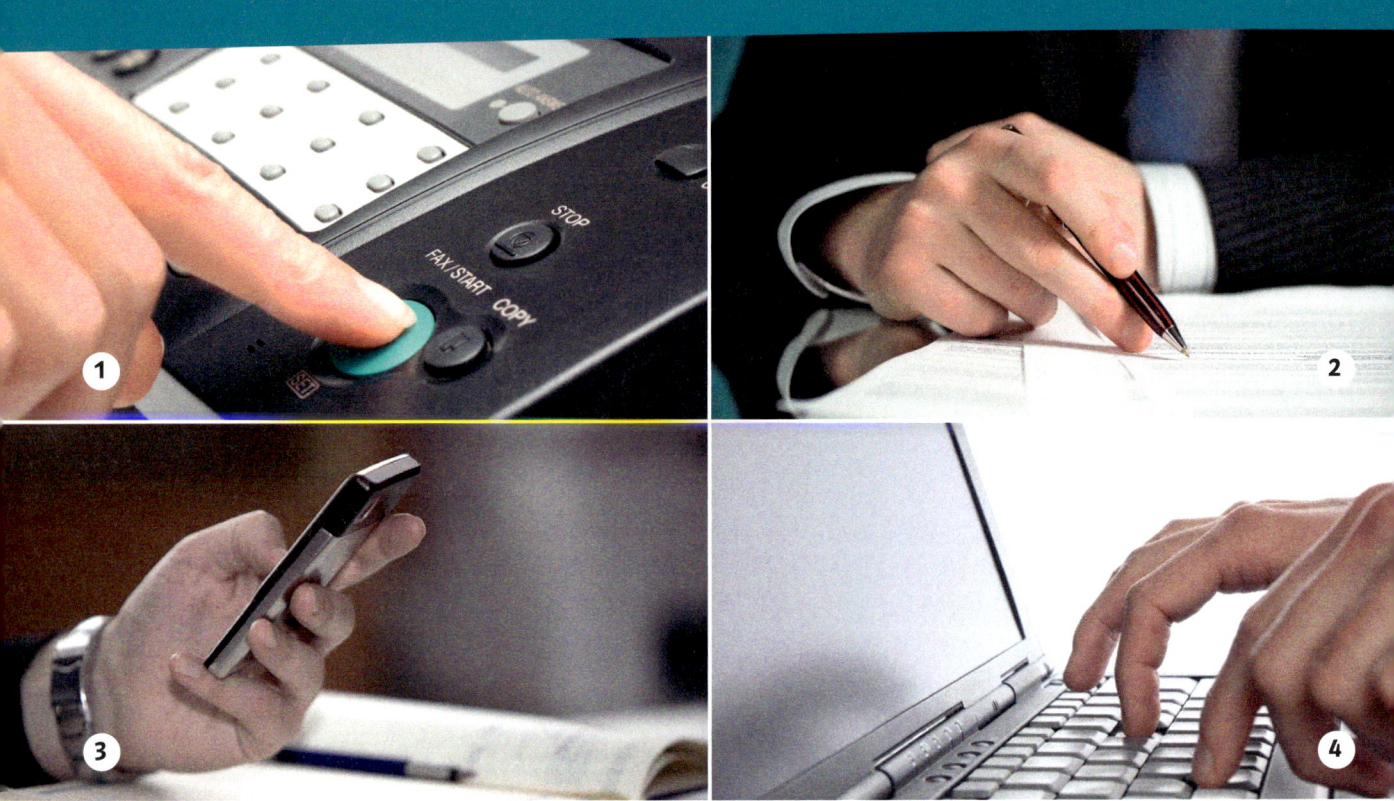

Unit 5
Business correspondence

Although the development of the Internet has created new means for communicating much more quickly and conveniently, such as e-mail, instant messaging and text messaging, letters and even faxes are in fact still widely used in many business contexts. A carefully written letter gives the recipient the impression that a certain
5 amount of effort went into writing it. This makes it more meaningful than an e-mail message. A letter can be more efficient than a phone call or an e-mail, because complicated and detailed information can be communicated in an effective and clearly structured form. Letters also have a more lasting effect, especially because, due to the pace of today's workplace, people tend to quickly forget the content of
10 voice-mail and e-mail messages.

However, faxes and e-mails do save a lot of time and money, as you can type your message on your PC and send it or fax it directly to the recipient without having to print it out, put it into an envelope and post it. The addressee in turn has the information immediately and can react more quickly, if they wish. Another advantage
15 of the fax is that it is usually less formal, which does not mean that it is less polite or friendly. A fax quite often looks like a memo and is sent with the company letterhead. Apart from that it also includes the date, the subject and the addressee. It also states how many pages are to be transmitted with a request to contact the sender if the specified number of pages sent have not been received.

20 The e-mail, which has become the most rapidly growing means of communication, is very economical and can be less formal than a letter. With respect to formality, some people seem to be under the illusion that they can write anything they want in an e-mail. But in the professional world this is not the case. An e-mail is not an "anything goes" chat line with a loose sentence structure, fragmented thoughts and incorrect

25 usage of grammar. Since e-mails are an important vehicle for communicating in business, their messages should be clearly written, tightly crafted, with the most important information contained in the first paragraph. Reference should also be made as to details from previous messages. Remember that every e-mail message has your name on it, so read it through carefully before hitting the "send" button.

P Exercise 1

Look at the pictures on page 70 and decide which means of communication you use most often at your place of work and why. Give examples of business situations for each of the types of communication shown.

R Exercise 2

Read the introductory text and decide whether the following statements are true or false.

1. Letters and faxes have become much less important in business communication.
2. Faxes and e-mails are much more cost effective and reach the addressee immediately.
3. A fax is less formal and polite than a letter or memo.
4. The e-mail is the most economic way of communicating.
5. E-mails should be written in a very personal and informal style.
6. When answering an e-mail, make sure to reread it before sending it off.

R Exercise 3

Complete the mindmap below (on a separate sheet of paper) with the information given in the box.

quick response • significant message • specific letter • invitation • new product • requesting info • providing info • announcing new policy • new programme • meeting • routine info • company news • introducing yourself • new location • customer service • complaint

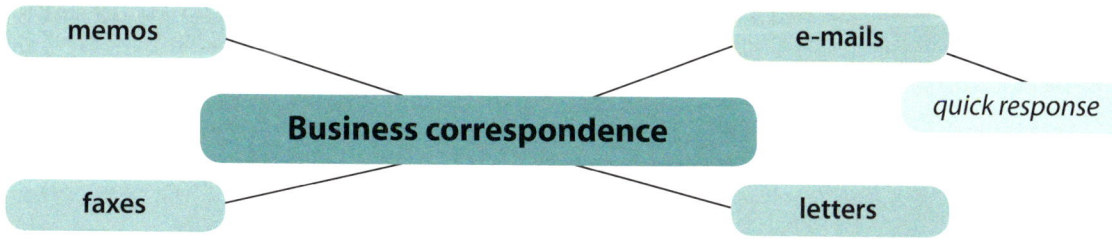

memos

e-mails

Business correspondence

quick response

faxes

letters

I Exercise 4

Work with a partner and discuss the advantages and disadvantages of the different types of written communication.

A Business letters

No matter how popular e-mails have become as a form of business correspondence, letter writing has kept its foremost position when it comes to communicating official and formal information between companies and between a company and its clients. With respect to style and layout, business letters, whether they are sent from one

5 company to another or to clients, are always written in a polite and friendly but formal style. Of course this applies to any form of first contact between a company and its business partners or clients, even by e-mail.

Once business partners or clients have had a lot of contact and have got to know and like each other, subsequent correspondence can then become less formal in style. In

10 fact, this kind of correspondence is usually sent by e-mail rather than 'snail-mail'. In terms of form and style, business letters have changed over the years and become a lot less formal, but they still include some very basic standard sections and phrases, as shown in the following table.

American business letter format	British business letter format
A Return address, sender's address, company letterhead	**A Return address, sender's address, company letterhead**
B Date September 10, 20_ (month – day – year) The month is given in letters, usually in full. However, it is fairly common to just write the first three letters of the month. There is always a comma between day and year. The year is always written out in full.	**B Date** 10 September 20_ (day – month – year) The month is given in letters, usually in full. However, it is fairly common to just write the first three letters of the month. The year is always written out in full.
C Return address, addressee Mr. Jack Finch Human Resources Savvy Corporation 805 Gladney Drive Monroe, LA 71236 U.S.A. Note that punctuation is still commonly used: Mr. (U.S.A.) Ms. is used when you do not know the marital status of a woman.	**C Return address, addressee** Mr Jack Finch Human Resources Excel Ltd 769 Highland Road Staines Middlesex TW18 3UP UK Use UK for Scotland, England, Wales and Northern Ireland if you are not sure where the city is. Ms is used when you do not know the marital status of a woman.
D Salutation Dear Mr. Finch, Dear Ms. Finch, Dear Dr. Finch, Dear Prof. Finch, Gentlemen: Dear Sir or Madam,	**D Salutation** Dear Mr Finch Dear Ms Finch Dear Dr. Finch Dear Prof. Finch Dear Sirs Dear Sir or Madam

Note that in US usage a colon is often used instead of the comma.

Open punctuation is not yet commonly used in the US. Closed punctuation is the norm.

Never combine titles such as Dr. or Prof. with Mr. and / or Ms – e.g. ~~Mr. Dr. Finch~~.

Note that in British usage open punctuation is commonly used.

Never combine titles such as Dr or Prof with Mr and / or Ms – e.g. ~~Mr Dr Finch~~.

E Subject line
In the USA the subject line is written above the salutation, just like in a German business letter. The subject line is usually written in bold letters.

E Subject line
In the UK the subject line is written between the salutation and the beginning of the letter. The subject line is usually written in bold letters.

F Body of the letter
There are usually three parts to a letter:
- the introductory line / sentence
- the body or main part of the letter
- the closing line / sentence

Note that the first word of the body of the letter is always capitalised!

F Body of the letter
There are usually three parts to a letter:
- the introductory line / sentence
- the body or main part of the letter
- the closing line / sentence

Note that the first word of the body of the letter is always capitalised!

G Complimentary close
The salutation and complimentary close should be in line with each other, meaning that if you write to someone whose name you don't know (e.g. Dear Sirs / Sir or Madam) you should close your letter with Sincerely yours. If you write to someone whose name you know you may close with Sincerely or Yours truly.

If you end your salutation with a comma or colon, you will have to put a comma after your complimentary close! This is called closed punctuation. Nearly everyone uses open punctuation these days, meaning that there is no punctuation at the end of the salutation or of the complimentary close.

G Complimentary close
The salutation and complimentary close should be in line with each other, meaning that if you write to someone whose name you don't know (e.g. Dear Sirs / Sir or Madam) you should close your letter with Sincerely yours. If you write to someone whose name you know you may close with Sincerely or Yours truly.

If you end your salutation with a comma or colon, you will have to put a comma after your complimentary close! This is called closed punctuation. Nearly everyone uses open punctuation these days, meaning that there is no punctuation at the end of the salutation or of the complimentary close.

H Signature block
This includes your signature (first and last name) and the job title and / or the department.

H Signature block
This includes your signature (given name and family name) and the job title and / or the department.

I Enclosures
Include this section if you have enclosed something with the letter. You may write "Enclosure(s)" or "Enc(s)".

I Enclosures
Include this section if you have enclosed something with the letter. You may write "Enclosure(s)" or "Enc(s)".

Exercise 1

Study the following letter and match the numbers in the letter with the words in the box.

> body • complimentary close • company address • date • enclosure • closing line • fax number • job title • website • introductory sentence • postcode • addressee's name • recipient's address • subject line • salutation • signature block • telephone number

---

THE COOPERATIVE BANK `1`

Freepost MR9473
Manchester
M4 8BA `2`
Phone: 0845 068 6727 `3`
Fax: 0845 068 6729 `4`

10 October 20_ `5`

Mr Douglas George `6`
13 Hammond Lane
Cardiff Cf1 2JW `7`

Dear Mr George `8`

Account No. 05668530242 `9`

I am sorry to inform you that you now have an overdraft of £168.93 on your current account. `10`

I allowed your last credit transfer to Homeowners Ltd to pass as you have a large credit balance on your deposit account. But I would like to point out that we cannot allow an overdraft facility unless you make a formal arrangement with the bank. If you would like to do this, please fill out the enclosed application form and return it to our main office by post. `11`

Thank you. We look forward to hearing from you soon. `12`

Yours sincerely `13`

Mike Jarrett `14`

Assistant Manager `15`

Enc.: Application form `16`

WWW.CO-OPCustomer.Services.COOPBANK:UK `17`

P Exercise 2

This is a letter from an engineering company enquiring about a staff pension scheme. Put the fragments in the right order and write out the letter.

a Please contact me if you have anything else you would like to discuss.

b The enclosed booklet, PS 134, will give you details of the type of policy I think would suit you. The minimum age for joining would be 18, with a retirement plan at 55 for woman und 60 for men.

c Thank you for writing us.

d I am replying to your letter of 15 September concerning a staff pension scheme for your employees.

e Human Resources Department
Global Engineering PLC
Sanei House
Sanei Street
Liverpool L2 2ET

f I can arrange for an agent to call on you at any time. He will be contacting you in a few days after you have had time to consider this proposal.

g Employee contributions could be arranged, and the policy includes life insurance and benefit payment in the event of death.

h Dear Mr Stewart

i Yours sincerely
Ralph Waters
Policies Manager
Encl.

j 10 September 20_

k Associated Pension Insurance
158 Creston Street
Liverpool L2 3EB1

P Exercise 3

Rewrite the following sentences so that they sound more polite.

1. We want a loan.
2. Send us your field force agent.
3. We want an overdraft.
4. We don't want our car insurance with your company any more.
5. Confirm the loan agreement.
6. You can't get an overdraft.

P Exercise 4

Your boss has asked you to make the necessary changes to the following sentences so that they sound much more formal and business-like. Rewrite the sentences using a polite form.

(…) Thanks for sending us 550 € the other week, but don't forget you still owe us 2.000 €, which we want you to pay before end of April. If you're having problems finding the money, why don't you give us a call? We could arrange a different way for you to pay us. (…)

Communicating across cultures: The tone of English business correspondence

What is considered polite differs in different cultures. For example, one-word answers such as "ja", "nein" are not impolite in German. If I say: "Sollen wir ins Kino gehen?", you could answer "Ja" in German. In English people would be more inclined to say "Yes, that would be nice / great". Thus, German business correspondence tends to be factual and to the point. Polite phrases are often considered superfluous. While this abrupt tone is generally accepted in Germany, it may seem rude to English-speaking people or sound as though you are not interested. That is why you ought to aim to make frequent use of expressions like: **We would like to** (inform you); **I would be grateful** (if you could help me), **I am afraid** (the system is not running smoothly); **We are very sorry** (to inform you); **Would you be so kind as** (to inform us in time) in your English correspondence. Do not forget to insert the word **please** whenever you make a request, e.g.: If we can be of further assistance **please** do not hesitate to contact us.

Note: Please do not say: ~~We kindly ask you~~ …, say **We would like to ask you** … instead.

R Exercise 5

⊚ 15 Listen to the dialogue between the loan advisor, John Files, and a customer, Jason Gray, and complete the sentences with the appropriate information.

1. Mr Gray wants to **1** his business.
2. In order to do so Mr Gray is asking the bank to **2** .
3. Mr Files cannot **3** but he might be able to arrange for a **4** .
4. Mr Gray needs **5** to buy those **6** .
5. He thinks he can repay the loan within **7** .
6. The **8** is the only security he can offer.
7. Mr Files has to consult with **9** first and will let Mr Gray know their decision **10** .

P Exercise 6

The head of your bank's loans department has told you that your client's loan would have to be covered by securities such as shares or bonds.
Write a letter to Mr Gray explaining that under the circumstances the credit has been refused, but advise him to try other sources, e.g. finance houses.

P Exercise 7

KMK Sie wurden gebeten die Anfrage eines englischsprachigen Kunden zu beantworten. Nehmen Sie dazu die folgenden Stichpunkte in Ihr Schreiben auf.

- Heutiges Datum, Anrede (Mr Fosh), Betreff (Erhöhung des Dispositionskredits)
- Bezugnahme auf ein Telefonat von gestern, in dem der Kunde um eine Erhöhung seines Dispositionskredits bat.
- Bitte um Erhöhung des Dispositionskredits von €3.000,00 auf €5.000,00 zum Zwecke eines Küchenkaufs gewähren.
- Hinweis geben, dass die Erhöhung nur kurzfristig ist.
- Rückzahlung innerhalb eines 12 Monatszeitraums anbieten und den Brief mit einem sinnvollen Schlusssatz beenden.

P/M Exercise 8

KMK Sie arbeiten bei einem großen Versicherungsunternehmen, der Herzog Versicherungs AG Karlsruhe. Ihr Vorgesetzter bittet Sie, einen Kurzbrief mit nachfolgendem Inhalt an einen englischsprachigen Kunden (Henry Smith) zu schicken.

- Betreff: Antrag für Gebäude- und Hausratversicherung
- Hinweis auf beigefügten Versicherungsantrag
- Bitte um umgehendes Ausfüllen des Vertrags, da der Hauskauf schon erfolgt ist
- Sofortige Rücksendung erwünscht, da ein Angebot frühestens innerhalb von drei Tagen nach Eingang Ihres Antrags möglich ist
- Bei Fragen telefonische Kontaktaufnahme

Herzog Versicherungs AG
Karlsruhe

Postfach 27034
76133 Karlsruhe
Tel. 0721 / 245 4323
http://www.Herzog-Versicherung.de

Kurzbrief

An: Henry Smith
        Karlstr. 116
        76130 Karlsruhe
        …

B E-Mails

E-mails are becoming the most common used form of business communication. They are easy to write, easy to send, even with a lot of data attached, can be sent to several people at the same time, are much cheaper than any other form of communication and, last but not least, they are time-zone friendly. You never have to worry about office hours. There are a few drawbacks which have to be mentioned: spam, worms, Trojans and viruses. That's where firewalls, filters, and a certain amount of caution in dealing with e-mails are called for.

M **Exercise 1**

One of your colleagues does not speak English very well. Explain the following instructions to him in German.

1. Think before using the Cc function to send a message to a group of people who don't know each other.
2. When replying to a message, don't start a new mail. Just reply leaving the original messages attached like a thread.
3. Keep your messages shorter than a page, so readers don't have to scroll. People don't like reading long messages.
4. If you want to communicate detailed and complicated information, send a letter or make a phone call.
5. Don't use exclamation marks or emoticons when writing a business e-mail.
6. Use punctuation in the same way as you would in a formal business letter.
7. Don't send personal e-mails from the office, because it is regarded as official company communication and systems administrators can usually read all mails.
8. Summarise the contents of your e-mail message in the subject line. Be as specific as possible.
9. Check your spelling and reread your message before sending it off.
10. Use capitalisation and address people the same way as you would in a business letter.

P **Exercise 2**

Which of the statements do you agree with? Give reasons.

Language and grammar: Typical mistakes in business correspondence
A few English verbs account for a large percentage of the mistakes Germans make when writing business correspondence in English:

apologize (sich entschuldigen)
We **apologize for** the delay.   wrong: ~~We excuse us for the delay.~~

excuse (verzeihen, entschuldigen)
Please **excuse** the delay.   wrong: ~~Please apologize the delay.~~

appreciate (schätzen, begrüßen, dankbar sein, anerkennen)
(a) We would appreciate **it** if you could assist us. (**"it"** is absolutely necessary here!)
(b) We would appreciate **receiving** the unit as soon as possible.
wrong: ~~We would appreciate to receive the unit as soon as possible.~~

P/R **Exercise 3**

Use the less formal phrases and short forms listed below (1.–10.) to replace the underlined phrases in the following two e-mails.

1. Feel free
2. See you tomorrow
3. Could Sally
4. Don't forget
5. I'm sorry to tell you
6. I can't make
7. Rgds
8. I have to
9. Can you
10. Re

From: Amy.Wheeler@goldmanbank.de
To: Asset Management Department
Cc:
Date: 20.01.2009   8:35
Subject: Monthly meeting 21.01.2009

Dear all,

<u>I would like to remind you</u> that we have a team meeting tomorrow afternoon at 14:00, as I told some of you yesterday. I've reserved the conference room on the third floor. You should receive the latest figures from Douglas this morning. <u>Don't hesitate to</u> request any additional information you require.

<u>I look forward to seeing you tomorrow.</u>

<u>Regards,</u>
Amy

Dear Amy,

<u>With reference to</u> your mail, <u>I regret to inform you</u> that <u>I will not be able to attend</u> the meeting tomorrow afternoon, as <u>it is necessary for me</u> to travel to our head office that day. <u>I would be grateful if you would</u> give us more notice in future, and inform us about meetings a few days in advance.

<u>I wonder if Sally could</u> attend the meeting instead?

Regards,
Joe

Match these abbreviations and symbols (1.–10.), which are widely used in e-mails and web addresses, with the words and phrases (a.–j.).

1.	:	a.	as soon as possible
2.	ABC	b.	back slash
3.	–	c.	frequently asked questions
4.	pls	d.	underscore
5.	asap	e.	colon
6.	/	f.	capitol letters
7.	THX	g.	minus
8.	_	h.	Thanks
9.	FAQ	i.	slash
10.	\	j.	please

R Exercise 5

Complete the following e-mail with words and expressions from the box.

> enquired • in order to • feel free to • would like • thank you very much • attached • reply

From:	sarah.winter@firstmercentilebank.com
To:	Tony.Slater@slatters.de
Date:	2009.14.08 10:15
Attachments:	Pensionscheme.pdf
Subject:	Enquiry about pension schemes

Dear Mr. Slater,

__1__ for your e-mail in which you __2__ about our private pension schemes. __3__ give you a brief overview of our services and products I have __4__ our brochure as a pdf-file.

Please __5__ call me anytime during our business hours if you should have any questions or if you __6__ to make an appointment. Of course you can also __7__ by e-mail.

Sincerely yours,

Sarah Winter
Financial consultant

P Exercise 6

**These are typical phrases from business correspondence but the words
are in the wrong order. Rewrite them correctly, adding capital letters and
punctuation where needed.**

1. if get back any problems to me filling out there are the application form
2. Monday next I forward you seeing in my to look office
3. forgot to sorry the attach I the proposal form
4. I'm claims report attachment sending the as an
5. requested make necessary policy as we in will your the changes
6. anything else you me there if know can I let for is do
7. thanks your in many for matter this help
8. would confirm tomorrow like to appointment at 10 pm I our

P Exercise 7

**Work with a partner to practise writing and exchanging e-mails. You may
change and add information to make your e-mail realistic. Use the situations
suggested below.**

Situation 1:

You have to make a presentation and you need help, e.g background
information, annual figures on …

Situation 2:

You have to complete a proposal, but you haven't got all the information
you need. You know that your colleague has the information. Ask him/her
for help.

Situation 3:

A colleague has sent you an e-mail asking for your help and advice in
dealing with a customer's account balance.

P Exercise 8

KMK **Sie arbeiten in einem international ausgerichteten Unternehmen und
erhalten den Auftrag, Ihre internationalen Kunden zu einer Informationsveranstaltung einzuladen. Bitte verwenden Sie hierfür den unten
vorgegebenen Inhalt.**

- Laden Sie den Kunden ein, an der Informationsveranstaltung über
  Vermögensberatung am 23.03. teilzunehmen.
- Verweisen Sie auf die ausführlichen Tagungsunterlagen im Anhang.
- Erklären Sie, dass das Tagungshotel im Zentrum von Düsseldorf liegt und
  mit öffentlichen Verkehrsmitteln erreicht werden kann, jedoch stehen
  auch beim Hotel Parkplätze zur Verfügung.
- Drücken Sie Freude aus über mögliche Zusage des Kunden.
- Finden Sie einen passenden Schlusssatz.

Phrases: Business correspondence – letter, e-mail

To refer to previous communication

Many thanks for your …	Vielen Dank für Ihr …
We thank you for your …	Wir bedanken uns für …
Referring to …	Bezugnehmend auf …
We refer to …	Wir beziehen uns auf …
Further to our discussion/phone call on …	Im Anschluss an unser Gespräch/Telefonat vom …

To apologise

We are very sorry to learn that …	Wir bedauern erfahren zu müssen, dass …
We regret the fact that …	Wir bedauern die Tatsache, dass …
We are very sorry, but …	Es tut uns sehr Leid, aber …
This was an error on our part.	Der Fehler liegt bei uns.
Please accept our apologies.	Wir bitten Sie, dies zu entschuldigen.

To ask for something

We would like to ask you to …	Wir möchten Sie bitten …
Would you please send us …	Bitte schicken Sie uns …
We must/would like to point out that …	Wir möchten darauf hinweisen, dass …
We would therefore be grateful if …	Wir würden uns freuen, wenn …
We would appreciate it, if you could/would …	Wir würden es begrüßen, wenn Sie … könnten/würden.
Please let us have (full/complete) details of …	Wir bitten Sie, uns die vollständigen Einzelheiten … zukommen zu lassen.
Please make sure that …	Bitte sorgen Sie dafür, dass …
Please arrange for …	Bitte veranlassen Sie …

To communicate good news

We are pleased to note that …	Wir freuen uns festzustellen, dass …
We are pleased to inform you that …	Wir freuen uns Ihnen mitteilen zu können, dass …
Our company will settle …	Unser Unternehmen wird … begleichen.
As requested, we will …	Wie gewünscht, werden wir …
We would also like to mention …	Wir möchten auch erwähnen …

To provide information to the customer

However, we must inform you that …	Wir müssen Ihnen jedoch mitteilen, dass …
We have examined the …	Wir haben … überprüft.
On the basis of the terms stated in …	Aufgrund der in … genannten Geschäftsbedingungen …
Having studied your application/claim we will …	Nach Überprüfung Ihres Antrags/Schadenfalles werden wir …
The invoice amount will be remitted.	Der Rechnungsbetrag wird überwiesen.
Enclosed you will find …	Beigefügt ist/sind …

To request that something is done

Please confirm this …	Bitte bestätigen Sie dies …
Please arrange for the data to be sent by e-mail/post to …	Bitte veranlassen Sie, dass die Daten per E-Mail/Post an … geschickt werden.

To refuse something

I'm afraid I cannot agree to this proposal.	Leider muss ich diesen Vorschlag ablehnen.
Much as we regret it, we have to say no.	Zu unserem großen Bedauern müssen wir eine abschlägige Antwort geben.
We regret that we are unable to assist you.	Wir bedauern Ihnen nicht behilflich sein zu können.

To make a suggestion

May we suggest that you inform the supplier.	Wir möchten vorschlagen den Lieferanten zu benachrichtigen.
It would be advisable to send the details by fax.	Es wäre gut, wenn Sie uns die näheren Angaben faxen könnten.

To end a correspondence on a friendly note

We look forward to hearing from you.	Wir freuen uns, von Ihnen zu hören.
We hope to hear from you soon.	Wir hoffen, bald von Ihnen zu hören.
We look forward to serving you again.	Wir freuen uns, Ihnen wieder helfen zu können.
We look forward to welcoming you as our customers.	Wir würden Sie gerne als neuen Kunden begrüßen.
We hope this proposal will be of interest to you.	Wir hoffen, dass dieser Vorschlag Ihr Interesse findet.
We hope this information will help you.	Wir hoffen, dass diese Auskunft für Sie hilfreich ist.

Unit 6
Banks and insurance companies – organisation and structure

P **Exercise**
Answer the following questions.

1. What is the name "Wall Street" synonymous with?
2. Why have London and Frankfurt become such important centres of financial activities?
3. What other major financial centres do you know? Make a list.
4. Why is Lloyds so well-known internationally?

A Types of banks

Banks come in a variety of forms ranging from small private banks to large investment banks, from publicly owned savings banks, municipal savings banks and cooperatives, as is quite often the case in Germany, to the super-sized, internationally active banks, which have a global reach with their subsidiaries and holding companies in many different countries throughout the world. Here are some of the major types of banks:

Types of banks

Private banks are sometimes still family owned. They focus on high net worth individuals and corporate clients with a substantial minimum income and assets. Many of them have been taken over by major commercial banks. Their exclusive and prestigious name suggests solidity and discretion and thus appeals to wealthy clients.

Investment banks (also called merchant banks) focus on raising money for companies from private investors or on the financial markets by finding buyers for their equity/stock (IPOs, share issues).

Co-operatives (associations) and **municipal savings banks** provide a range of retail services to private clients and businesses. Municipal banks and cooperative associations are usually restricted to a city or region.

Retail banks provide a wide range of services to mostly retail customers, also called private customers. These banking institutions offer services such as savings and checking accounts, mortgages, personal loans as well as debit cards and credit cards, the whole range of banking services. They also cater to business clients and usually have an asset management division as well. Commercial banks can be both banks which deal with corporations or large businesses only as well as banks that deal with the general public, the private customer. Commercial banks are not to be confused with investment banks.

M **Exercise 1**

Match the English expressions with their German equivalents.

1. municipal savings banks	a. Privatkunden
2. retail bank	b. Bank für Wertpapier- und Emissionshandel
3. retail customers	c. Stadtsparkassen
4. co-operative banks	d. Aktienemission
5. investment bank	e. Vermögensverwaltung
6. corporate customers	f. Genossenschaftsbanken
7. Wealth/Asset management	g. Firmenkunden
8. public limited company	h. Bank mit Schwerpunkt Privatkundengeschäft
9. share issue	i. Tochtergesellschaft
10. subsidiary	j. Aktiengesellschaft

I **Exercise 2**

Discuss the following questions with your partner and then present your results to the class.

1. Which banks in the town where you live are public limited companies?
2. Which banks in your town have a global presence?
3. How is your bank structured as a business organisation?
4. Do you know a private bank that caters exclusively to wealthy corporate or private clients? What do you know about it?

B Organisation and structure of a bank

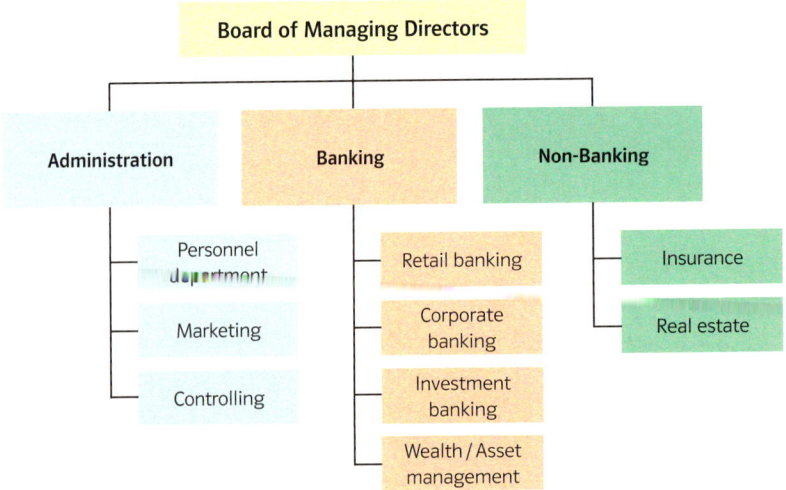

Any major bank is usually organised as a plc (public limited companies (BE)), or as an Inc. or Corp. (Incorporated, Corporation (AE)) and their organisation is based on functional divisions and departments which reflect the range of their activities and products.
The general range of business activities of a bank are broadly displayed in the structure above.

R **Exercise 1**
Match the departments of financial institutions with their main activities.

1. Corporate	a. provides insurance products in cooperation with the group's cooperating partner(s), e.g. life insurance, home and contents insurance, car insurance, credit insurance, etc.
2. Retail	b. recruits and trains staff and deals with employees' salaries, etc.
3. Personnel	c. offers the bank's own range of unit trusts (mutual funds) and other investment products
4. Investment	d. provides banking and finance solutions for companies
5. Wealth/Asset management	e. handles clients' current accounts, savings accounts, and deposit accounts
6. Real Estate	f. deals with matters relating to personnel, e.g. recruitment, training, salaries
7. Human Resources	g. helps clients to purchase suitable property and lines up financing
8. Insurance	h. caters to individuals and corporate clients with an income in excess of about £150,000 p.a., and liquid assets of £500,000 or more.

M **Exercise 2**

What are the German equivalents for these terms?

1. Corporate
2. Retail
3. Credit/Loan
4. Investment
5. Real Estate
6. Insurance
7. Human Resources
8. Wealth/Asset management

R **Exercise 3**

Use the information given in the box to complete the company profile of this international bank.

Company profile: Bank	
Type	
Founded	
Headquarters	
Key people	
Industry/Business	
Products and Services	
Net income	
Total assets	
Employees	*81 308*

81 308 • Finance and Insurance • Chief Executive Officer (CEO) • Frankfurt • Business banking • Private banking • Investment banking • Asset management • 1870 • €280.20 billion • €6.510 billion • Public (plc) • Chairman of the Supervisory Board

R **Exercise 4**

Complete this short presentation using the words in the box.

Financial products • headquartered • emerging countries • corporate • presence • expanding markets • finance hubs • fund • employs • is investing • private • revenues • wealth • retail

What is the name of this bank?

Our bank is an international bank, [1] in Frankfurt. The bank [2] more than 81,000 people in 76 countries, and has a large [3] in Europe, the Americas, Asia and the [4].

Our bank has offices in [5], such as London, Moscow, New York, Singapore, Hong Kong and Tokyo. Furthermore, the bank [6] in [7] such as the Middle East, Latin America, Central & Eastern Europe and Asia Pacific.

Our bank offers [8] and services for [9] and Institutional clients along with [10] clients. Services include sales and trading of debt and equity, mergers and acquisitions (M&A), risk management, corporate finance, [11] management, [12] banking and [13] management.

The bank is in terms of its [14] one of the top three investment banks in the world and is listed on the Frankfurt and New York stock exchanges.

Exercise 5

Work in small groups and draw an organisational diagram of the company where you work. Present your results to the class.

I
KMK **Exercise 6**

Work with a partner and act out the following dialogue. Use the role cards.

Role card: Student A   (see role card Student B on page 150)

In Ihrer Bank beginnt Sandy O'Neil aus Schottland mit der Arbeit. Sie möchte ein Jahr in Ihrer Abteilung arbeiten. Die firmeninterne Ausbildung hat sie in Schottland beendet.

- Begrüßen Sie sie herzlich als zukünftige Kollegin. Fragen Sie, ob Sie mit ihr Englisch reden können, weil Sie dazu ohnehin wenig Möglichkeit haben.
- Beginnen Sie den Dialog mit allgemeinen Fragen, z. B. wie lange sie schon in Deutschland ist und wo sie in Deutschland wohnt.
- Erkundigen Sie sich nach Größe und Organisation ihres Unternehmens in Schottland und nach der Tätigkeit in den Abteilungen.
- Informieren Sie sie über die Abteilungen Ihrer Bank und weisen Sie sie in die Tätigkeit in Ihrer gemeinsamen Abteilung ein.
- Erklären Sie, dass Sie sich auf eine gute Zusammenarbeit freuen.
- Finden Sie einen sinnvollen Schluss zu diesem ersten Gespräch.

Info: Types of companies and job titles

Some of our biggest banks and insurance companies are certainly international companies, which means they do business in many countries around the world. Quite often staff in a country is faced with the problem of not knowing what type of firm their subsidiary is and what ranks and titles of its management they are dealing with. The following list may be of help:

Germany	Great Britain	USA
Aktiengesellschaft (AG)	Public Limited Company (PLC)	Stock Corporation (Inc. Corp.)
GmbH	Private Limited Company (Ltd)	Closed Corporation
Genossenschaft / Verband	Cooperative (Association)	Cooperative (Association)
Vorstand, Aufsichtsrat	Board of Directors	Board of Directors
Vorstandsvorsitzender	Chairman of the Board of directors	Chairman of the Board of Directors
Präsident	President	President
Direktor	Director / Manager	Manager
Stellvertretender Direktor	Deputy Director / Assistant Manager	Assistant Manager
Geschäftsführender Direktor	Chief Executive Officer (CEO)	Chief Executive Officer (CEO)
Leiter der Personalabteilung	Head of the Personnel Department / Human Resources	Head of Personnel Department / Human Resources

C Structure of insurance companies

In Germany insurance companies as we know them today have been around for more than 160 years. In the UK even longer than that, starting with marine and fire insurance in the 16th century when the UK, a nation of seafarers, was beginning to develop into one of the greatest global empires. The need for insurance, particularly marine
5 insurance, evolved as a "natural necessity", making the UK the cradle of European insurance. Lloyd's of London, a world-famous insurance market, which is neither a company nor a stock corporation, did not get started as a marine underwriter until the late 17th and early 18th century, yet still considers marine insurance as one of their most important sources of premium income.

10 In Germany the first insurance companies were founded in Hamburg, first providing marine coverage, soon to be followed by fire insurance. Other classes of insurance e. g., life, liability and health were to follow at a later date. Most of the original underwriters were restructured and reorganised in the course of the last hundred years, some of them merged with others in order to grow, while others were swallowed up through take-
15 overs or acquired by their competitors. With deregulation opening the European market up for companies to expand their business easily across national borders, mergers and take-overs gave the German insurance market an international make-over.

R Exercise 1
Answer the following questions on the text.

1. Why did insurance become so important so quickly in the UK?
2. Which classes of insurance were first offered in both countries?
3. What did competition force most German insurance companies to do?
4. Explain the term deregulation and describe how it changed the insurance market.
5. What makes Lloyds so special?

R **Exercise 2**

Use the information given in the box below to complete the company profile of this international insurance company (on a separate sheet of paper).

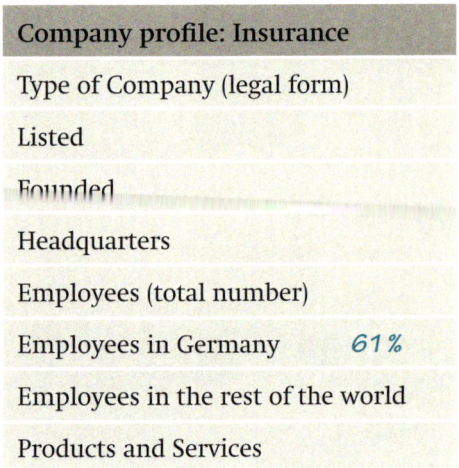

Company profile: Insurance	
Type of Company (legal form)	
Listed	
Founded	
Headquarters	
Employees (total number)	
Employees in Germany	*61 %*
Employees in the rest of the world	
Products and Services	

1889 • Life / Health insurance •
182 171 • Holding company •
Property-casualty insurance •
European Company SE •
DAX / NYSE • *39 %* • *61 %* •
Banking • Asset Management •
Munich

R **Exercise 3**

Complete the company profile below using the information in the box.

Stock corporations • presence • asset managers • employees •
headquartered • serves • global services provider • customers •
parent company • revenues • life • insurance

Company Profile

Our company is one of the leading **1** in insurance, banking and asset management. With 182,171 **2** worldwide, our group **3** more than 80 million **4** in about 70 countries. On the **5** side, our company is the market leader in Germany with respect to **6** insurance and has a strong international **7**. In the past fiscal year our group achieved total **8** of over 102 billion euros. We are also one of the world's largest **9**, with third-party assets of 765 billion euros.

In 2006 our **10** became the first company in the EURO STOXX 50 index to adopt the legal form of a Societas Europea (SE), which is a new European legal form for **11**. We are **12** in Munich.

R **Exercise 4**

www Find out more about structure and organisation of some German companies by checking the web. Organise your results and complete a table with your information as shown below. Present your results to the class.

Companies (Legal form)	Products/services (Divisions / Departments)	Facts/figures	Growth/outlook

R **Exercise 5**

Complete the following sentences using information from the text below.

1. In the USA Corp. or Inc. stands for ? .
2. In Great-Britain a plc is a ? .
3. Public limited companies offer ? to the public.
4. At the ? shareholders elect a ? .
5. The ? makes decisions on company policies.
6. The board appoints a ? , who is responsible for carrying out the ? for the ? of the company.

Communicating across cultures: Forms of business organisations in Britain and the US

The structure and organisation of British and American companies is different from what we have in Germany. It is therefore not always easy to find English equivalents for many German expressions and job titles, and some can simply not be translated. There is, for example, no "Prokurist" in Britain or America, which means you will have to give a lengthy explanation.

In the United States a public limited company is called a corporation (Corp) or (Inc). In South Africa and Australia it is called a proprietary company (Pty). In Britain a public limited company is called a plc. The shares of a public limited company (plc) are offered to the public.

In a limited company or corporation the general meeting of shareholders elects a board of directors headed by the chairperson of the board. It has the same supervisory function as a supervisory board in Germany, but in addition to this it also acts as an executive board by making decisions on company policies and objectives. The members of the board of directors are therefore on the one hand executive members of the board who are executives of the company, and on the other hand non-executive members from outside.

The board appoints a chief executive officer (CEO) also called managing director in Britain or president in America, and a number of senior executives (directors or vice presidents) who are normally responsible for various function areas of the company. They carry out the board's decisions and run the daily operations of the company. In many cases the chief executive officer is also the chairperson of the board.

D Changes and innovation in financial services

Changes in banking services

Banks like other labour-intensive service industries are under constant pressure to reduce costs. As branches and their staff account for over half of their overheads banks are concerned where to
5 reduce the number of branches they operate. One way of doing this is to merge with or acquire a bank with a similar or at least overlapping network of branches. This is part of an ongoing process of consolidation in most European countries.

10 For a time shedding branches was regarded as a priority. Banks encouraged their customers to use ATMs, bank online or use telephone banking hoping that they would be able to close branches as a result. If one considers that it has been estimated
15 that a payment effected by a cashier costs $1.27 whereas a computerised payment costs 1 cent, there is obviously a strong argument in favour of reducing the number of cashiers (and branches) and encouraging people to bank online. Thanks
20 to lower overheads many online savings and deposit accounts offer better rates of interest than conventional accounts. There are now a number of banks which have no branches and operate entirely via the internet.

Despite the fact that an increasing number of
25 customers are happy to bank online and take advantage of the ease with which they can compare interest rates and transfer deposits from one account to another at the click of a mouse, surveys show that a majority of customers still want a physical
30 branch and that those happy to bank online or by telephone form a small minority. Many older people, who either have no internet access or feel dubious about online savings and deposit accounts, want the feeling of security offered by a branch
35 operated savings account with passbook.

There has, however, been a serious change of heart. Branches are no longer simply regarded as a cost factor. The banks now see the branches as a source of income. Many banks have bought
40 insurance companies, have a major stake in them or cooperate closely with them. The branches are now seen as an outlet for insurance and other products. Financial advisors can sign customers up for new products and boost overall sales. At the same time
45 retail accounts generate a steady stream of fee income and branches have the important function of attracting deposits. Banks are now more interested in luring customers into their branches and poaching customers from each other by making it
50 easy for customers to switch banks. There is intense competition for retail customers. At the same time there is an attempt to design more attractive branches. Some banks – like a national chain of bookshops – have experimented with franchising,
55 e.g. introducing Starbucks or Costa coffee shops in some of their banks. Industry analysts expect banks to give even greater consideration to branch design, location and staffing in the future.

In a parallel development lines are being blurred
60 between different types of retail outlets. Supermarkets increasingly offer a range of insurance policies, personal loans and even mortgages. They also assume some banking functions, offering their own debit cards or store cards. They also routinely
65 offer cash back free of charge.

521 words

M **Exercise 1**

KMK The text on page 92 describes the most common changes in banking services in recent years. Read the text and find suitable answers to the following questions in German. Use a dictionary if necessary.

1. Wie entstehen die hohen fixen Kosten der Banken?
2. Wie können die Banken Kosteneinsparungen erreichen?
3. Wie können Banken die Zahl ihrer Filialen reduzieren, ohne Kunden zu verlieren?
4. Inwieweit wird der Abbau von Bankfilialen heute noch als Priorität angesehen?
5. Welche Vorteile hat Online Banking aus der Sicht des Kunden?
6. Wie wollen die meisten Bankkunden ihre Bankgeschäfte erledigen?
7. Warum gibt ein herkömmliches Sparkonto mit Sparbuch vielen Kunden ein Gefühl der Sicherheit?
8 Warum sehen Banken ihre Filialen heutzutage in einem positiveren Licht?
9. Auf welche Weise versuchen manche Banken, ihre Filialen einladender zu gestalten?
10. Inwiefern werden die Grenzen zwischen Einzelhandelsunternehmen, Banken und Versicherungen heute verwischt?

I **Exercise 2**

Get into groups and discuss the pros and cons of online banking, telephone banking and banking at a branch. Present your results to the class.

R **Exercise 3**

Form nouns from the words in this box and use them to fill the gaps in the following sentences.

> advertise • close • compete • convenient • insure • lose • produce • reduce • sell • solve

1. Banks use ? on TV or in the press to market their services.
2. Closing branches can result in a ? of customers.
3. Many people value the ? of home-banking.
4. A franchise system could be a good ? .
5. Banks and building societies are ? in the market.
6. Local managers know best which ? their customers will buy.
7. Lloyds is a British ? market.
8. A ? in the number of branches gives banks a bad press.
9. Franchising has been shown to increase ? considerably.
10. Barclays announced 171 ? of bank branches on a single day.

R **Exercise 4**

◎ 16 Listen to this radio advertisement praising the innovative ideas of an international bank. Make a grid and complete it with information from the advertisement.

Exercise 5
Fill in the missing prepositions.

1. It is difficult to find a solution [?] this problem.
2. One major bank is planning to close 200 branches [?] 2012 at the latest.
3. For many people a visit [?] their local branch is preferable to banking online.
4. Banks hope that customers will spend more money [?] financial products.
5. Banks are [?] keen competition [?] other financial services providers.
6. Banks can increase their branch network [?] sharing branches.
7. Branches should get rid [?] dark and uninspiring colours.
8. Franchising can increase sales [?] 20 %.
9. She is assistant [?] the chairman of the board.
10. For some British banks a further reduction [?] the number of branches is [?] the question.

Language and grammar: Tricky prepositions

by / until   bis
I need the report **by** Monday means that you must get it on Monday (or sooner) because from then on you will need it for your work. Example: The goods must reach us **by** the end of next week.

I need the report **until** Monday means that you need it only until Monday and will then be finished with it.

Example: The import licence is valid **until** 31 August. (You say: until **the thirty-first of** August.)

from ... to   von ... bis
This year's shoe fair will take place **from** 30 June **to** 4 August. (You say: ... from **the thirtieth of** June to **the fourth of** August.)
Wrong: from 30 June ~~until~~ 4 August

from, of , by   von / vom
The date of a communication is preceded by "of" or "dated":
Example: We refer to your offer **of** 2 November. (You say: ... of **the second of** November)
Wrong: We refer to your offer ~~from~~ 2 November.

Where the communication came from is expressed by "from":
Example: We received a complaint **from** one of our customers.
Wrong: We received a complaint ~~of~~ one of our customers.

The author is introduced by means of the preposition "by":
Example: This is shown in a report **by** an independent study group.
Wrong: This is shown in a report ~~of~~ an independent study group.

Phrases: Banks and insurance companies – organisation and structure

Banks range from small private banks to large commercial banks.	Banken reichen von kleinen Privatbanken bis hin zu großen Geschäftsbanken.
The structure is based on functional departments/divisions.	Die Struktur basiert auf funktionalen Geschäftsbereichen.
The structure reflects their various business activities.	Die Struktur spiegelt die unterschiedlichen Geschäftsaktivitäten wider.
Human Resources is responsible for …	Die Personalabteilung ist für … zuständig.
High Street banks cater for/to both retail and corporate customers.	Die großen Geschäftsbanken betreuen sowohl Privatkunden als auch Firmenkunden.
Private banks were often originally family owned.	Die Privatbanken waren ursprünglich häufig in Familienbesitz.
Banks frequently offer an asset/wealth management service.	Zu den Dienstleistungen der Banken gehört oft die Vermögensverwaltung.
Nowadays banks generally offer a wide range of insurance products.	Heutzutage bieten Banken in der Regel eine breite Palette von Versicherungsprodukten an.

Departments and responsibilities

He has recently completed a traineeship/apprenticeship.	Er hat gerade eine Ausbildung abgeschlossen.
I gather you are doing an internship here.	Ich habe gehört, dass Sie hier ein Praktikum machen.
Financial advisors give clients investment advice.	Finanzberater bieten Klienten eine Anlageberatung.
Loan/credit advisors are in charge of personal loans.	Darlehensberater sind für die Vergabe von Privatdarlehen zuständig.
I'm responsible for …	Ich bin verantwortlich für …
I'm in charge of …	Ich bin zuständig für …
Harry reports directly to Sally.	Harry ist Sally direkt unterstellt.
Borrowers need to provide the necessary collateral/security.	Darlehensnehmer müssen die nötigen Sicherheiten bereitstellen.
A mortgage is secured on a property.	Eine Hypothek wird durch eine Immobilie abgesichert.
The bank offers the whole range of insurance products.	Die Bank bietet die gesamte Palette von Versicherungsprodukten an.
Our bank provides customers with its own real estate service.	Unsere Bank bietet Ihren Kunden ihre eigenen Immobiliendienstleistungen an.

Unit 7
Banks

The term bank covers a wide range of financial institutes which have taken over various tasks in our economic system. Retail banks arrange payments for consumers and private people, investment banks focus on different forms of placing their customers' money, while central banks have the task of maintaining sound financial
5 conditions to ensure price stability and to keep inflation at bay.

The first modern banks, founded in the 15th century, mainly catered for the needs of merchants. Nowadays banks are important players in financial markets, which grew strongly especially after regulations were lifted in the US at the end of the last century. In Europe, the growth period led to stronger cooperation between banks and
10 insurance companies, so that many banks now offer insurance as well as real estate services to their clients. In the course of the worldwide credit crisis, the banking trade will go through further changes – so every single institute will be faced both with major risks and chances.

I/P **Exercise 1**
Brainstorm with your partner on one of the following topics:

1. Different banks in Germany
2. The role of banks in consumers' daily lives
3. The social role of banks

R Exercise 2

Match the following texts with the pictures on page 96.

A. Thank you so much for speaking English to us. It was quite hard for us to walk into a German bank, because we don't understand the language and apart from that we didn't know how we'd ever manage to open an account.

B. I have just started my apprenticeship today. My colleagues are very friendly and I like my job, but nevertheless it was an exhausting day.

C. The European Central Bank came into being on 1 June 1998. The introduction of the Euro seven months later was a historic moment for Europe.

D. This man founded a bank on a really amazing idea. He gave loans to really poor people. Experts all over the world shook their heads about the idea. But his bank has survived and in 2006 he was even awarded the Nobel Peace Prize.

A Working in a bank

Most young people consider working in a bank to be a very attractive job. It requires a high level of education, it pays well and offers a wide range of perspectives after completing an apprenticeship. These perspectives include a professional working environment, a very demanding atmosphere and the opportunity to participate in a relatively high benefit system.

P Exercise 1

Use the building blocks in the box below to make sentences describing retail banks, their employees and their clients.

Example: Bankers explain bank products in detail.

		detailed information.
	ask for	*bank products in detail.*
	offer	starting salaries of about 20,000.
Bankers	pay back	current and savings accounts for their customers.
	explain	
Clients	keep	debt in monthly instalments.
	have	in different areas, such as HR and IT.
Retail banks	build up	loans and accumulate more and more debts.
	receive	services to small businesses.
	work	branches on the high street.

Exercise 2

Read the following text about British students starting work at a bank. What are the differences between the situations in Britain and Germany?

All the way to the bank

Graduates fresh out of university have usually accumulated considerable debts. So they will be looking for a well-paid job that will enable them to pay off their student loans and their overdrafts as
5 quickly as possible. After several years of always being short of money and constantly begging the bank manager for yet another overdraft extension, the very thought of banks might well induce a nervous sweat in most graduates. But in
10 fact the UK retail banking sector, which employs over 330,000 people and looks after a good 130 million bank accounts, could be a very attractive proposition for these young career-seekers.

So what exactly is retail banking? The traditional
15 image is of banks with branches on the high street that offer financial services to individuals and small businesses. Due to technological developments in recent years there are also quite a few stand-alone internet retail banks. But the main focus of
20 the sector is still looking after customers' current and savings accounts, mortgages and, of course, overdrafts.

Graduates who are losing sleep about their overdrafts will be interested to learn that many of
25 the retail banks offer graduate training schemes with starting salaries of around £20,000, of course enhanced with bonuses and benefits. Even more interesting is the fact that trainees will also have access to preferential rates on highly relevant
30 bank products, for example graduate loans.

When imagining working at a bank, most people only think of the "frontline" employees, like cashiers and account managers, that they have encountered in their daily lives. In fact,
35 the retail banking sector offers a huge range of potential positions. In addition to classic roles like bank manager and cashier, there are all sorts of jobs requiring individual skills. Banks need IT specialists, specialists in law, people with
40 HR skills, and especially people with customer service skills.

Nowadays, more and more customers are changing the way they handle their accounts and moving to internet and telephone banking. Many
45 banks have recognised this trend and have realised that the role of the branch is changing. Branches will increasingly be places where people go to get information on financial products and advice, and consequently the employees in them will have
50 much more sales-focussed roles. In view of this changing focus, graduates who are interested in finding jobs in the retail banking sector should prioritise customer services skills. (...)

Retail banking offers attractive salaries, excellent
55 benefits and a wide choice of challenging positions that do not necessarily have anything to do with explaining to students why they can't extend their overdraft for the tenth time this week.

437 words

Exercise 3

Choose one of the two topics below and sum up the information on it that you can find in the text above.

1. The situation of the British graduates who are interested in a job in a bank
2. Working conditions and perspectives in a bank in Britain

R Exercise 4

Complete the following sentences with words from the text on page 98.

1. An [?] is a short-term loan available on current accounts.
2. The most common products in [?] are savings and current accounts, mortgages, personal loans, debit and credit cards.
3. After graduating many students look forward to receiving a high starting [?].
4. If you want to practise at a high level in certain jobs you not only need theoretical knowledge, you also require individual [?].
5. With our range of ATM, [?] and telephone banking you can access your account anytime.
6. I cannot understand this brochure about investments at all, I'll have to go to my bank's local [?] and talk to somebody there.

B Tasks and services of retail banks

Retail banks cater for the needs of private consumers and small businesses. They supply the traditional bank services people rely on in their daily life. When wages are transferred to accounts, telephone bills are paid and credit cards are debited, retail banks are always involved. Since retail banks are so representative of end-consumer banking business in Germany, many investment banks do not even offer apprenticeships as bank clerks any more. Look at the following phrases, which describe some of the most common products.

Banks	open keep close	current accounts. savings accounts. deposit accounts. safe custody accounts.
	offer	bank cards. credit cards.
	transfer money by arrange a set up a	direct debit. credit transfer. standing order.
	provide customer service advise clients attend to consumers' needs	in the branch. via telephone banking. via online banking.
	arrange	personal loans. corporate financing.
	act as an intermediary and	sell insurance products. provide access to the stock market. offer forms of investment.

P Exercise 1

Use the table above and describe the products and services offered by your bank.

Exercise 2

Translate the following sentences. Use the table on page 99.

1. Es ist eine gute Idee, einen Dauerauftrag für die Miete einzurichten.
2. Ich möchte ein Girokonto eröffnen, denn ich muss einige Überweisungen tätigen.
3. Es ist gut, wenn Kunden das Telefonbanking benutzen, aber wenn ich ein Konsumentendarlehen gewähre, möchte ich einen Kunden in der Filiale beraten.
4. Banken verwalten Depotkonten und gewähren Zugang zur Börse.

P **Exercise 3**

Have a look at these two people and choose some products from the table on page 99 that they might be interested in. Give reasons for your choice.

Ray Burton
He is originally from the US, and has just come to Stuttgart to work here for two years. He is single and has rented a flat for the two years. After that he will very probably go back to America. He has never entered a German bank and does not know how to make payments in Germany.

Dorothy Williams
She came to Germany six months ago, and now her probation period in her hotel has come to an end. She has decided that she will stay in Germany permanently. In Britain she had some savings schemes where she invested about 200 pounds every month.

R **Exercise 4**

🎧 17 **Listen to Ray's dialogue and take notes of what Ray opted for.**

1. Ray wants to transfer his rent by	a) standing order. b) direct debit.
2. He needs	a) a bank card. b) a credit card.
3. He will apply for	a) online banking. b) telephone banking.

R **Exercise 5**

🎧 18 **Listen to Dorothy's dialogue and answer the following questions.**

1. Where did Dorothy find information on savings accounts?
2. What is the difference between a notice account and an instant access account?
3. What kind of account does Dorothy decide for?
4. What is the interest rate on this type of savings account?
5. What is so special about this account at this moment of time?

Language and grammar: False friends

Some German words are frequently confused with similar English words which have a very different meaning.

aktuell	current, topical	actual	tatsächlich, wirklich
bekommen	to get	to become	werden
Chef	boss	chef	Koch, Köchin
		chief*	Häuptling
eventuell	perhaps, possible/bly	eventual	schließlich, letztendlich
Kritik	criticism	critic	Kritiker(in)
prüfen	to examine, check, test	to prove	beweisen
selbstbewusst	self-confident	self-conscious	schüchtern, gehemmt
sensibel	sensitive	sensible	vernünftig
Warenhaus	department store	warehouse	Lagerhaus

M **Exercise 6**

Translate these statements into English.

1. Momentan arbeite ich in der Kreditabteilung.
2. Dieses Programm wird eventuell in unserer Bank eingeführt.
3. Mein Chef ist leider ziemlich selbstbewusst und nicht sehr sensibel.
4. Meine Kollegin kann keine Kritik an ihrer Arbeit ertragen.
5. Ich bekomme ungefähr 5 Kontoanträge in der Woche.
6. Diese Formulare müssen noch einmal überprüft werden.
7. Unsere Marketingabteilung beobachtet die aktuellen Trends sehr genau.
8. Mit dieser Karte können Sie in den meisten Warenhäusern bezahlen.

Communicating across cultures: Writing and talking about sums of money

Especially in online communications, be careful how you specify the currency. Well over twenty countries have a "dollar", for example, and there are many countries with a "peso", a "dinar" or even a "pound". For e-mails, the only internationally reliable currency symbol on your keyboard is the dollar sign. Other currency symbols may not be interpreted correctly by a foreign e-mail system. The safest solution is always to use the ISO 4217 currency abbreviations of the international banking community (EUR, USD, GBP, etc.).

Officially, the idea that an English billion has 12 zeros while an American billion has only 9 zeros is considered outdated. The BBC and the British government now use the word "billion" (and "trillion") in the same way as the USA. However, some people in the UK are still insecure about possible misunderstanding of the word "billion" and prefer to speak of "a thousand million". The big problem is, of course, that the German words "Billion" and "Trillion" have a different meaning, and the word "milliard", although it can still be found in older English dictionaries, is unfamiliar to most people in the UK and the USA.

C Banking theory – financial intermediation

Within our economic system, which is based on the flow of capital, banks play a crucial role – as suppliers and administrators of money. They make sure that whoever wants to save or invest money can do so – and they also make sure that whoever needs money, for example to found a company or just to buy a car, can take out a loan. Without banks people in need of money would have to look for investors. This task of coordinating the demand for money and the influx of funds is called financial intermediation.

P **Exercise 1**
Look at the pictures below. They are taken from some bank advertisements.

1. Describe what you see and what product might be advertised here.
2. Match the following slogans with the pictures.

    A **Your competent advisor in any financial situation**

    B *Whatever sum you want us to handle – it won't be peanuts to us*

    C LOOKING INTO A BRIGHT FUTURE

M Exercise 2

Find the translations for these German terms in the text below.

> 1. Einlagen • 2. Darlehen • 3. Zwischenhändler • 4. Dauer •
> 5. Risiken einschätzen

Explaining the theory of financial intermediation

Banks have taken on the task of organising the flow of money – they do this by taking in money as deposits and by giving out money in the form of loans. This task can be differentiated into separate functions concerning the size, duration and risk of operations:

Lot size transformation

The bank changes the size of the sums it operates with. This means that, for example, many private people want to put their money into the bank while several major companies are looking for loans to finance their investments. In this case banks act as intermediaries when they bundle many small deposits into several major loans.

Period transformation

The bank transforms the duration of loans and deposits according to their clients' needs. A long-termed loan for example is financed by several short-termed deposits, such as savings accounts, etc.

Risk transformation

Banks have greater experience and also easier access to information regarding investment and granting loans. So customers prefer to let banks work with their money and estimate the risks rather than doing it themselves.

R Exercise 3

Match the following examples (a.–c.) with the three functions of lot size, period and risk transformation described above.

1. Lot size transformation	a. A bank has noticed that many of its clients are still leaving a lot of money in their savings accounts because they can't think of a better way to invest it. So the bank targets these people with a campaign to promote security-oriented equity funds.
2. Period transformation	b. The company Smith Tyre Ltd applies for a loan of several million Euro to open a new plant. Their bank grants this loan and finances it by issuing new bonds.
3. Risk transformation	c. The Milestones Bank typically has a high proportion of short-termed loans, such as overdrafts and consumer loans, in its balance. The bank also offers several savings plans with an average duration of seven years.

D Tasks of the European Central Bank

The banking system does not only consist of retail and investment banks, both of which look after the needs of individual people and businesses, but also of central banks, which have a more general function. They guard and maintain the stability of the entire economic system.

R Exercise
Complete the following text using the words from the box below.

> circulating • conducts • coordinate • covering • decision making • defend •
> ensure • functioning • issues • maintain • oversees • purchasing •
> protected • preserve

The European Central Bank

The European Central Bank (ECB) is an institution with some unique characteristics partly because it 1 an area whose
5 borders extend over those of a single state. Yet it still fulfils the role of any other central bank. First and foremost its task is to 2 price stability. It is the ultimate guardian of the value of money. (…)

10 Today (…) money derives its value from its 3 power, the value of the goods you can buy with it, so the job of a modern central bank is mainly to make sure that the amount of money 4 in an economy is properly balanced against the value of
15 the goods it can purchase. In that way the value of the currency can be 5 . But a modern economic system is enormously complicated and the ECB, like other central banks, is involved in a wide range of activities to 6 that it all works.

20 The ECB defines and conducts monetary policy within the Euro area. It 7 banknotes. It 8 operations in the foreign exchange market, buying and selling currencies as it deems appropriate, and it holds and manages reserves of foreign
25 currencies. It also helps to make sure all credit institutions are sufficiently sound and trustworthy and to 9 the stability of the whole financial system.

Furthermore it ensures the smooth 10 of payment systems throughout the Euro area, so the
30 transactions between banks can be conducted swiftly and effectively. The ECB does all this in close cooperation with the national central banks of the Euro area. Together they form what is called the Eurosystem. In fact the governors of these
35 national central banks together with the six members of the ECB's executive board form the governing council of the ECB, its supreme 11 body.

The members of the Eurosystem meet regularly to 12 and discuss their activities in a number of
40 committees made up of experts from departments within the ECB and the national central banks. The national central banks are also the ECB's shareholders. Shares are distributed according to the population and GDP of each country. But this
45 does not mean that larger member states have a greater say in ECB decisions than smaller ones. In fact the ECB is a truly supranational institution. Its staff and board members are not there to 13 the interest of any individual member
50 state, but to make the best decisions in the interest of all Euro area citizens.

Having a single central bank for such a vast area 14 different states with different traditions has never been done before. And yet the
55 Euro is a reality and prices within the Euro area remain stable just as the treaty on the European Union demands.

E Alternative models of banking

In Bangladesh, an alternative bank was founded in 1976 which not only aims at profits but also at social development of poor people. The Grameen Bank has since turned out to have both very successful social aims and highly profitable business figures. In 2006, Muhammad Yunus and the Grameen bank were awarded the Nobel Peace Prize.

Microcredits – A way out of the vicious circle of poverty and inequality

The Grameen Bank in Bangladesh is renowned for having introduced the microcredit system – a system of granting small loans to poor people. In its
5 early years, the concept was considered to be rather exotic and not very viable by conventional bankers, but its success in the meantime has attracted international attention and admiration. All the
10 more reason to take a closer look at this alternative approach to banking, which has enabled the bank to cater for people who would never have been considered creditworthy by traditional banks, and
15 which has become a structural means of fighting poverty in Bangladesh.

The basic system underlying microcredit operations is that borrowers are organised into groups of five debitors. The members of these groups are respon- 20 sible for supporting and monitoring each other – so each borrower is under moral pressure to pay back the loan. In practice, at first just two members of the group are granted loans. Only after 25 they have paid back their loans are the next two members allowed to apply for loans. As soon as these have paid back their loans, the fifth person may also apply for a loan. In this way, collateral 30 in the form required by conventional banks is no longer needed; it is replaced by mutual support and peer pressure.

Loans are granted to people who can present a viable project with a perspective of generating income to pay back the loan. Groups eligible for a loan are selected, supervised and supported by so-called "bicycle bankers", who act as close partners to the groups. There are regular meetings between group members and bankers where ceremonies are held and various topics are discussed. The loans are paid back in 50 weekly instalments. In this way the bank not only provides financial means but also supports social stability and contributes to the success of the borrowers' projects.

The success of this system has broad effects on the social structure. Poor people are enabled to set up their own businesses and to find a way of looking after themselves. But there is a second aspect which fundamentally affects society. Most of the Grameen Bank's borrowers are women. They improve their own and their families' financial situation and thus also raise the general educational and nutritional standards.

Furthermore the relationship between the female and the male sectors of society becomes more balanced as women accumulate more economic means. The Grameen Bank reports female borrower rates of 94 per cent.

Traditional objections to lending money to poor people have been disproven by the microcredit system. Poor people are often considered to be lazy, badly trained or not intelligent enough to find an occupation. To traditional bankers this also implies that the poor lack the necessary discipline to save money or pay back loans. Such prejudices have been discredited by the Grameen Bank, which quotes repayment rates of 97 per cent on their microcredit loans.

Through its success the microcredit system has served as a model worldwide. Its international recognition was crowned by the Nobel Peace Prize, which was awarded to the bank and to its founder in 2006.

528 words

R Exercise 1
Read the text above and answer the following questions.

1. How does the Grameen Bank make sure loans are paid back?
2. What activities do members finance with their loans?
3. How do the loans improve women's situations?
4. Which prejudices against poor people have been disproven?

M Exercise 2
KMK Sie arbeiten in einer Filiale der Milestones Bank Deutschland. Ihr Abteilungsleiter, Herr Müller, wird zu einer Wohltätigkeitsveranstaltung Ihrer Bank gehen, bei der auch eine Rede über die Perspektiven der Mikrokredite in Lateinamerika gehalten wird. Herr Müller bittet Sie, ihm in einer kurzen E-Mail die Grundidee der Mikrokredite laut Muhammad Yunus zu erläutern.

P Exercise 3
www There are also voices criticising the Grameen Bank and the system of microcredits. Find points of criticism on the Internet.

Phrases: Banks and their products and services

Working in a retail bank

I am very interested in the graduate training schemes offered by the MS Bank.	Ich habe großes Interesse an den Traineeprogrammen der MS Bank für Universitätsabsolventen.
The starting salary is not very important to me. With bonuses, benefits and preferential rates a job in a bank is very attractive anyway.	Das Anfangsgehalt ist nicht sehr wichtig für mich. Mit Boni, Vergünstigungen und Vorzugsangeboten ist eine Stelle in der Bank ohnehin sehr attraktiv.
Being a bank clerk does not automatically mean working at the counter or being a bank manager.	Bankangestellter zu sein bedeutet nicht automatisch, am Schalter zu arbeiten oder Bankdirektor zu sein.
Today there is a wide range of different jobs requiring individual skills, for example in the fields of human resources and customer service.	Heute gibt es viele verschiedene Stellen, die individuelle Fähigkeiten voraussetzen, beispielsweise im Bereich der Personalführung und des Kundendienstes.
For me the most important aspects of working in a bank are a demanding work atmosphere, challenging positions and good career perspectives.	Für mich sind die wichtigsten Aspekte der Arbeit in der Bank eine anspruchsvolle Arbeitsatmosphäre, herausfordernde Stellen und gute Karriereaussichten.

Products of retail banks

Our bank offers several kinds of account. You can open current/savings/safe custody accounts here.	Unsere Bank bietet verschiedene Kontenarten an: Sie können hier Giro-/Spar-/Depotkonten eröffnen.
There are two kinds of card available for this current account. A bank card will be ordered automatically, but you can also apply for a credit card.	Für dieses Girokonto sind zwei Kartenarten verfügbar. Eine Bankkarte wird automatisch bestellt, aber Sie können auch eine Kreditkarte beantragen.
You can transfer money by direct debit/credit transfer/standing order.	Sie können Geld per Einzugsverfahren/ Überweisung/Dauerauftrag transferieren.
To make transactions you can contact us in the branch/use telephone banking/use online banking.	Um Transaktionen vorzunehmen können Sie uns in der Zweigstelle kontaktieren/Telefonbanking benutzen/Online-Banking benutzen.
We also arrange personal loans as well as corporate financing.	Wir arrangieren auch Konsumentendarlehen und Firmenkredite.
Furthermore we sell insurance products, provide access to the stock market and we offer various forms of investment.	Zudem vertreiben wir auch Versicherungen, gewähren Zugang zur Börse und bieten verschiedene Investmentarten an.

Unit 8
Insurance

Insurance in some form or other has been around for many centuries – in fact, marine insurance was developed about 3000 years ago by the Phoenicians, who were great seafaring traders. The oldest example of an insurance policy dates back to a Mediterranean voyage in 1347 A. D.

5 Private property insurance – which was initially to protect against damage by fire – appeared in England after the Great Fire of London, which destroyed a large percentage of the city's buildings in 1666. Over the centuries, the insurance industry has grown steadily and nowadays plays an essential role as part of the overall economy in industrialised countries.

10 Some kind of insurance cover is a must for most individuals and organisations in our society. If you have property – for example, a house, a flat, a car, a home entertainment system or jewellery – you need insurance. If you have dependants, you need insurance. Certain types of insurance are even obligatory. One example of this is motor insurance; driving without it is a crime. Before a car is even allowed on the road, the owner must
15 be able to provide documentation of liability insurance coverage.

I/P **Exercise**
The pictures above show some typical situations where insurance is needed. Work in pairs and make a list of other examples. Compare your lists and discuss them in class.

A   Managing risk

R **Exercise 1**
Complete the following text using the prepositions from the box.

> of (5 x) • by (3 x) • against (2 x) • to (2 x) • from • for • at (2 x) •
> in (2 x) • on

Insurance is a way 1 managing risk. We are exposed to risk 2 almost everything we do, whether travelling or 3 home. Without insurance, the potential consequences caused 4 the risks we face 5 everyday life would be so great that we would never have peace 6 mind or security. For example, every time there is a storm, thousands of households are 7 risk of equipment failure due 8 electrical surge.

We use insurance to protect 9 the possibility 10 loss, usually financial. When we buy insurance, we transfer our risk 11 the insurance company in exchange 12 a payment, known as a premium. Then, if we suffer a loss which is covered 13 our insurance policy, we make a claim and the insurance company pays compensation.

Insurance works and is affordable because insurance companies group together a large number of people who are all exposed to the same possible circumstances. The company calculates that, in any one year, the total premium collected 14 this group of people should cover the cost 15 any claims made 16 the few who actually suffer a loss.

Another way of managing risk is to take precautions 17 worst case scenarios becoming reality. Insurance companies insist 18 certain reasonable precautions being taken, especially in household insurance, otherwise the policy could become invalid. It is also sensible to find some way 19 marking valuable property so that you can identify it if it is stolen.

M **Exercise 2**
Find the English equivalents of the following German words and terms in the text above.

1. (die Versicherung) in Anspruch nehmen
2. wertvoller Besitz/wertvolles Eigentum
3. durch eine Versicherung abdecken
4. Verlust
5. Versicherungsprämie
6. Vorsichtsmaßnahmen treffen
7. ungültig
8. Schadenersatz leisten
9. Überspannung
10. bezahlbar

With a partner, brainstorm a) precautions which you can take to try to prevent the following risks from becoming reality and b) precautions which you can take to help you to report and identify stolen goods more accurately.

Example: *a) lock valuable items up in a safe place*
               b) take photos of valuable items

Risks: 1. Burglary from a private house or flat   3. Electrical surge
         2. Fire in the home   4. Car theft or vandalism

R/M Exercise 4

Read the text below (Reinsurance) and put the following German information (Rückversicherung) into English.

Reinsurance

The above shows ways in which individuals and companies can protect and insure themselves against risk. But what happens if a hurricane comes along, such as hurricane Gustav in 2008,
5 or, even worse, hurricane Katrina, which caused devastation along the north central Gulf Coast of the US in 2005? Many people lost their lives and property in Katrina, in what was then the costliest natural disaster in US history and the worst natural disaster that the insurance industry had ever 10 handled. Millions of claims followed. Taking all this into account, along with the possibility that another catastrophe of a similar size could have happened in the same year, it is not surprising that insurance companies themselves need insurance. 15 This is called reinsurance. This is how insurers manage their own risks – by insuring themselves against these risks. This is done through a contract between the insurer and a reinsurer – there is no link between the insured person and a reinsurer. 20

Lloyd's of London is the world's leading specialist insurance market. One third of all its business is reinsurance.

Rückversicherung

Rückversicherung ist die Versicherung der Versicherer. Durch die Rückversicherung schützt sich der Erstversicherer vor der Gefahr, durch sehr hohe Einzelrisiken oder Katastrophen wie Orkane oder Erdbeben, nicht kalkulierbare Vermögensschäden zu erleiden. Andererseits gibt die Rückversicherung dem Erstversicherer die Möglichkeit, Wagnisse zu versichern, die wegen ihrer Höhe oder ihrer Gefährlichkeit seine wirtschaftliche Kraft übersteigen würden. Rückversicherer betätigen sich als Einkäufer von Risiken weltweit.

I/P Exercise 5 ☞ **Unit 3 Presentations**

www Internet project: Finding out about insurance, part 1.
Go to Lloyd's of London's website. In small groups, prepare a short presentation of the history of Lloyd's and how its market operates in the world today.

B The insurance industry

Nowadays a wide variety of general insurance contracts is available to cover us against the various perils with which we, our property and our wealth are faced in our everyday lives. The German Insurance Association (GDV) has well over 400 members. Each resident in Germany spends on average approximately 2000 € a year on private insurance.

As the level of wealth in a country rises, so does the level of private insurance coverage. This has a positive knock-on effect – the insurance industry in Germany is a very significant employer in the job market, providing work for many hundreds of thousands of people.

P/R Exercise 1
www Internet project: Finding out about insurance, part 2.

The German Insurance Association (GDV), which represents about 97% of the insurance market in Germany, has a lot of interesting facts on its website.
Type GDV into your search engine and go to its homepage. Follow the link to its English language site and then to its current yearbook published in English and further to its opening pages, "Insurance industry at a glance" and "Contents".

- **Answer the following questions:**
1. What is the average premium paid per household? Do households pay more or less than in the previous year?
2. How many classes of insurance are written by GDV members? What are they?
3. Which is the largest class of insurance in terms of premiums?
4. Which is the smallest class?

- **Turning to "The insurance industry as job provider" in the GDV's current English language online yearbook, find the following information:**
1. For approximately how many people in total does the insurance industry provide employment?
2. Make a list of the types of staff and workers that this includes.
3. Has the total number of employees risen or fallen over the past 3 years? What reasons are given for this?
4. What facts are reported about part-time workers?
5. Which are the five largest insurance centres in Germany?

I/M Exercise 2
Working with a partner, find the German translations for the classes of insurance you have found on the GDV website.

 **Exercise 3**

www **Internet project: Finding out about insurance, part 3.**

The following text, taken from the US Department of Labor, Bureau of Labor Statistics, describes working conditions and work environment in the United States. How do these compare with those of the German insurance industry?

Working in small groups, find out the answers through, for example, internet research and asking questions of your co-students, teacher and your sponsoring company. Be prepared to report back to the class. There will not be one correct answer, as many companies will have differing conditions

---

Working Conditions

Hours

Many workers in the insurance industry – especially those in administrative support positions – work a 5-day, 40-hour week. Those in executive and managerial occupations often do more than 40 hours. There are several occupations in the insurance industry where workers may work irregular hours outside of office settings. Those working in sales jobs need to be available for their clients at all times. This may result in these individuals working 50 to 60 hours per week. Also, call centers operate 24 hours a day, 7 days a week, so some of their employees must work evening and weekend shifts. The irregular business hours in the insurance industry provide some workers with the opportunity for part-time work. Part-time employees make up 8 percent of the labor force.

Work environment

Insurance employees working in sales jobs often visit prospective and existing customers' homes and places of business to market new products and provide services. Others working in the industry may need to leave the office frequently to inspect damaged property, and at times can be away from home for days, traveling to the scene of a disaster – such as a tornado, flood, or hurricane – to work with affected policyholders and government officials.

A small but increasing number of insurance employees spend most of their time on the telephone working in call centers, answering questions and providing information to prospective clients or current policyholders. These jobs may include selling insurance, taking claims information, or answering medical questions.

R **Exercise 4**

There are no spelling mistakes in the above text, but some of the words are spelt the American way. Can you locate them?

C Insurance fraud

Insurance fraud refers to either dishonest – i.e. fraudulent – claims or exaggerated claims. Such claims are a major problem for the insurance industry. They can range from small deceptions to spectacular lies; their purpose being to deceive the insurance company into paying more than it otherwise would.

5 For example, someone involved in a car collision could claim that more damage was done in that collision than was really the case. This way the owner could get pre-existing damage repaired at the cost of the insurance company. The more spectacular cases often involve life insurance, where an insured person fakes their own death so that the life insurance policy is paid out.

10 Some, normally law-abiding, average members of society, feel that a fraudulent claim is a "victimless crime" but this is not the case. Fraudulent claims can lead to a rise in premiums, which affects both honest and dishonest policyholders alike.

M **Exercise 1**
Summarise the above text in German.

R **Exercise 2**
Which word or phrase taken from the text and shown in the box below is best illustrated by the following situations.

Example:
2. He did this so that his wife could collect his life insurance. (fraud)

pre-existing damage	inconsistent statement	faked death	evidence
fraud	*law-abiding*	*exaggerated*	*deception*

1. Mr. Bridgley pretended to have fallen overboard and drowned at sea.
2. *He did this so that his wife could collect his life insurance.*
3. Mrs. Bridgley also claimed for damages to the sailing boat, although some of them had occurred during a storm the previous winter.
4. Although Mrs. Bridgley told her next-door neighbour that she had last seen her husband on Thursday 14th, she told the police that it was on Wednesday 13th.
5. Mr. Bridgley changed his appearance and moved to the north of the country where he got a job using a false identity.
6. Mr and Mrs Bridgley's son, James, found out what was going on and went to the police.
7. Mr Bridgley pretended that he had lost his memory, but the police found papers which proved that he had been preparing his "death" for a long time.
8. It was reported in the press that Mrs. Bridgley had originally received £250000 from the life insurance, but actually it was only £150000.

I **Exercise 3**
Why do some people consider insurance fraud not to be a true act of crime? Discuss in class.

D Quote, choice, claim

1 Quote

Frank Bendel, a doctor from Baden Württemberg, is moving to King's Lynn in east England for a few years to work in a practice there. He has bought a house near the coast and now needs to get building and contents insurance.

R Exercise 1

◎ 19 **Listen carefully to the following telephone conversation between Dr Bendel and the insurance broker from North Norfolk Insurance. Look at the information that they wrote down after the conversation and correct it if necessary.**

Frank Bendel has written:	The insurance broker has written:
Amon Gardner, Vilbeaforce Road, Dowhan Market, Appointment at 10:30	fbendel@t.online.de

P Exercise 2

Write the broker's e-mail to Dr Bendel incorporating the following points. Refer back to Unit 6 if you need help.

1. Danke für die Anfrage.	(Annahme Checkliste) und
2. Anhang	c) einige Infoblätter
a) Versicherungsantrag,	3. Rufen Sie an, falls es Fragen gibt.
b) "Assumptions checklist"	4. Freue mich auf nächsten Dienstag.

R Exercise 3

> **Why use a broker?**
>
> North Norfolk Insurance Brokers is a leading home insurance broker. This means that we compare home insurance quotes from a specially selected panel of over ten leading insurance providers in the UK to find you the very best quote we can. Whether you're looking for separate buildings and contents cover or a combined buildings and contents policy, we can help you – and save you a lot of time.
>
> Our search is tailored to your needs, which means that whether you're a new customer looking for a quote, or an existing customer renewing your insurance, we'll find you a great deal each time we search for your home insurance.

One of the information sheets is entitled "Why use a broker?" Read the information above and answer the following questions.

1. What does a broker do?
2. Why might you want to use a broker?
3. Do you have to buy buildings and contents insurances separately?
4. What two kinds of customers do North Norfolk Insurance Brokers deal with?

R/M Exercise 4

Before Dr Bendel could fill in the assumptions checklist, he needed to look up some words in the dictionary. Read the checklist and then match the words in the list below (1.–12.) with their German translation (a.–l.).

Assumptions checklist	correct	incorrect
You are the property owner.		
Your home is not left unoccupied for more than 30 consecutive days.		
Your home is your permanent residence, i.e. it is not used as a weekend or holiday home.		
Your home is in a good state of repair and will always be maintained as such.		
Your home is not used in any way as part of a business, trade or profession.		
Your home is built of standard construction (i.e. brick, stone or concrete walls, and a tiled, slate, concrete or asphalt roof), and has no building work in progress.		
Your home has not suffered from flooding in the last 10 years.		
Your home has never shown any signs of subsidence, landslip or heave. You are not aware that your home is in an area where there has ever been evidence of subsidence, heave or landslip.		
You or any person living in the home have never had insurance refused or had terms imposed.		
You or any person living in the home have never been convicted of any criminal convictions, and do not have any criminal prosecutions pending.		

1.	assumption	a.	Schiefer
2.	consecutive	b.	ausstehend
3.	to maintain	c.	Erdrutsch
4.	trade	d.	Strafverfolgung
5.	tile	e.	aufeinanderfolgend
6.	slate	f.	Verwerfung
7.	subsidence	g.	aufrechterhalten
8.	landslip	h.	Annahme
9.	heave	i.	Vorstrafe
10.	criminal conviction	j.	Handel
11.	criminal prosecution	k.	Dachziegel
12.	pending	l.	Erdsenkung

R **Exercise 5**

◉ 20 **Dr Bendel picks up the telephone. Listen carefully to the conversation between him and Eamonn Gardener. Then say whether the following statements are true or false and correct them if necessary.**

1. Frank received Eamonn's original e-mail without problems.
2. Forms like this are difficult for some English native speakers too.
3. Answering "incorrect" to a statement on this assumptions checklist makes buying the insurance more complicated.
4. Knowing geological information about the land that property stands on is important for insurance purposes.
5. Giving wrong information on a proposal form can make the policy invalid.
6. Eamonn wants Frank to fill in the forms and fax them back.

I **Exercise 6**

In their first telephone conversation, Eamonn assumes that Frank is going to "shop around", i.e. check different insurance providers and get quotes from them, before he makes a final decision.
Now you are going to do a role play, working with a partner. Act out your role play, using your own words. Use the phrases for politely disagreeing and / or partially or reluctantly agreeing, given below.

Role card: Buying Insurance – Student A (see role card Student B on page 151)

You are Frank's new colleague, Doctor Allsopp.
You are in favour of Frank shopping around before he makes a final decision.

Your reasons for this are:
1. If Frank doesn't shop around, he may be spending more money than necessary and he will have no idea if he has a good deal or not.
2. Frank's English is good enough for him to work as a doctor in England, so his worry about the new vocabulary is unnecessary.
3. North Norfolk Insurance Brokers work with only 10 providers. They probably earn good commission from them so are not really independent.
4. If Frank goes on the internet and finds a comparison site, he can fill in his information just once and they will find him a number of different quotations.

Add any other reasons you can think of.

Language and grammar: Agreeing and disagreeing

Politely disagreeing
- I don't really agree with you on that.
- I'm not so sure about that.
- I'm afraid I can't agree with that.
- But surely, you can see that …
- Do you really think so? I think …
- I'm sorry, but I have a different opinion.
- I'm sorry but I don't agree.

Partially / Reluctantly agreeing
- I agree with you up to a point, but …
- I agree with you in principle, but in this case …
- Well, yes and no …
- That's quite true, but …
- I suppose you could be right.
- Well, I'll give you that point, but …

R Exercise 7

The following Tuesday, Frank is sitting in Eamonn's office. Complete their conversation by filling in the gaps using the words and phrases given below.

> no claims bonus • all risks cover • lump sum • legal responsibility • personal possessions • total value • extend • accidental damage • fixed glass • storm damage • new for old • occupants • household contents • upper limit • standard • quotes • individual items • coverage

Eamonn:	Right, I think we have everything now, Dr. Bendel. Can you think of anything else?
Frank:	No, I think you've asked me every question under the sun!
Eamonn:	Not quite! Well if this is all right with you, I'm going to recap what we've just said about ▮1▮. That will help us decide if we've forgotten anything.
Frank:	Fine with me.
Eamonn:	Here goes then. Firstly, there are going to be four ▮2▮ in the house. You, your wife and your two children, who are three and five years old. That's right, isn't it?
Frank:	Yes, that's right.
Eamonn:	A ▮3▮ household insurance policy covers most of your possessions, for example, furniture, domestic equipment, electrical appliances, furnishing, clothing, food and drink, some valuables and cash up to a certain limit. It also covers damage to your possessions caused by fire, flooding, and ▮4▮, as well as theft. You told me that you want to ▮5▮ your policy to cover ▮6▮ to all of the contents of your home, which is going to cost extra. Otherwise, the only contents that would be covered against accidental damage would be mirrors and ▮7▮ in furniture and televisions. Right?
Frank:	Yes, I'd like ▮8▮ against accidental damage.
Eamonn:	OK. Now, there's usually what's known as 'new for old' cover. This means that you get the full cost of replacing an old item with a new one if it is damaged or stolen. The exception here is clothing and bedding – they aren't covered on a ▮9▮ basis.
Frank:	Sounds good so far.
Eamonn:	The ▮10▮ you've put on your household contents is £55 000. This includes two paintings, valued at £2 500 each and some jewellery, in total valued at £5 900.
Frank:	And an antique desk, about £2 000.
Eamonn:	Oh yes, the desk. You'd better take photos of the ▮11▮, just in case. Now, did you say you wanted cover for ▮12▮ taken out of the home, for example, cameras, jewellery or sports equipment? That will cost extra too. This is called ▮13▮. There is usually an ▮14▮ on the value of any single item. I'll have to check.
Frank:	Yes, I'd like that too.
Eamonn:	Right, the final thing is that household contents insurance usually also provides cover for payment of a ▮15▮ of money if

you or your wife die as a result of a fire, theft, or an accident in the home. It can also cover your ⬛16 if someone is injured or dies when they visit your property. Most companies will also give you a ⬛17 – that's a discount for not making a claim – when you renew.

Frank: My head is spinning. No, joking aside, it all sounds fine. Thank you for the detailed explanation. When do you think you'll be able to give me some ⬛18 ?

Eamonn: Will the day after tomorrow be soon enough? I normally get four quotes.

Frank: That quickly? That's excellent. Then I can talk it over with my wife and give you our decision by the end of the week.

Exercise 8 ☞ **Phrases**

Act out a role play with a partner. One of you is the insurance broker, the other is a potential client finding out about contents insurance.

2 Choice

Exercise 1

Eamonn Gardener sends these four quotes to Frank Bendel. With a partner, discuss and decide which quote gives Dr Bendel the best deal.

Insurance companies	East Midlands	Safe Hands	Bradley & Barnes	Isle of Derry
Annual premium	£410	£435	£460	£430
No claims bonus after 1 year	10%	15%	15%	15%
Building coverage	Up to £500000	Up to £500000	Up to £1 million	Up to £500000
Household contents coverage				
Excess	£100	£50	£50	£100
New for old	yes	yes	yes	yes
All risks (personal possessions taken out of the home)	yes	yes	yes	yes
Accidental damage	yes	yes	yes	yes
High risk items	up to £12000	up to £15000	up to £20000	up to £15000
High risk single item	£2000	£2500	£3000	£2500
Freezer contents	Up to £750	£1000	£1000	£1000
Plants in the garden	£0	£1000	£1000	£1000
Theft from outbuildings (sheds, garages)	£2500	£2500	£2000	£2000
Money in the home	£350	£1000	£750	£350
Alternative accommodation in case of flood or fire	equivalent accommodation up to £7500	equivalent accommodation up to £7500	equivalent accommodation up to £5000	equivalent accommodation up to £7500

M Exercise 2

KMK Dr. Bendel möchte seine Frau in seine Entscheidung miteinbeziehen. Schreiben Sie seine E-Mail an seine Frau. Fassen Sie die wesentlichen Informationen auf Deutsch zusammen.

M Exercise 3

Mrs Bendel has a question about the length of the contract. She gets out a copy of a household contents insurance policy that she has in Germany and reads the relevant paragraph over the phone to her husband. Dr Bendel now has to ask Eamonn Gardener if the same rule applies in England. Translate the paragraph into English.

> **„Vertragsdauer"**
>
> „Versicherungsverträge mit mind. einjähriger Vertragsdauer verlängern sich jeweils um ein Jahr, wenn nicht drei Monate vor dem jeweiligen Ablauf der anderen Partei eine schriftliche Kündigung zugegangen ist."

R Exercise 4

Eamonn Gardener replies by e-mail. Read his e-mail and answer the questions below.

Dear Dr Bendel,

Thanks for your enquiry.
The way you describe renewal of a policy in Germany is what we call a "tacit renewal provision". In the UK it is different, although recently a few insurance providers have begun to change over to the German way. The way it works here is that I will write to you a few weeks before your insurance is due to expire and ask you if you would like to renew. I will enclose a summary of your current cover so that you can decide if you would like to make any alterations. I will also let you know how much the premium will be. You will need to inform me of your decision in advance of the renewal date and then arrange to pay the premium to ensure that there is no break in cover.
I hope that this answers your question satisfactorily and look forward to hearing from you

Kind regards,
Eamonn Gardener
North Norfolk Insurance Brokers

---

1. What exactly is a "tacit renewal provision"?
2. What is the main difference between insurance renewal in the UK and in Germany?
3. What do you think are the advantages or disadvantages of each procedure?

3 Claim

In the end, Dr Bendel chooses Safe Hands Insurance Company. Three months after he moves into his new house, while he and his wife are in Stuttgart visiting family, his house is broken into and the two paintings, the jewellery and some cash are stolen. On return from holiday, he discovers the burglary and calls Eamonn Gardener.

I **Exercise 1**

Read the following dialogue between the insurance broker and Dr Bendel.

Eamonn:	North Norfolk Insurance Brokers, Eamonn Gardener speaking. How may I help you?
Frank:	Oh Eamonn, it's Frank Bendel here. We've had a burglary! The burglar got in through the French doors!
Eamonn:	Hello Frank. Oh dear – I'm so sorry. What a terrible welcome to the country. What did you lose?
Frank:	I'm not quite sure yet; we've only just got back from Stuttgart. My wife's looking around now. The paintings have definitely gone as well as all her jewellery and some cash she left in the kitchen.
Eamonn:	Let me make a suggestion – look around carefully, and see what's missing. Then report it to the police. When you've done that, call me back. In the meantime I'll find the copy of your policy and have a look. I'll have quite a lot of questions for you to answer I'm afraid, but I'll fill in the claim form for you and deal with the insurance company.
Frank:	That will be a big help. Right, I'll do that. I'll speak to you later this afternoon probably Eamonn. Goodbye.
Eamonn:	Goodbye Frank.

I/P **Exercise 2**

Frank has said he will have quite a lot of questions. What will he need to know? Discuss this with a partner and make a list of questions he will probably ask.

P **Exercise 3**

Using your list of questions explain why they might be significant for the success of Dr Bendel's claim.

P **Exercise 4**

The insurance company has decided to pay Dr Bendel's claim in full. A supervisor has asked Janette Atkins, a trainee in the claims department, to prepare a short letter, based on the notes below. Write the letter to Dr Bendel.

> Household contents policy No. 1794958/66
> Reference claim AZ 1963-C from 13 August – claim for stolen valuables, broken glass door. Sorry to hear of burglary. Pleased to inform – successful claim – settle in full. Payment of £ 8.200 less excess. Need bank account details. Happy we were of service!

E Complaining

In Germany, the style of complaints tends to be direct: you state the facts bluntly and require action in no uncertain terms. This is accepted and nobody takes offence. As you may expect from your experience in practising agreeing and disagreeing, complaints in the English-speaking world are formulated in a different way. The style is more indirect, polite and conciliatory. Nothing is gained by antagonizing the other party; he or she will simply be less cooperative. So remember to express your complaint in a friendly and understanding manner. You will still get your point across.

Writing:
I am writing with reference to …
~~I want to complain about …~~
I'm afraid that her manner left something to be desired.
~~She was rude.~~
There must have been an error / a mix-up on your part / somewhere.
~~You are wrong.~~
I would be (most) grateful if you would deal with this matter (immediately). ~~Do it now!~~

Speaking:
I'm sorry to bother you, but …
Excuse me, but …
I'm afraid I have to make a complaint …
I'm afraid there may be a misunderstanding …
I understand it's not your fault, but …
Sorry to say this, but …
I think you might have forgotten to …
Actually, I don't think that …

P **Exercise**

Using the following notes and referring to the phrases above in the writing section, write the letter of complaint which prompted the following answer.

sent claim form Sep 4th • spoke to someone in claims department Oct 3rd • assured that claim OK • letter dated Oct 21st refusing settlement • phoned – person in claims department very unfriendly • now notice policy no. on letter is different from mine • feel sure mistake has been made • pls deal with matter asap

Dear Sir,

Your letter of 9th November

I am writing with reference to the above-mentioned letter. Firstly, I should like to apologise for the inconvenience caused you by our error. Your policy number was indeed confused with another customer's, leading to this unfortunate misunderstanding. We do usually take great care to ensure that claims are properly handled and on this occasion an acceptable standard has clearly not been met.
Your claim has now been assessed and will be settled in full. I have given instructions for an immediate payment to be made.
Once again, I should like to offer my apologies for the annoyance caused. Please don't hesitate to contact me if I can be of any further help.

Yours sincerely,
Dora Wheaton
Manager – Claims Department

Phrases: Insurance

Customer consultation – the insured

Can I speak to an insurance broker?	Kann ich mit einem Versicherungsmakler sprechen?
I'd like more information on …	Ich hätte gerne nähere Information zu …
Can you give me a quote for contents insurance?	Können Sie mir ein Angebot für eine Hausratversicherung machen?
Which items are classed as contents/valuables?	Welche Gegenstände zählen zum Hausrat/zu den Wertsachen?
Is my bicycle covered?	Ist mein Fahrrad mitversichert?
What is covered in glass breakage?	Was ist bei Glasbruch versichert?
What isn't covered by contents insurance?	Was ist nicht über die Hausratversicherung versichert?
There's a big price difference between buying insurance from you and buying it online.	Es gibt einen großen Preisunterschied zwischen dem Versicherungsabschluss bei Ihrer Firma und dem Online-Abschluss.
What must I do if I want to make a claim?	Was ist im Falle eines Schadens zu tun?
When does coverage start?	Ab welchem Zeitpunkt besteht der Versicherungsschutz?
Is there an excess?	Gibt es eine Selbstbeteiligung?
Will I get a no-claims-bonus next year if I haven't made a claim?	Werde ich im nächsten Jahr einen Schadenfreiheitsrabatt bekommen, wenn ich keinen Anspruch geltend gemacht habe?
Can you explain the small print to me?	Können Sie mir das Kleingedruckte erklären?
How is the premium calculated?	Wie wird der Beitrag/die Prämie berechnet?
What are the cancellation options?	Welche Möglichkeiten der Kündigung gibt es?

Customer consultation – the insurer

I promise you a detailed consultation.	Ich verspreche Ihnen eine ausführliche Beratung.
We distinguish ourselves from the competition not only through price but also through our benefits.	Wir unterscheiden uns von der Konkurrenz nicht nur im Preis, sondern auch in den Leistungen.
Coverage could start today.	Der Versicherungsschutz könnte ab heute bestehen.
Each contract contains certain standard cover which can be extended as desired/on request.	Jeder Vertrag beinhaltet einen gewissen Standard, der auf Wunsch erweitert werden kann.
Of course then the premium increases too.	Natürlich steigt dann auch die Prämie.

If you want your bicycle to be insured, you'll have to take out extra cover.	Wenn Sie wollen, dass Ihr Rad mitversichert ist, müssen Sie zusätzlichen Versicherungsschutz abschließen.
We have two tariffs/rates of charge.	Wir haben zwei Tarife.
You have to inform us of any damages immediately and in writing.	Sie müssen uns über etwaige Schäden unverzüglich schriftlich informieren.
In this case, we would take over repair costs.	In diesem Fall würden wir die Reparaturkosten übernehmen.
There is an excess of 75 euros.	Es gibt eine Selbstbeteiligung von 75 €.
You don't have to keep receipts of low-priced items.	Bei niedrigpreisigen Gegenständen brauchen Sie nicht jeden Beleg aufzuheben.
If you decide to take out insurance with us, I can promise you excellent service!	Falls Sie sich entscheiden, die Versicherung bei uns abzuschließen, kann ich Ihnen ausgezeichneten Service versprechen!
Please call me if you think of any other questions!	Rufen Sie mich bitte an, falls Sie weitere Fragen haben.
Don't leave it too long to decide!	Warten Sie mit Ihrer Entscheidung nicht zu lang!
Don't decide immediately. Sleep on it!	Entscheiden Sie sich nicht sofort. Schlafen Sie eine Nacht darüber!

Making a claim

What exactly caused the damage?	Was genau hat den Schaden verursacht?
How long was the house unoccupied?	Wie lang war das Haus unbewohnt?
You will have to provide evidence of the value of the damaged property.	Sie müssen den Wert des beschädigten Hausrats nachweisen.
Do you have original receipts?	Haben Sie die Originalbelege?
Your contents insurance does not cover you in this particular case.	Ihre Hausratversicherung deckt diesen besonderen Fall nicht ab.
It's written quite clearly in the small print.	Es steht ganz deutlich im Kleingedruckten.
Unfortunately you'll lose your no-claims bonus.	Leider werden Sie Ihren Schadenfreiheitsrabatt verlieren.
When will compensation be paid?	Wann wird die Entschädigung ausgezahlt?
How long will it be before I know the result of my claim?	Wie lange dauert es, bis der Schaden endgültig abgewickelt ist?
Will my renewal premium be affected?	Hat das Auswirkungen auf meine Folgeprämie?
I've already informed the police.	Ich habe die Polizei schon verständigt.
I'd like to cancel.	Ich möchte kündigen.

Unit 9
Job application

Even with all the resources available nowadays, it is still difficult to find an apprenticeship, a trainee position or a first job, particularly one that matches your expectations. Most companies advertise their openings in various newspapers across the country and sometimes even abroad. However, the internet is increasingly becoming the forum for
5 job adverts. The advantage here is that you have a choice of national and international companies and destinations to choose from. All you need to do is write an e-mail and you will receive quick notification if there is a vacancy. Jobcentres and private recruitment centres can also help you find a position, and if you are a self-confident type you might even try sending an unsolicited application to major companies on
10 the off-chance that they might just be looking for people to hire. However, no matter which path you follow, the biggest obstacle your application has to overcome is the initial selection process, which takes place in the personnel department.

P **Exercise 1**
Describe the pictures above.

R **Exercise 2** ☞ **Phrases**
Read the text above. Can you think of any other way of looking for a job?
How did you find your apprenticeship / job?

Advert 3

Job Description

Friendly? Polite? Enjoy talking to people? You will be joining a lively team working with insurance clients in the heart of Cheltenham. We offer a comfortable team working environment with thorough training to insure your success. Your role will predominantly be to call customers and talk to them about the benefits of an insurance policy.

Qualifications

Dealing with customers on the phone, maintaining an accurate set of accounts and files, dealing with inquiries from customers, administering cash paid and received and documenting financial transactions. Insurance or financial services experience will be an advantage, but the key qualification is a polite and professional approach to dealing with clients.

Job Title	Customer Service Representative / Insurance Adviser / Account Handler
Job Type	Permanent
Location	United Kingdom, Swindon
Salary	14,000 – 15,500 (GBP) per annum plus company benefits

Advert 4

Job Description

Tellers needed! Would you like to be part of a dynamic winning team? Come join the leader amongst the global payments companies. We are known around the world as one of the most successful businesses and one of the best places to work. We are looking for tellers who strive to deliver the ultimate in service to our elite customers, servicing clients in a banking environment, with foreign currency exchange, foreign drafts, US and foreign travellers cheques and card member account payments.
Teller and foreign currency experience required.

Qualifications

Excellent oral and written communication skills, strong customer service background a must. Ability to maintain a high degree of accuracy while working under pressure in a team environment. Product marketing a plus. Knowledge of Microsoft Office required. Good command of English, foreign languages a plus.

Job Title
Financial Service Representative / Teller
Job Type
Full Time Employee
Location
New York, New York, USA
Salary
Competitive

Benefits
such as Medical, Dental and Vision insurance, generous vacation plan, paid training programs, tuition reimbursement and ongoing education, Legal Assistance, Life and Disability insurance

M **Exercise 4**
KMK Wählen Sie eine der oben aufgeführten Stellenanzeigen aus und stellen Sie ihre Wahl der Klasse auf Deutsch vor. Beachten Sie dabei die wichtigsten Detailpunkte des Unternehmens: Stellenbeschreibung, Anforderungen, Gehalt und Leistungen.

B CV / Résumé

If you write a CV in English it should be in tabular form and fairly short – two pages at the most. As it is an essential part of your job application, you should only give the facts and figures. Your motivation and your particular qualifications for the job should be pointed out in the cover letter, not in the CV. You should mention the following
5 points in a British-style CV:

1. personal details (name, date of birth, nationality, marital status, home address)
2. education (including the names of the schools, dates and places)
3. work experience
4. language proficiency
10 5. leisure activities

In the UK a lot of emphasis is put on outside interests and personal achievement, such as hobbies, extra-curricular activities at school and leadership positions. Do not forget to include them in your CV. Make sure you state your qualities clearly, do not overstate or understate them.

15 It is becoming quite common these days for British employers to accept a résumé instead of a CV. A résumé is an American-style professional history which details the main aspects of your career. It is shorter than a CV and less structured. One of the most important aspects is your career objective. This should contain information about the function and the level of responsibility you are aiming for as well as the
20 type of company you would like to work for. The career objective is followed by a chronological résumé, starting with what you have done most recently. This reverse chronological order is common with both the CV and the résumé. Never include a photograph in any international CV or résumé.

Always remember to use various different verbs which describe your skills and
25 qualifications. Do not only use "was" and "did" in your CV. Use verbs such as "carried out", "distributed", "evaluated", etc. to identify the various skills you can provide.

M **Exercise 1** Aufgabe zur Hinführung auf die KMK-Prüfung „Leseverstehen"
KMK **Lesen Sie den oben aufgeführten Text und beantworten Sie die folgenden Fragen auf Deutsch.**

1. Worauf sollten Sie beim Schreiben eines Lebenslaufes (CVs) auf Englisch besonders achten?
2. Welche Inhalte sollte er auf jeden Fall enthalten?
3. Auf welche Inhalte legt man im Gegensatz zu einem deutschen Lebenslauf in Großbritannien besonderen Wert?
4. Worin unterscheidet sich ein amerikanischer Lebenslauf von einem britischen Lebenslauf?
5. In welcher chronologischen Reihenfolge sollte man sowohl den britischen als auch den amerikanischen Lebenslauf schreiben?
6. Was sollte auf einem internationalen Lebenslauf nie erscheinen?
7. Auf was sollte man beim Schreiben des Lebenslaufes besonders achten?

A German CV / Tabellarischer Lebenslauf

Persönliche Angaben

Name	Mandy Bauer
Adresse	Stuttgarter Str 36 B
	71332 Waiblingen
	Tel. 07151 4689132
	E-Mail: mandy.bauer@t-online.de

Staatsangehörigkeit	deutsch
Geburtstag	12.02.1990
Geburtsort	Karlsruhe
Familienstand	ledig

Schulbildung

Mai 2006	Tulla Realschule, Karlsruhe
	Abschluss: Mittlere Reife
Mai 2009	Zertifikatsprüfung Englisch für kaufmännische Berufe, Niveau III
Sept 2006 – Juni 2009	Kaufmännische Schule West, Stuttgart
	Abschluss: Bankkauffrau

Beruflliche Ausbildung und Erfahrung

Sep 2006 – Juli 2009	Ausbildung zur Bankkauffrau bei der Sparkasse Stuttgart, Stuttgart
	Schwerpunkte: allgemeine Kundenbetreuung, Kontoeröffnung, Kontoschließung, Zahlungsverkehr, Fremdwährungen, Kreditkartenbetreuung
	Abschlussprüfung: Bankkauffrau IHK
Sept 2009 – heute	Privatkundenbetreuung, Sparkasse Stuttgart

Sprachkenntnisse	Deutsch: Muttersprache
	Englisch: fließend in Wort und Schrift (B2)
	Spanisch: gut in Wort und Schrift (B1)
Sonstige Kenntnisse	MS Office (Windows, Excel, Powerpoint), Linux
Interessen	Volleyball, Lesen, Reisen

M **Exercise 2**
Study the English version of a CV on page 130 and rewrite Mandy's CV in English using the vocabulary in the box below.

> Vocational training and job experience • other skills • nationality • bank clerk • marital status • personal details • education • secondary school leaving certificate • apprenticeship • private customer service • payments • opening an account • emphasis on

PERSONAL DETAILS

Name	Stephan Hammer
Address	Am Berg 27
	34870 Wetzlar, Germany
	Tel.: +49 (0)177 588 67 24
	E-mail: Stephan.Hammer@gmx.de

Nationality	German
Date of Birth	14 February, 1987
Place of Birth	Wetzlar, Germany
Marital Status	Single

Education

Sept 2006 – Aug 2009	Friedrich-List-Schule Karlsruhe, Germany, as part of an apprenticeship within the dual system of learning in cooperation with: Allianz Lebensversicherungs-AG
	Kriegsstr. 117
	76135 Karlsruhe
	Germany
Sep 2009	Certified Management Assistant / Insurance
May 2006	Gymnasium Hohenwalde, Wetzlar, Germany
	Abitur, a university entrance qualification

Work Experience

Dec 2006 – Mar 2009	Worked with the field force of a tied agency of Allianz, and distributed private insurance policies
Dec 2006 – Dec 2007	Allianz Lebensversicherungs-AG, Karlsruhe, Germany
	Assisted the head of the Human Resources Department
	Maintained contacts to clients in the Private Clients Department
	Dealt with clients in the Risk Management Department

Other Skills and Interests	Analysed, processed and assessed records
	Filed forms

Language Skills	German: native speaker
	English: good working knowledge (B1)
	French: basic communication skills (A2)

Computer Skills	Microsoft Office (Word, Excel, Power Point)

Hobbies	Playing football
	Listening to and playing music

M **Exercise 3**

Read the CV on page 130 and find the English translation for the following German words and expressions.

1. Allgemeine Hochschulreife
2. Wirtschaftsassistent (Schwerpunkt Versicherung)
3. gute Englischkenntnisse
4. Akten analysieren und beurteilen
5. Kontakt mit Kunden pflegen
6. jemanden unterstützen
7. im Außendienst arbeiten
8. duale Ausbildung in Zusammenarbeit von Betrieb und Hochschule

P **Exercise 4**

Match each verb on the left with an equivalent on the right and make example sentences for the verbs (1.–8.). *Example:*

6.	maintain	h. keep up

Example sentence: It is essential to maintain good customer relations.

1.	process	a. evaluate
2.	file	b. study
3.	organise	c. set up
4.	distribute	d. deal with
5.	analyse	e. sell
6.	*maintain*	f. add to the records
7.	assess	g. examine carefully
8.	review	*h. keep up*

P **Exercise 5**

You have chosen one of the positions advertised on pages 126–127 in this unit. Now write your own CV using vocabulary from Unit 1 and a dictionary.

> **Communicating across cultures: Job applications**
>
> You should *not* include references from previous employers in your application when applying in Britain. You will usually be asked to give the names and addresses of possible referees so that the company can approach them directly. In your covering letter you may indicate that you are prepared to provide names of referees on request.
>
> You should *not* include a photo in your application when applying in the USA or Britain nor make any reference to your religion or race, unless specifically asked to do so.

C Writing a letter of application

Even in our age of instant communications a cover letter is still very important and should be written with particular attention to detail. These are the basic elements:

Your Name
Your Address
Your E-mail Address
Your Phone Number

Date

Contact's Name
Contact's Job Title
Contact's Department
Company Name
Company Address

Dear Ms/Mr CONTACT

The first paragraph states why you are contacting the person, then mentions either your connection with that person or where you read about the job. It may also briefly state who you are. Next you demonstrate some knowledge of the company. This shows that you are a sincere and worthy applicant.

In the second and third paragraph you give more details about yourself. Summarise why you are what they are looking for. The aim is to show that you are the ideal candidate for the job advertised.

The last paragraph is your goodbye. Thank the reader for his or her time. Don't forget to state that you look forward to receiving their reply, or give a time when you will be getting in contact with them by phone.

Yours sincerely

Signature

Enclosure

Info: Cover letter

Keep in mind that the idea of a cover letter is not to rewrite your résumé or CV. The main purpose is to tell them where you learned about the ad, why you are the right person for the job, and how they can reach you.
In terms of online applications, there are also conventions for an e-mail cover letter. According to the recruiting experts, your cover letter should have the same format and quality even if it is being submitted over the Internet. When you send your e-mail, attach it as a PDF file. If you really want the job, follow up an e-mailed cover letter and CV/résumé with a hard copy by post. A hard copy gives your application a greater chance of being noticed.

M Exercise 1

Lesen Sie die informellen Anweisungen bezüglich eines Bewerbungsschreibens auf Seite 132 und beantworten Sie bitte die folgenden Fragen:

1. Wie soll das Schreiben gegliedert sein?
2. Welche Inhalte sollen in den unterschiedlichen Absätzen enthalten sein?
3. Was soll das Schreiben auf jeden Fall nicht enthalten?
4. Was soll man beachten wenn man das Begleitschreiben als E-Mail schreibt?

R Exercise 2

Read Mandy Bauer's cover letter below and find those sentences and parts of the letter which contain the following information:

- date
- contact's address
- where you saw the ad
- your job experience
- why you are qualified for the job
- closing remarks

Mandy Bauer
Stuttgarter Str. 36 B
71332 Waiblingen
Germany

12 April 2009

Mr Evans
Personnel Manager
Commerce Bank
704 Gladney Drive
Birmingham SE 1285
United Kingdom

Dear Mr Evans

I am writing in response to your Commerce Street News advertisement for a bank customer service representative. High quality service is vital in banking and that is exactly what I will provide if you hire me.
As my CV indicates, I have worked in financial services for more than three years, which means I will not need any extensive training in this field at extra expense to you.
In addition I have learned how to deal with a wide variety of people. In each case I assess their individual needs and how the bank can address these more efficiently. The majority of my customers have been very pleased with my service and, most importantly, they have returned to do business with us again.
I hope you will give me a call or contact me by post or e-mail so that we can meet. Thank you for the opportunity to discuss my qualifications.

Yours sincerely

Mandy Bauer

P Exercise 3 ☞ Phrases

Write a cover letter based on your CV to apply for one of the adverts you chose on pages 126–127 in this Unit.

D Preparing for a job interview

Mandy was put on a shortlist and has been invited to a job interview. A friend of hers has brought her some important information to help her prepare for the interview.

What are companies looking for?

All the different questions an interviewer is asking you are supposed to help him or her answer the two basic decisive questions:

1. Will you fit in well with this company?
5 2. Do both the position and the company fit well with your skills, interests, personality and work values?

This implies, of course, that the more you know about your prospective employer, the more able you will be to perform well in an interview. Know as much as possible about the company's products, services and objectives. It will make it easier for you to respond well to
10 any question that may come up. Other interests, hobbies, or experience mentioned in your CV can also be a source of follow-up questions. Think in advance how you would respond.

However, you should not only think of what they may ask you, but also what you want to ask them when that famous moment comes up and they ask you: "Do you have any questions?" You might think beforehand about a few issues that are important to you, e.g.
15 opportunities for further training or the use of your language skills. It all depends on your prior information about the company and the job advertised.

If the interview is conducted in English prepare answers to some of the most commonly asked questions beforehand by writing out possible answers. It will help you become familiar with the questions that an interviewer may ask you.

20 Do not underestimate your personal appearance. Those so-called "soft skills" are of great importance. Don't take any risks wearing jeans, T-shirts, sweatshirts and sneakers. Try to look and act like a professional.

Be on time, have an open smile on your face, greet your interviewer with a firm handshake, speak clearly and keep eye contact with your interviewer. Don't cross your arms and legs as
25 it shows you are nervous and closed up. On the other hand don't be too cool and relaxed. Always stay friendly and polite and don't make any negative comments about others or yourself.

Last but not least, thank the interviewer for the chance to be invited for the interview. Don't make any comments until you are out of hearing range.

R Exercise 1
Read the text on page 134 and answer the following questions.

1. What is the most important information an interviewer is trying to find out about you?
2. How can you prepare to deal with these questions?
3. Why should you think in advance about the other interests you mentioned in your CV?
4. How can you prepare for the inevitable "Do you have any questions?"
5. Why should you write out answers to possible questions put in English? Find reasons in the text and give your own personal reasons.
6. What advice is given concerning your personal appearance and attitude?

I Exercise 2
KMK **Bereiten Sie sich mit den folgenden Vorgaben auf ein Rollenspiel mit Ihrem Partner vor. Ein Schüler spielt die Rolle des Personalentwicklers und der andere die von Mandy. Sie haben zehn Minuten Zeit zur Vorbereitung.**

> **Role card: Student A**   (see role card Student B on page 151)
>
> Sie sind Mandy Bauer aus Waiblingen und haben sich auf die Anzeige in der Commerce Street News beworben. Man hat Sie nach Birmingham zum Vorstellungsgespräch bei der Commerce Bank eingeladen.
>
> Begrüßung und Small Talk (freie Antworten)
>
> Die Hinweise und Beispiele zum Bewerbungsschreiben und zum tabellarischen Lebenslauf in dieser Unit helfen Ihnen bei der Beantwortung der Fragen.

I/R Exercise 3
◎ 21 **Listen to the extract of a job interview and discuss the interview in class.**

> **Language and grammar: Use of capital letters**
>
> **Capitalize all geographical names and geographical adjectives:**
> * We have customers in **N**ew **S**outh **W**ales in **A**ustralia.
> * There is a growing market in **S**outh **E**ast **A**sia.
> * Our **B**ritish and **I**talian subsidiaries are quite successful.
> * Prices are falling on the **E**uropean markets.
>
> **Capitalize all calendar days, months and holidays:**
> * The meeting will be held next **F**riday.
> * We start stocking up for **C**hristmas in **S**eptember.
> * **N**ew **Y**ear's **D**ay is a public holiday.
>
> **Capitalize titles when they are used as part of people's names. Titles used after a person's name are generally not capitalized:**
> * The report was presented by **V**ice-**P**resident Brian Laurel.
> * The commission will be chaired by **S**ir Francis Drake.
> * John Hardy, chairman of Media Clusters, agreed to the proposal.
> * Fanny Harville, chief financial officer, refused to step down.

Phrases

Referring to the source of address

I saw your advertisement in …	Ich habe Ihre Anzeige in … gesehen.
I saw this vacancy advertised on the … website.	Ich habe diese Stellenanzeige auf der … Webseite gefunden.
I would like to apply for the position advertised in the …	Ich möchte mich für den in der … ausgeschriebenen Posten bewerben.
I have been given your address by … who told me that you have a vacancy for …	Ich habe Ihre Anschrift von … bekommen, der mich darauf aufmerksam machte, dass bei Ihnen die Stelle eines … frei geworden ist.
I am applying on the off-chance that you may have a vacancy.	Ich erlaube mir, Ihnen eine Initiativbewerbung zu schicken, für den Fall, dass bei Ihnen eine Stelle frei ist.

Giving reasons for applying

In my present position as …	In meiner derzeitigen Stelle als …
I have just completed an apprenticeship as …	Ich habe gerade meine Ausbildung als … beendet.
I completed my apprenticeship two years ago.	Vor zwei Jahren habe ich meine Ausbildung abgeschlossen.
I am presently employed as …	Ich bin zur Zeit als … angestellt.
I would welcome the opportunity to …	Ich würde mich über die Möglichkeit freuen …
In addition I have learned how to deal with …	Ich habe zudem gelernt, mit … umzugehen.
I enjoy working with people.	Ich arbeite gerne mit Menschen zusammen.
I am eager to use my knowledge of English.	Ich möchte gerne meine Englischkenntnisse anwenden.
I have experience in …	Ich habe Erfahrung im/in …

Referring to qualifications

I passed my … three years ago.	Vor drei Jahren machte ich mein/e …
I did my apprenticeship with the … in banking/insurance).	Ich habe eine Ausbildung bei der Firma … (im Banken-/Versicherungsbereich) gemacht.
I spent three months in the … department.	Ich war drei Monate in der … Abteilung.
I have got good accounting and communication skills.	Ich verfüge über gute Kenntnisse in der Buchhaltung und Kommunikation.
I have good administration and bookkeeping skills.	Ich verfüge über gute Kenntnisse und Fertigkeiten in der Verwaltung und Buchhaltung.
I have been working with … since/for …	Ich arbeite schon seit … bei …

Referring to certificates, diplomas, degrees and references

I enclose copies of my …	Kopien/Zweitschriften meiner … sind diesem Schreiben beigefügt.
I took my Abitur two years ago.	Vor zwei Jahren machte ich das Abitur.
A university entrance qualification	Abitur
From … to … I attended …	Von … bis … besuchte ich …
Primary (UK)/Elementary School (US)	Grundschule
Secondary School	Realschule
Comprehensive School	Gesamtschule
Vocational School	Berufsschule
Vocational Grammar School	Berufliches Gymnasium
General Grammar School	Gymnasium
I have trained as a …	Ich bin gelernte/r …
I have completed an apprenticeship in …	Ich habe eine Ausbildung als … abgeschlossen.
I did my apprenticeship with …	Ich habe eine Ausbildung bei … gemacht
In … I passed the Chamber of Commerce examination for banking/insurance professions.	Im Jahre … legte ich die IHK-Prüfung für Bank-/Versicherungsberufe ab.

Referring to starting date and relocation

I would be able to start at short notice.	Ich kann kurzfristig anfangen.
I would have to give the usual notice at my present firm.	Ich müsste die übliche Kündigungsfrist einhalten.
I could start on 1 August.	Ich könnte am 1. August anfangen.
I would be prepared to move to …	Ich wäre bereit nach … umzuziehen.

Closing the letter

I would be happy to provide the names of references.	Gerne gebe ich Ihnen Referenzen an.
I look forward to hearing from you.	Ich freue mich auf Ihre Antwort.
I would be grateful if you would consider my application.	Ich würde mich freuen, wenn Sie meine Bewerbung berücksichtigen würden.
I hope you will give me the opportunity to present myself at an interview.	Ich hoffe, dass Sie mir die Möglichkeit geben, mich bei Ihnen persönlich vorzustellen.

Unit 10
Globalisation and global markets

Globalisation is a process which has become possible thanks to developments in the past few decades in the fields of information technology, transport, commercial liberalisation and employee qualification. Companies which previously operated on a national basis are now working on an international scale. International trade has
5 broad effects on the operating procedures and business planning of companies, on employees, on consumers and also on national governments. There are major risks in this worldwide competition. Jobs may be lost, production plants transferred to other countries and national problems might develop into a global crisis. But companies do not have much of a choice, because the risks involved in not taking part in the
10 globalised market are greater than those involved in taking part in it. Against the background of the financial crisis that hit the world in 2008 there are now more voices calling for stricter regulation – which may change the face of globalisation yet again.

P **Exercise 1**
Look at the pictures above. Give a brief description of the situations.

P **Exercise 2**
What products have you used this week that were not produced in Germany? Where do you think were they produced? Make a list.

A Defining globalisation

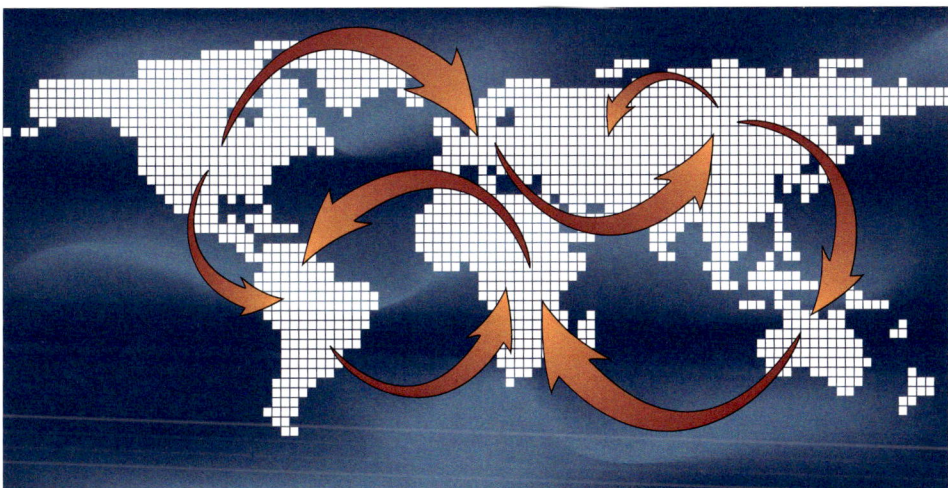

Globalisation is not just a simple economic fact. It is a worldwide development with effects on work, consumption, investment and laws in every country and on every person, regardless of whether they are employees, employers, consumers or investors. Before talking further about the nature and development of globalisation, it is important to define the term and clarify its basic characteristics.

R **Exercise 1**
Complete the following text using the words from the box.

> poverty • world • technologies • effects • globalisation • challenges •
> benefits • movement • barriers • infrastructure

There are many different definitions of **1** , but most acknowledge the greater **2** of people, goods, capital and ideas due to increased economic integration which in turn is propelled by increased trade and investment. It is like moving towards living in a borderless **3** .

There has always been a sharing of goods, services, knowledge and cultures between people and countries, but in recent years improved **4** and a reduction of **5** means the speed of exchange is much faster. Globalisation provides opportunities and **6** . Bigger markets can mean bigger profits which leads to greater wealth for investing in development and reducing **7** in many countries. Weak domestic policies, institutions and **8** and trade barriers can restrict a country's ability to take advantages of the changes. Each country makes decisions and policies that position them to maximise the **9** and minimise the challenges presented by globalisation.

The issues and perceived **10** of globalisation excite strong feelings, tempting people to regard it in terms of black and white, when in fact globalisation is an extremely complex web of many things.

P Exercise 2

Use the description of globalisation above and think about what globalisation means to these people. Organise your notes in a table.

	Consumers	Employees	Investors	Politicians
Benefits/ Problems	*exchange of cultures*			

P Exercise 3

Discuss the following statements with your partner and compare the results in class.

Global trade has always been there, it has not changed during the last decade.

Global competition has improved the situation of employees in Europe.

Consumers can only benefit from globalisation. The range of products is getting bigger and prices are falling due to the fierce competition.

Communicating across cultures: Cross-cultural misunderstandings

As soon as several people from different countries are involved in a business process it becomes very important to understand the impact cultural differences may have on human interaction. If the people involved are not aware of these difficulties, communications may go wrong, with quite serious consequences for a company. The following examples illustrate the potential dangers in cross-cultural communications.

- Cameron Diaz had to apologise to the people of Peru because, on a visit to the Andes, she carried a bag with a slogan that reminded the people of an insurgency which claimed many lives.
- An international incident occurred when, as a joke, Prince Harry wore a nazi symbol on his fancy dress at a party. This caused uproar in the newspapers and required hard work by diplomats of both countries involved to appease the situation.
- A Japanese employer has severe difficulties in giving explicit criticism to his American employee for being badly organised. Since the American employee is accustomed to straight and open criticism, he simply cannot understand why his employer is talking to him in such a friendly manner.

P Exercise 4

www Find more situations on the net where intercultural differences are involved. The search words "cross-cultural" and "blunder" may help you.

M Exercise 5

Your German boss is going to Japan. Think about what he can do to avoid making intercultural mistakes and sum up your results (in German) in an e-mail to your boss.

B How do companies globalise?

Globalisation not only stands for good opportunities and advantages for businesses. It also means that businesses have to react faster to meet the market's demands faster than their competitors. Business and investment strategies are becoming more and more important in this process. Companies are constantly undergoing changes in their fight for the best position on the markets.

R Exercise 1
Match each term with the correct explanation.

Term	Explanation
1. Acquisition or Takeover	a. One company passes on a process to another company in order to save costs or to focus on their core competence. Example: Some companies pass on their customer service to external call centres.
2. Foreign Direct Investment	b. This term means that a part of a company is moved abroad because labour is cheaper or there is a pool of skilled workers in the new country. During the IT boom, many German companies opened new departments abroad due to a lack of able programmers at home.
3. Joint Venture	c. This means investing in a company abroad because it has large potential or because the government offers attractive incentives. A national parent company controls an international affiliate by holding at least 10% of its shares.
4. Merger	d. A company enters a new market and creates a new company together with a domestic company to gain expert knowledge or because of laws which demand this. Chinese law, for example, only accepts this form of entering the Chinese market.
5. Offshoring	e. Companies that are relatively equal in size join together to create a new company with new advantages. Usually both parties benefit from this. In 1998 Chrysler Corp. merged with Daimler Benz to form DaimlerChrysler. In this way, Chrysler planned to access more European markets while Daimler Benz intended to open new markets in North America.
6. Outsourcing	f. One smaller company is purchased by a much larger one. This can have benefits for both companies, but since the one company is bought by the other, its consent is not required, so the action may be either friendly or hostile.

Exercise 2

Complete the following articles from a business magazine using the prepositions from the box below.

against • between • by • for • in (2x) • into • of • on (3x)

Article A

Greenhouse MS launches bid for Morphsys

Due to the low capitalisation of Morphsys **1** the stock market, their rivals Greenhouse MS have launched a surprising bid **2** the company. Last night the board of Morphsys held an emergency meeting to discuss defence tactics. After a long night the spokesman of Morphsys announced: "This bid is extremely unattractive and **3** the interest of our employees and shareholders we will find ways to defend ourselves and to fight back."

Article B

EGA announcing focus on third world countries

The famous Economic Growth Agency (EGA), founded **4** former World Bank leader Jochen Buse, has announced its focus on promoting investment **5** third world countries. "In our partner countries we have encountered both highly qualified and motivated staff as well as an advanced infrastructure, so companies planning to establish overseas subsidiaries may fall back **6** our expertise in the field of international investment," their spokesman said.

Article C

Owners of Milestones and Prosper banks begin talks

The owners **7** the two renowned financial institutes have started talks that could lead to the creation of a new bank which would be the country's biggest bank. The deal **8** Milestones and Prosper would transform the entire public banking sector, with 12 million private customers and 1,400 branches embracing the potential of being Europe's biggest bank. Shares of the two banks would be exchanged **9** a new company stock issued in their place.

Article D

> ### Muranmen going public
>
> Muranmen's CEO Manuel Muran today unveiled an initiative which introduces a phase of further streamlining of Muranmen in order to prepare the company for going public. In the following 12 months, certain production steps will be passed on to partner companies in the field of automotive production. In this way Muran wants to bring the company's main fields `10` focus. He also intends to increase the return `11` assets. "This program will lead to a more focused business model that provides us with the flexibility to deliver value to our customers and superior growth to our future shareholders."

R **Exercise 3**
The articles report on a hostile takeover, a foreign investment, a merger and a case of outsourcing. Can you tell which is which?

P **Exercise 4**
Work with a partner. Pick one of the following cases and

1. decide what might be the best step to solve each company's problem;
2. write a fictitious newspaper article, pointing out the advantages both for the company's value and for its employees.

Example:
1. Bayern Bier: huge profits last year – invest profits – expand company
Last year, Bayern Bier made huge profits and they need to invest the profits to expand the company. – I think they might acquire a smaller company, maybe a competitor or a supplier.

Case 1:	*Bayern Bier:* *huge profits last year – invest profits – expand company*
Case 2:	**Modern Porcelain Co.:** enter Russian market – no local market knowledge – small Russian porcelain company's stock market value is very low
Case 3:	**Saarland Pneumatics:** production too expensive – renowned production centres in China
Case 4:	**Baden-Baden Autos:** would like to integrate tyre company – few resources
Case 5:	**Kiel Software:** produce software – no skilled programmers available in home country
Case 6:	**Stuttgart Computers:** have thousands of customers – call centre is too expensive

C Global financial markets

On global financial markets, people can invest in various kinds of assets to make a profit, to lower risk, to hedge against potential losses or to secure a reliable source of raw materials.

R **Exercise 1**
Complete the following text using the words from the box below.

> bonds • commodities • creditor • currency • foreign exchange • gold • shareholders • shares • stocks

1 are loans with a fixed sum which has to be paid back after a set period of time – so here the investor is a **2** of the issuing organisation, which is either a company or a state.

3 are assets that have tangible properties, such as oil, metals and agricultural products. These are used both for the production of goods as well as for speculation purposes. **4** for example is a very popular investment in insecure times – while the price of crude oil is an indicator of worldwide economic development.

5 are also referred to as **6** or equities and represent a unit of ownership in a corporation. **7** do not have influence on the business's day-to-day operations, but they are entitled to an equal share in any dividends.

8 trading is a monetary business which is based on converting the **9** of one country into that of another country. These currency deals are executed between governments or businesses of different countries.

R **Exercise 2**

The people on the left (1.–4.) are asking for advice. The people on the right (a.–d.) are giving advice. Match the numbers with the letters.

1. The situation on the car market is getting harder every day. As you know, we would like to take over a competitor abroad to access bigger markets.	a. I'd use a foreign exchange option. Option means that you settle a contract today that in three months time you will do a trade at set conditions. So if you choose a foreign exchange option today, you'll already know how many Euros you will receive for your bill to be paid in US$.
2. I have many shares in my portfolio – I am really worried that they might all go down one day. I'd like to have something to lower the risk.	b. I would consider making a commodity future with your coal deliverer in Western Australia. This means that you agree with your supplier on the price and quantity you will get in six months. This way you secure your company against a possible higher quotation of coal prices in a mid-term perspective.
3. I am head of finance of a machine manufacturer. Since my company is very dependent on the international export markets I am losing sleep over this exchange rate turbulence. How can I make sure I know what I'll get for my machinery when the invoice is paid three months later? My client is paying me in US$ but my company is located in Germany.	c. Since the situation on the stock market reflects this development, the market capitalisation of car companies is quite low. What about buying their shares on the stock market to start a takeover?
4. I am an executive manager in procurement for a big German steel company. For our production, we need to purchase Australian coal. As the development of industry in China increases its pace, we are having trouble calculating end consumer prices because coal prices on the world market are rising very quickly.	d. I'd surely recommend you to buy AAA state bonds. Bonds generally don't correlate with shares – which means that bonds may go up while shares are going down.

D Financial markets and their risks: The subprime crisis

"I THOUGHT WE WERE JUST BUYING A HOUSE!"

P Exercise 1

Describe the cartoon and explain how it relates to the subprime crisis.

R Exercise 2

21 Tim Brand is thinking about buying a flat. With all the talk of the subprime crisis and the collapse of the American housing market, he is wondering how this might affect him. He phones the Global Markets department of the Milestones Bank in London and asks his friend Vincent Hannah how the subprime crisis came about.
Listen to the dialogue and take notes on the causes and effects of the credit crunch. Use the table below.

Interest rates	Banks	House owners	Rating agencies	Housing market
were low in 2001				
	invented new products – subprime loans			

R Exercise 3

22 **Can you think of the missing word? Complete the following sentences. Listen to the dialogue once more to check your results.**

1. Subprime loans are loans to people who have a poor ? .
2. During the housing bubble the ? of property rose by about ten per cent every year.
3. The banks had much more ? for credit than they could supply.
4. Subprime loans were mixed with ? loans to improve the rating of the subprime loans.
5. The house owners default on their loans and the houses are ? by the banks.
6. Loans are expensive and house prices are falling, so the entire housing market ? .

E A perspective on globalisation

Where will globalisation take us? Even before the subprime crisis, capitalism and globalisation were being widely discussed. In his book, "Making Globalisation Work", Nobel Peace Prize winner Joseph Stiglitz has tried to give an answer to this question by describing both the current problems and the perspectives of globalisation.

P/R **Exercise 1**
Read the text and find a key word which best describes the content of each paragraph. Sum up the text in your own words with the aid of these key words.

Joseph Stiglitz

Making globalisation work

This book reflects my faith in democratic processes; my be-lief that an informed citizenry is more likely to provide some
5 checks against the abuses of the special corporate and fi-nancial interests that have so dominated the globalisation process; that ordi-nary citizens of the advanced industrial countries,
10 as well as of the developing world, share a com-mon interest in making globalisation work. (…)

I also hope to show that while globalisation's critics are correct in saying it has been used to push a particular set of values, this need not be
15 so. Globalisation does not have to be bad for the environment, increase inequality, weaken cultural diversity, and advance corporate interests at the expense of the well-being of ordinary citizens. In Making Globalisation Work, I attempt to show
20 how globalisation, properly managed, as it was in the successful development of much of East Asia, can do a great deal to benefit both the developing and the developed countries of the world. (…)

Economists who place less importance on
25 reducing income inequality are more prone to think that the actions governments might take to reduce that inequality are too costly, and may even be counterproductive. These "free market" economists are also more inclined to believe that
30 markets, by themselves, without government intervention, are efficient, and that the best way

to help the poor is simply to let the economy grow – and, somehow, the benefits will trickle down to the poor. (…)

On the other hand, those who, like me, think that 35 markets often fail to produce efficient outcomes (producing too much pollution and too little basic research, for instance) and are disturbed by income inequalities and high levels of poverty, also believe that reducing that inequality can cost 40 less than the conservative economists predict. Those who worry about inequality and poverty also see the enormous costs of not dealing with the problem: the social consequences, including alienation, violence, and social conflict. (…) 45

Globalisation, like development, is not inevitable – even though there are strong underlying political and economic forces behind it. (…) If globalisation leads to lower standards of living for many or most of the citizens of a country, and 50 if it compromises fundamental cultural values, then there will be political demands to slow or stop it. (…)

Open, democratic processes can circumscribe the power of special interest groups. We can bring 55 ethics back into business. Corporate governance can recognize the rights not only of shareholders but of others who are touched by the actions of the corporations. An engaged and educated citizenry can understand how to make globalisation work, 60 or at least work better, and can demand that their political leaders shape globalisation accordingly. I hope this book will help make this vision a reality.

Exercise 2

What is Joseph Stiglitz' criticism of globalisation as it exists today?
Take notes from the text.

Exercise 3

Which statements would Joseph Stiglitz agree with?

1. The interests of companies and financial institutions will always determine the face of globalisation.
2. Globalisation will always have a negative effect on the environment.
3. Cultural differences will automatically disappear with global trade.
4. Many economists believe that politics should not interfere with capitalism.
5. The people of a country have the right and the influence to change the course of globalisation.
6. Society has to accept the fact that there will always be people who lose out through globalisation.
7. It is very important that people are well informed so they can make choices.

Exercise 4

Talk to your partner. Choose a statement you absolutely disagree with and give reasons for your choice.

Exercise 5

Draft a statement about globalisation that expresses your opinion. Include five of the following seven words in your statement.

politician • citizen • poor • corporation • financial • cultural • society

Language and grammar: Conditional clauses

Bedingungssätze (conditional clauses) werden im Englischen nach einem relativ festen Schema gestaltet. Es gibt drei Grundtypen von Bedingungssätzen:

Hauptsatz Nebensatz der Bedingung	Nebensatz der Bedingung
1. I will buy shares (FUTURE) (Ich **werde** …)	if the indices continue to rise like that tomorrow. (PRESENT TENSE)
2. He would be a very rich man (CONDITIONAL) (Er wäre …)	if the Dax climbed to over 9000 points. (SIMPLE PAST)
3. We would have been able to buy our competitor (CONDITIONAL PERFECT) (wir wären … gewesen …)	if our revenues had doubled last year. (PAST PERFECT)

Ferner gilt das Schema, wenn der Nebensatz durch eine andere Konjunktion eingeleitet wird: z. B. *unless*, *provided (that)*, *on condition (that)*:

There will be severe coordination problems	unless we update our computer program.

Phrases: Globalisation

Company strategies

Outsourcing means that one company passes on a process to another company to save costs.	Auslagerung bedeutet, dass eine Firma einen Prozess an eine andere Firma auslagert um Kosten zu sparen.
In a foreign direct investment a company controls an international affiliate and holds at least 10% of its shares.	Bei einer Auslandsdirektinvestition kontrolliert eine Firma eine internationale Tochter und hält mindestens 10% der Anteile.
A joint venture is a strategy to enter a new market by creating a new company together with a domestic company.	Ein Joint Venture ist eine Strategie, einen neuen Markt zu erreichen, indem mit einer lokalen Firma eine neue Firma gegründet wird.
In a merger two companies join together to create a new company for the benefit of both.	Bei einer Fusion schließen sich zwei Firmen zusammen, um zum beiderseitigen Vorteil eine neue Firma zu erschaffen.
Offshoring means that a part of a company is moved abroad because labour costs are lower.	Eine Standortverlegung bedeutet, dass ein Teil einer Firma aufgrund niedrigerer Lohnkosten ins Ausland verlegt wird.
In a takeover one company purchases another one – in a friendly or hostile action.	Bei einer Übernahme kauft eine Firma eine andere – durch eine freundliche oder feindliche Aktion.

Financial instruments

Bonds are loans with a fixed sum which has to be paid back after a set period of time.	Anleihen sind Darlehen in festgelegter Höhe, die nach einer festgelegten Zeitdauer zurückgezahlt werden müssen.
Commodities are assets with tangible properties, e.g. crude oil or rice.	Rohstoffe sind Anlagegüter, die berührt werden können, zum Beispiel Rohöl und Reis.
Shares represent a unit of ownership in a corporation, profits are distributed in dividends.	Aktien stellen eine Besitzeinheit an einer Aktiengesellschaft dar, Gewinne werden in Dividenden ausgezahlt.
Foreign exchange trading is based on converting the currency of one country into that of another country.	Der Devisenhandel basiert auf dem Umtausch der Währung eines Landes in die eines anderen Landes.

Globalisation

Globalisation stands for a greater movement of people, goods, capital and ideas through increased economic integration.	Globalisierung steht für eine höhere Mobilität von Menschen, Gütern, Kapital und Ideen aufgrund verstärkter wirtschaftlicher Integration.
Globalisation may increase inequality and weaken cultural diversity, but it does not need to be like that.	Globalisierung kann eine ungleiche Verteilung erhöhen und kulturelle Vielfalt verringern, aber dies muss nicht notwendigerweise so sein.

Role cards Partner B

Unit 4 A – Exercise 1

Role card: Student B – Peter Davidson's diary	(see role card Student A on page 55)

Monday	13.00:	appointment with finance director of Eutechnics plc
Tuesday	9.00:	Internal meeting/economic data July
	10.00:	Telephone conference with Dr Raith/Frankfurt
	15.00:	meeting with unit trust managers
Wednesday	9.00 – 9.30:	appointment with John Baker/Lonsdale plc
	20.00:	Royal Opera House
Thursday	9.45:	Meeting/changes in bank regulations
	13.00:	Edit quarterly report
Friday	9.00:	meeting with Judith Armitage/CEO Novoil Investments.

Unit 6 B – Exercise 6

Role card: Student B	(see role card Student A on page 88)

Sie sind Sandy O'Neil aus Schottland und wollen für ein Jahr in einer deutschen Bank arbeiten.

- Sie lernen jetzt einen neuen Kollegen/eine neue Kollegin kennen. Sagen Sie, dass Sie gern Englisch reden möchten, da es für Sie noch schwierig ist, immer Deutsch zu sprechen.
- Beantworten Sie die Fragen Ihres Partners zu allgemeinen Dingen.
- Freie Antworten
- Beschreiben Sie die Abteilungen, in denen die Arbeit besonderen Spaß machte oder die besonders interessant waren.
- Drücken Sie Interesse an der zukünftigen Arbeit und Zusammenarbeit aus.
- Antworten Sie entsprechend.

Beenden Sie das Gespräch und drücken Sie die Hoffnung auf eine weitere Gelegenheit zum Erfahrungsaustausch aus.

Unit 8 D – Exercise 6

Role card: Buying Insurance – Student B   (see role card Student A on page 116)

You are Frank's new colleague, Doctor King.
You think that Frank should buy his insurance from North Norfolk Insurance Brokers and not shop around.

Your reasons for this are:
1. Eamonn Gardener will help Frank fill in the forms. He is also a local man and can help Frank if he has any questions.
2. There is a difference between being good at a language when talking about your own industry or profession or when using general English and understanding the special terms in other industries.
3. Frank may pay a little extra for this insurance but he will get good service and help if he has to make a claim. Service is more important than price.
4. Frank doesn't have much time.

And any other reasons you can think of.

Unit 9 D – Exercise 2

Role card: Student B   (see role card Student A on page 135)

Sie sind der Leiter der Personalabteilung, der das Vorstellungsgespräch führt. Beginnen Sie das Gespräch mit allgemeinen Fragen nach z. B.: Begrüßung, Flug, Wetter …

Führen Sie das Gespräch fort, indem Sie die Anforderungen in der Anzeige nochmals kurz zusammenfassen:
• Teamfähigkeit
• Sprachkenntnisse
• Kundenbetreuung

Fragen Sie nach der beruflichen Erfahrung:
• Dauer
• Arbeitsgebiet
• Computerkenntnisse

Erkundigen Sie sich nach den Gründen für einen Ortswechsel nach Birmingham.
Gehen Sie auf die Interessen ein und erkundigen Sie sich nach der Mobilität der Bewerberin.
Versprechen Sie, innerhalb einer Woche Bescheid zu geben.
Verabschieden Sie die Bewerberin.

Unit 1

Introducing yourself and your place of work

superior [suːˈpɪərɪə]   der/die Vorgesetzte
polite [pəˈlaɪt]   höflich
rude [ruːd]   unhöflich
relationship [rɪˈleɪʃnʃɪp]   Beziehung
to determine [dɪˈtɜːmɪn]   bestimmen
gesture [ˈdʒestʃə]   Geste
facial expression   Gesichtsausdruck
[ˌfeɪʃl ɪkˈspreʃn]
Exercise
customer service assistant   Kundenberater/-in
[ˌkʌstəmə ˈsɜːvɪs əˌsɪstənt]

A Talking about yourself

Exercise 1
briefly [ˈbriːflɪ]   kurz und knapp
apprenticeship [əˈprentɪsʃɪp]   Lehre, Ausbildung
quite a lot [ˌkwaɪt ə ˈlɒt]   ziemlich viel
classmate [ˈklɑːsmeɪt]   Klassenkamerad/-in
local [ˈləʊkl]   lokal, örtlich
bank clerk [ˈbæŋkˌklɑːk]   Bankkaufmann/-frau
originally [əˈrɪdʒɪnəlɪ]   ursprünglich
Exercise 3
investment banking   Kapitalanlagenberatung
[ɪnˈvestməntˌbæŋkɪŋ]
Exercise 4
Communicating across cultures
customary [ˈkʌstəmərɪ]   gebräuchlich
Exercise 5
marital status [ˌmærɪtl ˈsteɪtəs]   Familienstand
occupation [ˌɒkjʊˈpeɪʃn]   Beruf
divorced [dɪˈvɔːst]   geschieden
post code [ˈpəʊstˌkəʊd]   Postleitzahl
Exercise 6
insurance clerk   Versicherungskaufmann/-frau
[ɪnˈʃɔːrənsˌklɑːk]
insurance agent   Versicherungsvertreter/-in
[ɪnˈʃɔːrənsˌeɪdʒənt]
insurance broker   Versicherungsmakler/-in
[ɪnˈʃɔːrənsˌbrəʊkə]
investment consultant   Anlagenberater/-in
[ɪnˈvestmənt kənˌsʌltənt]
customer service officer   Kundenberater/-in
[ˌkʌstəmə ˈsɜːvɪsˌɒfɪsə]
loan advisor [ˈləʊn ədˌvaɪzə]   Darlehensberater/-in

B Talking about your work

Exercise 2
claim [kleɪm]   Schadensfall
application form   Antrag
[ˌæplɪˈkeɪʃnˌfɔːm]
records [ˈrekɔːdz]   Unterlagen, Akten

Exercise 3
Tapescript Track 1
customer service area   Kundenberatungsbereich
[ˌkʌstəmə ˈsɜːvɪsˌeərɪə]
cashier [kæˈʃɪə]   Kassierer/-in
deposit [dɪˈpɒzɪt]   Einzahlung
direct debit [daɪˌrekt ˈdebɪt]   Lastschrifteinzug
standing order   Dauerauftrag
[ˌstændɪŋ ˈɔːdə]
bank transfer   Banküberweisung
[ˈbæŋkˌtrænsfɜː]
need [niːd]   Bedürfnis
tailor-made [ˌteɪləˈmeɪd]   maßgeschneidert
solution [səˈluːʃn]   Lösung
corporate customer   Großkundenabteilung
department
[ˌkɔːpərət ˈkʌstəmə dɪˌpɑːtmənt]
asset management   Vermögensberatung
[ˈæset ˌmænɪdʒmənt]
legal department   Rechtsabteilung
[ˈliːgl dɪˌpɑːtmənt]
administrative offices   Verwaltungsbüros
[ədˈmɪnɪstrətɪvˌɒfɪsɪz]
human resources   Personalabteilung
department
[ˌhjuːmən ˈriːsɔːsɪz dɪˌpɑːtmənt]
in house training   firmeninterne
[ˌɪnhaʊs ˈtreɪnɪŋ]   Weiterbildung
to assess [əˈses]   beurteilen
real estate department   Immobilienabteilung
[ˈriːlɪˌsteɪt dɪˌpɑːtmənt]
regional branch office   regionale Zweigstelle
[ˌriːdʒənl ˈbrɑːntʃˌɒfɪs]
owner occupied flat   Eigentumswohnung
[ˌəʊnə ˌɒkjʊpaɪd ˈflæt]
property [ˈprɒpətɪ]   Grundstück, Besitz, Eigentum

Exercise 6
Tapescript Tracks 2 and 3
field force [ˈfiːldˌfɔːs]   Außendienst
consultation [ˌkɒnsʌlˈteɪʃn]   Beratungssitzung
to retrieve [rɪˈtriːv]   abrufen

Exercise 7
real estate assistant   Immobilienverkäufer/-in
[ˈriːlɪˌsteɪt əˌsɪstənt]
corporate business advisor   Firmenkundenberater/-in
[ˌkɔːpərət ˈbɪznɪs ədˌvaɪzə]
Exercise 8
to handle [ˈhændl]   bearbeiten, erledigen

C Helping foreign customers

cash [kæʃ]   Bargeld
cash dispenser   Geldautomat
[ˈkæʃ dɪˌspensə]

direct debit authorization [daɪˌrekt ˈdebɪt ɔːˌθəraɪˌzeɪʃn] — Lastschrifteinzugsermächtigung

statement [ˈsteɪtmənt] — Kontoauszug

statement printer [ˈsteɪtmənt ˌprɪntə] — Kontoauszugsdrucker

Exercise 1

withdrawal [wɪðˈdrɔːəl] — Abhebung

bill [bɪl] — Rechnung

Exercise 2

salary [ˈsæləri] — Gehalt

account [əˈkaʊnt] — Konto

D Taking care of foreign visitors

Exercise 3

luggage [ˈlʌgɪdʒ] — Gepäck

Exercise 7
Tapescript Track 5

corporate loan department [ˌkɔːpərət ˈləʊn dɪˌpɑːtmənt] — Abteilung für Firmendarlehen

to signpost [ˈsaɪnpəʊst] — ausschildern

Unit 2
Telephoning

to encourage [ɪnˈkʌrɪdʒ] — ermutigen, ermuntern, fördern

pressure [ˈpreʃə] — Druck

savings account [ˈseɪvɪŋz əˌkaʊnt] — Sparkonto

deposit account [dɪˈpɒzɪt əˌkaʊnt] — Festgeldkonto

to operate [ˈɒpəreɪt] — abwickeln

rate of interest [ˌreɪt əv ˈɪntrest] — Zins, Zinssatz

access [ˈækses] — Zugang

landline [ˈlændlaɪn] — Festnetzanschluss

A Telephoning in English

Exercise 1
Info:

comeback [ˈkʌmbæk] — Reaktion

unavoidable [ˌʌnəˈvɔɪdəbl] — unvermeidbar

embarrassment [ɪmˈbærəsmənt] — Verlegenheit

justified [ˈdʒʌstɪfaɪd] — gerechtfertigt

despair [dɪˈspeə] — Verzweiflung

Exercise 3

at your fingertips [ət jɔː ˈfɪŋgətɪps] — parat, verfügbar

to catch (caught, caught) [kætʃ] — mitbekommen, verstehen

to put (s.o.) through (put, put) [pʊt ˈθruː] — (jmdn.) durchstellen, verbinden

extension [ɪkˈstenʃn] — Durchwahl

appointment [əˈpɔɪntmənt] — Termin

urgently [ˈɜːdʒəntli] — dringend

to finalise [ˈfaɪnəlaɪz] — zum Abschluss bringen

major [ˈmeɪdʒə] — wichtig, groß

to get back (to) (got, got) [get ˈbæk tə] — zurückrufen

to leave a message (left, left) [ˌliːv ə ˈmesɪdʒ] — eine Nachricht hinterlassen

area code [ˈeərɪə ˌkəʊd] — Ortsvorwahl

to omit [əˈmɪt] — weglassen

to assume [əˈsjuːm; əˈsuːm] — annehmen

to switch off [ˌswɪtʃ ˈɒf] — ausschalten

If all else fails [ɪf ˌɔːl els ˈfeɪlz] — wenn alle Stricke reißen

Communicating across cultures

suitable [ˈsuːtəbl] — geeignet

to get down to business (got, got) [get ˌdaʊn tə ˈbɪznɪs] — zur Sache/zum Geschäftlichen kommen

to come across (came, come) [kʌm əˈkrɒs] — wirken

B Receiving and redirecting calls

Exercise 1

accounts [əˈkaʊnts] — Buchhaltung

convenient [kənˈviːnɪənt] — günstig, passend

Exercise 2

on behalf of [ɒn bɪˈhɑːf əv] — im Auftrag von

to postpone [pəsˈpəʊn] — verschieben

to chair [tʃeə] — den Vorsitz haben

with regard to [wɪð rɪˈgɑːd tə] — hinsichtlich, bezüglich

interference [ˌɪntəˈfɪərəns] — Störung

to consider [kənˈsɪdə] — betrachten, in Betracht ziehen

C Taking messages

Exercise 1
Info:

to take down (took, taken) [teɪk ˈdaʊn] — notieren

essential [ɪˈsenʃl] — wichtig

failure [ˈfeɪljə] — Versagen, Unterlassen

Exercise 2

to make up (made, made) [meɪk ˈʌp] — erfinden

Exercise 5

hyphen [ˈhaɪfən] — Bindestrich

dash [dæʃ] — Gedankenstrich

colon [ˈkəʊlɒn] — Doppelpunkt

slash [slæʃ] — Schrägstrich

stroke [strəʊk] — Schrägstrich

backslash [ˈbækslæʃ] — umgekehrter Schrägstrich

understroke [ˈʌndəstrəʊk] — Unterstrich

Exercise 6

grid [grɪd] — Tabelle, Raster

loan [ləʊn]   Darlehen
to assure [əˈʃʊə]   versichern
at the latest [ət ðə ˈleɪtɪst]   spätestens
disruption [dɪsˈrʌpʃn]   Störung

Exercise 8
to dispatch [dɪˈspætʃ]   versenden, verschicken
in stock [ɪn ˈstɒk]   vorrätig

D Making telephone calls
Exercise 1
provisional [prəˈvɪʒənl]   vorläufig
accommodation   Unterbringung, Unterkunft
[əˌkɒməˈdeɪʃn]
agenda [əˈdʒendə]   Tagesordnung
premises [ˈpremɪsɪz]   Geschäftsräume,
                                     Firmengelände
chairman (chairmen)   Vorsitzender (Vorsitzende)
[ˈtʃeəmən]
requirement [rɪˈkwaɪəmənt]   Bedarf
Exercise 3
term (life) assurance   Risikolebensversicherung
[ˈtɜːm (ˈlaɪf) əˌʃɔːrəns]
to take out insurance   eine Versicherung
(took, taken)   abschließen
[ˌteɪk aʊt ɪnˈʃɔːrəns]
insurance cover   Versicherungsdeckung
[ɪnˈʃɔːrəns ˌkʌvə]
to secure a loan   ein Darlehen absichern
[sɪˌkjʊərˌə ˈləʊn]
beneficiary [ˌbenəˈfɪʃəri]   Begünstigte/-r
premature [ˈpremətʃə]   vorzeitig
to stipulate [ˈstɪpjəleɪt]   vereinbaren, festlegen
asset [ˈæset]   Vermögenswerte
annual [ˈænjʊəl]   jährlich

**E Leaving messages on an
answering machine**
concise [kənˈsaɪs]   knapp und präzise

Exercise 1
to finalise [ˈfaɪnəlaɪz]   endgültig festlegen
funding [ˈfʌndɪŋ]   Finanzierung, Förderung

Exercise 2
joint [dʒɔɪnt]   gemeinsam

Unit 3
Presentations
to require [rɪˈkwaɪə]   benötigen
to range from … to …   reichen von … bis …
[reɪndʒ]
to scare [skeə]   erschrecken

audience [ˈɔːdɪəns]   Publikum
ability [əˈbɪləti]   Fähigkeit
oral [ˈɔːrəl]   mündlich
key skill [ˌkiː ˈskɪl]   Schlüsselqualifikation,
                                     -fertigkeit
to acquire [əˈkwaɪə]   erreichen, erlangen
essential [ɪˈsenʃl]   wesentlich, unbedingt
                                     erforderlich
preparation [ˌprepərˈeɪʃn]   Vorbereitung
Exercise
brief [briːf]   kurz

**A What makes a good
presentation?**
Exercise 3
content [ˈkɒntent]   Inhalt
aim [eɪm]   Ziel
in advance [ɪn ədˈvɑːns]   im Voraus
to bore [bɔː]   langweilen
conclusion [kənˈkluːʒn]   Schluss
to refer (to) [rɪˈfɜː]   sich beziehen auf
visual aids [ˌvɪʒʊəl ˈeɪdz]   visuelle Hilfsmittel
delivery [dɪˈlɪvəri]   Vortrag(-sweise)
manner [ˈmænə]   Art und Weise
to rehearse [rɪˈhɜːs]   proben
performance [pəˈfɔːməns]   Aufführung
to keep, kept, kept   ständig tun
(+ doing) [kiːp]
Exercise 4
**Communicating across
cultures**
to appreciate [əˈpriːʃieɪt]   schätzen
to respond [rɪˈspɒnd]   reagieren
sincerity [sɪnˈserəti]   Aufrichtigkeit
invasion of privacy   Verletzung der Privatsphäre
[ɪnˌveɪʒn əv ˈprɪvəsi]
unaware [ˌʌnəˈweə]   nichtsahnend
Exercise 7
apprenticeship [əˈprentɪʃɪp]   Ausbildung, Lehre
major [ˈmeɪdʒə]   Haupt-, bedeutend
insurance [ɪnˈʃɔːrəns]   Versicherung

B Preparing a presentation
1 Selecting the content
objective [əbˈdʒektɪv]   Ziel
to gather [ˈgæðə]   sammeln
Exercise 1
current [ˈkʌrənt]   gegenwärtig, aktuell
Exercise 2
to prioritise [praɪˈɒrɪtaɪz]   priorisieren, Schwerpunkte
                                     bilden
bold [bəʊld]   fett gedruckt
2 Structuring the content
vital [ˈvaɪtl]   entscheidend, wesentlich

Exercise 2
Tapescript Track 11

insurance broker [ɪnˈʃɔːrəns ˌbrəʊkə]	Versicherungsmakler/-in
to conclude [kənˈkluːd]	schließen, zum Schluss kommen

Exercise 3

to brief [briːf]	kurz informieren

Exercise 4

to refocus [ˌriːˈfəʊkəs]	sich neu konzentrieren
in conclusion [ɪn kənˈkluːʒn]	schließlich, zum Schluss
to sum up [sʌm ˈʌp]	zusammenfassen
issue [ˈɪʃuː]	Frage, Problem

3 Visual aids

visual [ˈvɪʒʊəl]	visuell
aid [eɪd]	Hilfsmittel
to enhance [ɪnˈhɑːns]	verbessern
to arouse (interest) [əˈraʊz]	(Interesse) wecken
to double [ˈdʌbl]	eine doppelte Funktion erfüllen
handout [ˈhændaʊt]	Informationsblatt
flowchart [ˈfləʊtʃɑːt]	Ablaufdiagramm, Flussdiagramm
cue [kjuː]	Stichwort, Hinweis
upper and lower case letters [ˌʌpər nˌləʊəkeɪs ˈletəz]	Groß- und Kleinbuchstaben

Exercise 2

pie chart [ˈpaɪ ˌtʃɑːt]	Tortendiagramm
bar chart [ˈbɑː ˌtʃɑːt]	Balkendiagramm
line graph [ˈlaɪn ˌgrɑːf]	Liniendiagramm
organigram [ɔːˈgænɪgræm]	Organigramm

Exercise 3

in relation to [ɪn rɪˈleɪʃn tuː]	in Beziehung zu

4 Equipment
Exercise
Info:

in working order [ɪn ˌwɜːkɪŋ ˈɔːdə]	in betriebsfähigem Zustand
well rested [ˌwel ˈrestɪd]	ausgeschlafen
confidence [ˈkɒnfɪdəns]	Vertrauen

5 Prompt cards

pre-tax profits [ˌpriːtæks ˈprɒfɪts]	Vorsteuergewinn
to revise downwards [rɪˌvaɪz ˈdaʊnwədz]	nach unten korrigieren
real estate [ˈrɪəl ɪˌsteɪt]	Grundbesitz, Immobilien
forecast [ˈfɔːkɑːst]	Vorhersage
estimate [ˈestɪmət]	Schätzung
revision [rɪˈvɪʒn]	Korrektur

Exercise

policy [ˈpɒləsi]	Police (Versicherung)
cash benefit [ˌkæʃ ˈbenəfɪt]	Barleistung
self-employed [ˌselfɪmˈplɔɪd]	selbstständig
disabled [dɪˈseɪbld]	arbeitsunfähig, behindert
renewable [rɪˈnjuːəbl]	erneuerbar

deferred period [dɪˌfɜːd ˈpɪəriəd]	Karenztage
lump sum [ˌlʌmp ˈsʌm]	Einmalzahlung, Pauschale
limb [lɪm]	Glied, Gliedmaße

C The language of presentations
Exercise 2

to rise, rose, risen [raɪz]	steigen
to peak [piːk]	den Höchststand erreichen
to decline [dɪˈklaɪn]	zurückgehen, fallen, sinken
to increase [ɪnˈkriːs]	zunehmen
to bottom out [ˌbɒtəm ˈaʊt]	den Tiefstand erreichen
to decrease [dɪˈkriːs]	abnehmen
to drop [drɒp]	fallen
to rocket [ˈrɒkɪt]	in die Höhe schießen
to remain stable [rɪˌmeɪn ˈsteɪbl]	sich (stabil) halten
to plummet [ˈplʌmɪt]	stürzen, absacken
to level off [ˌlevl ˈɒf]	sich einpendeln, sich stabilisieren

Exercise 3

to modify [ˈmɒdɪfaɪ]	ändern, verändern
securities [sɪˈkjʊərətiz]	Wertpapiere, Effekten

Exercise 4

policyholder [ˈpɒləsiˌhəʊldə]	Versicherungsnehmer/-in

Exercise 5
Tapescript Track 12

axis [ˈæksɪs]	Achse
stage [steɪdʒ]	Stufe
to acquire [əˈkwaɪə]	akquirieren
substantial [səbˈstænʃl]	beträchtlich
sharply [ˈʃɑːpli]	hier: steil (ansteigen)
to peak [piːk]	den Höchststand erreichen

Exercise 6

share [ʃeə]	Anteil
percentage [pəˈsentɪdʒ]	Prozentsatz
to make up, made, made [ˌmeɪk ˈʌp]	ausmachen

Exercise 7

life assurance [ˌlaɪf əˈʃɔːrəns]	Lebensversicherung
household contents (insurance) [ˌhaʊshəʊld ˈkɒntents]	Hausrat(versicherung)
personal liability [ˌpɜːsənl laɪəˈbɪləti]	Privathaftpflicht
legal (insurance) [ˈliːgl]	Rechtschutz(versicherung)

Exercise 8

to swap [swɒp]	tauschen

D Delivering the presentation

senior staff [ˌsiːniə ˈstɑːf]	leitende Angestellte, Führungskräfte

Exercise 1

to state [steɪt]	angeben

Tapescript Track 13

tight [taɪt]	knapp
imposing [ɪm'pəʊzɪŋ]	beeindruckend
stake [steɪk]	Aktienanteil
merger ['mɜːdʒə]	Fusion
buoyant ['bɔɪənt]	lebhaft, steigend

Exercise 2

to bear in mind, bore, borne [ˌbeə ɪn 'maɪnd]	bedenken, beachten

Exercise 3

evaluation [ɪˌvæljʊ'eɪʃn]	Bewertung, Beurteilung
to evaluate [ɪ'vælʊeɪt]	bewerten, beurteilen

Exercise 4

to assess [ə'ses]	beurteilen, bewerten
to award [ə'wɔːd]	vergeben, verleihen
to substantiate [səb'stænʃieɪt]	begründen
appropriate [ə'prəʊprɪət]	geeignet, angemessen
repetitive [rɪ'petətɪv]	monoton, sich wiederholend
lively ['laɪvlɪ]	lebendig, spritzig

E Public speaking strategies

to terrify ['terɪfaɪ]	in Schrecken versetzen
respondent [rɪ'spɒndənt]	Befragte/-r
well-tailored [ˌwel'teɪləd]	zugeschnitten
supportive [sə'pɔːtɪv]	unterstützend
twitch [twɪtʃ]	Zucken
jerky ['dʒɜːkɪ]	ruckartig

Exercise 1

hesitation [ˌhezɪ'teɪʃn]	Verzögerung
repetition [ˌrepə'tɪʃn]	Wiederholung
deliberately [dɪ'lɪbrətlɪ]	absichtlich
to catch out (caught, caught) [kætʃ 'aʊt]	erwischen
to incorporate [ɪn'kɔːpəreɪt]	einbauen
coherently [kəʊ'hɪərəntlɪ]	zusammenhängend

Phrases

gist [dʒɪst]	das Wesentliche
furthermore [ˌfɜːðə'mɔː]	überdies, außerdem

Unit 4
Meetings and negotiations

negotiation [nɪˌgəʊʃɪ'eɪʃn]	Verhandlung
essential [ɪ'senʃl]	sehr wichtig, unbedingt erforderlich
objective [əb'dʒektɪv]	Ziel
succinctly [sək'sɪŋktlɪ]	kurz und bündig, prägnant

A Making an appointment

Exercise 1

PA (Personal Assistant) [ˌpiː'eɪ] [ˌpɜːsnl ə'sɪstənt]	Chefsekretär/-in
unit trust [ˌjuːnɪt 'trʌst]	Investmentgesellschaft
CEO (Chief Executive Officer) [ˌsiːiː'əʊ] [ˌtʃiːf ɪɡˌzekjʊtɪv 'ɒfɪsə]	Vorstandsvorsitzende/-r, Firmenchef/-in

Exercise 2

Communicating across cultures

supplementary [ˌsʌplɪ'mentərɪ]	zusätzlich
charge [tʃɑːdʒ]	Gebühr

B Preparing agendas, meetings and conferences

Exercise 2

to draw up (drew, drawn) [drɔː 'ʌp]	entwerfen, erstellen
in advance [ɪn əd'vɑːns]	im Voraus
familiar [fə'mɪlɪə]	vertraut
to appoint [ə'pɔɪnt]	benennen, bestimmen, ernennen

Exercise 3

draft [drɑːft]	Entwurf

Exercise 4

approval [ə'pruːvl]	Billigung, Einverständnis

Exercise 6

beverage ['bevərɪdʒ]	Getränk
whiteboard ['waɪtbɔːd]	Weißwandtafel
in working order [ɪn ˌwɜːkɪŋ 'ɔːdə]	in betriebsfähigem Zustand

C Taking the minutes

proceedings [prə'siːdɪŋz]	Handlungsverlauf
to keep an account (kept, kept) [ˌkiːp ən ə'kaʊnt]	Buch führen

D Negotiations

Exercise 3

fall-back position ['fɔːlbæk pəˌzɪʃn]	Rückzugsposition
bottom line [ˌbɒtəm 'laɪn]	Untergrenze
scope [skəʊp]	Raum, Umfang
to concede [kən'siːd]	einräumen, gewähren

Exercise 4
Tapescript Track 14

rural ['rʊərəl]	ländlich
turnover ['tɜːnˌəʊvə]	Umsatz
mortgage ['mɔːgɪdʒ]	Hypothek
to skip [skɪp]	überspringen, auslassen
to fix [fɪks]	festlegen (Termin)

Communicating across cultures

profoundly [prəˈfaʊndlɪ]	tief, hochgradig
outcome [ˈaʊtkʌm]	Ergebnis
to convey [kənˈveɪ]	vermitteln
confidence [ˈkɒnfɪdəns]	Vertrauen
obtrusive [əbˈtruːsɪv]	aufdringlich
trusting relationship [ˌtrʌstɪŋ rɪˈleɪʃnʃɪp]	Vertrauensverhältnis
slap [slæp]	Klaps, Schlag
hug [hʌg]	Umarmung
to go down well (went, gone) [ˌgəʊ daʊn ˈwel]	gut ankommen
to address [əˈdres]	anreden
reluctance [rɪˈlʌktəns]	Widerwille
counterpart [ˈkaʊntəpɑːt]	das Gegenüber, der Gegenpart
to underestimate [ˌʌndərˈestɪmeɪt]	unterschätzen
investigative [ɪnˈvestɪɡətɪv]	erforschend
approach [əˈprəʊtʃ]	Ansatz
value judgment [ˈvæljuː ˌdʒʌdʒmənt]	Werturteil

Unit 5
Business correspondence

conveniently [kənˈviːnɪəntlɪ]	bequem
recipient [rɪˈsɪpɪənt]	Empfänger/-in
lasting [ˈlɑːstɪŋ]	dauerhaft
letterhead [ˈletəhed]	Briefkopf
to transmit [trænzˈmɪt]	übertragen
to request [rɪˈkwest]	bitten
fragmented [fræɡˈmentɪd]	unzusammenhängend
vehicle [ˈvɪəkl]	(Hilfs)mittel
previous [ˈpriːvɪəs]	vorherig

A Business letters

subsequent [ˈsʌbsəkwənt]	darauf folgend
section [ˈsekʃn]	Teil, Abschnitt
common [ˈkɒmən]	üblich
marital status [ˌmærɪtl ˈsteɪtəs]	Familienstand
salutation [ˌsæljʊˈteɪʃn]	Anrede
subject line [ˈsʌbdʒekt ˌlaɪn]	Betreffzeile
bold [bəʊld]	fett gedruckt
body of the letter [ˌbɒdɪ əv ðə ˈletə]	Textteil des Briefes
to capitalise [ˈkæpɪtəlaɪz]	groß schreiben
complimentary close [ˌkɒmplɪmentrɪ ˈkləʊz]	Grußformel im Brief
signature block [ˈsɪɡnətʃə ˌblɒk]	Name und Unterschrift
enclosure [ɪnˈkləʊʒə]	Anlage (Brief)

Exercise 1

postcode [ˈpəʊstkəʊd]	Postleitzahl
overdraft [ˈəʊvədrɑːft]	Überziehung

current account [ˌkʌrənt əˈkaʊnt]	Girokonto
credit transfer [ˈkredɪt ˌtrænsfɜː]	Überweisung
deposit account [dɪˌpɒzɪt əˈkaʊnt]	Einlagenkonto
overdraft facility [ˈəʊvədrɑːft fəˌsɪlətɪ]	Überziehungskredit
application [ˌæplɪˈkeɪʃn]	Antrag

Exercise 2

pension scheme [ˈpenʃn ˌskiːm]	Versorgungsplan
retirement plan [rɪˈtaɪəmənt ˌplæn]	Altersvorsorgeplan
contribution [ˌkɒntrɪˈbjuːʃn]	Beitrag
policy [ˈpɒləsɪ]	(Versicherungs-)Police
benefit [ˈbenəfɪt]	Leistung, Nutzen

Exercise 3

field force agent [ˈfiːldfɔːs ˌeɪdʒənt]	Außendienstmitarbeiter/-in
loan agreement [ˈləʊn əˌgriːmənt]	Darlehensvereinbarung

Communicating across cultures

to be inclined (was, been) [bɪ ɪnˈklaɪnd]	geneigt sein zu
factual [ˈfæktjʊəl]	sachlich
superfluous [suːˈpɜːfluəs]	überflüssig

Exercise 5
Tapescript Track 15

to extend [ɪkˈstend]	erhöhen, erweitern
bridging-loan [ˈbrɪdʒɪŋ ˌləʊn]	Überbrückungskredit
revenue [ˈrevənjuː]	Erlös, Ertrag
security [sɪˈkjʊərətɪ]	Sicherheit

B E-Mails

drawback [ˈdrɔːbæk]	Nachteil

Exercise 3

to hesitate [ˈhezɪteɪt]	zögern
to require [rɪˈkwaɪə]	benötigen

Exercise 5

appointment [əˈpɔɪntmənt]	Termin

Exercise 7

account balance [əˈkaʊnt ˌbæləns]	Kontostand

Unit 6
Banks and insurance companies – organisation and structure
A Types of banks

subsidiary [səbˈsɪdɪərɪ]	Tochtergesellschaft
holding company [ˈhəʊldɪŋ ˌkʌmpənɪ]	Kapitalbeteiligungsgesellschaft, Dachgesellschaft

net worth [ˌnet ˈwɜːθ] — Reinvermögen, Gesellschaftskapital

prestigious [presˈtɪdʒəs] — angesehen, renommiert
solidity [səˈlɪdɪti] — Zuverlässigkeit, Solidität
discretion [dɪˈskreʃn] — Verschwiegenheit
to appeal [əˈpiːl] — ansprechen
IPO (Initial Public Offering) [ˌaɪpiːˈəʊ] — Börsengang
share issues [ˈʃeə ˌɪʃuːz] — Aktienemission
to cater to [ˈkeɪtə tuː] — abzielen auf, sich kümmern um
asset management division [ˈæset ˈmænɪdʒmənt dɪˌvɪʒn] — Vermögensverwaltungssparte

B Organisation and structure of a bank
broadly [ˈbrɔːdli] — weitgehend
Exercise 1
unit trust [ˌjuːnɪt ˈtrʌst] — offener Investmentfond
to purchase [ˈpɜːtʃəs] — kaufen
Exercise 4
emerging countries [ɪˌmɜːdʒɪŋ ˈkʌntriz] — Schwellenländer
presence [ˈprezəns] — Präsenz
hub [hʌb] — Mittelpunkt, Zentrum, Basis
revenue [ˈrevənjuː] — Erlös, Einnahmen, Einkünfte
equity [ˈekwɪti] — Eigenkapital, Stammaktien

C Structure of insurance companies
to merge [mɜːdʒ] — fusionieren
take-overs [ˈteɪkˌəʊvəz] — Übernahmen
to acquire [əˈkwaɪə] — erwerben
deregulation [ˈdiːreɡjʊˈleɪʃn] — Deregulierung, Öffnung der Märkte

Exercise 3
services provider [ˈsɜːvɪsɪz prəˌvaɪdə] — Dienstleister
fiscal year [ˌfɪskl ˈjɪə] — Geschäftsjahr
third-party assets [ˌθɜːdpɑːtɪ ˈæsets] — Fremdvermögen
Exercise 5
to appoint [əˈpɔɪnt] — ernennen

D Changes and innovation in financial services
to shed [ʃed] — abwerfen
dubious [ˈdjuːbɪəs] — unsicher
to lure [ljʊə] — ködern
to poach [pəʊtʃ] — abwerben
Exercise 3
to compete [kəmˈpiːt] — wetteifern
convenient [kənˈviːnɪənt] — günstig, praktisch, bequem
to value [ˈvæljuː] — schätzen
Exercise 4
to praise [preɪz] — anpreisen

Tapescript Track 16
to dispose of sth. [dɪˈspəʊz] — etwas entsorgen
offshore [ˌɒfˈʃɔː] — im Ausland

Exercise 5
keen (competition) [kiːn] — heftig, heiß (Wettbewerb)

Unit 7
Banks
retail bank [ˌriːteɪl ˈbæŋk] — Privatkundenbank
to place [pleɪs] — investieren
to cater for [ˈkeɪtə fɔː] — sich kümmern um
real estate [ˈrɪəl ɪˌsteɪt] — Immobilien
Exercise
exhausting [ɪɡˈzɔːstɪŋ] — anstrengend
amazing [əˈmeɪzɪŋ] — unglaublich
Nobel Peace Prize [ˌnəʊbel ˌpiːs ˈpraɪz] — Friedensnobelpreis

A Working in a bank
Exercise 1
instalment [ɪnˈstɔːlmənt] — Ratenzahlung
HR (Human Resources) [ˌeɪtʃˈɑː] [ˌhjuːmən ˈriːsɔːsɪz] — Personalwesen
to accumulate [əˈkjuːmjəleɪt] — ansammeln
Exercise 2
graduate [ˈɡrædʒʊət] — Hochschulabsolvent/-in
overdraft [ˈəʊvədrɑːft] — Kontoüberziehung
to induce [ɪnˈdjuːs] — herbeiführen
stand-alone [ˌstændəˈləʊn] — eigenständig
current account [ˌkʌrənt əˈkaʊnt] — Girokonto
savings account [ˌseɪvɪŋz əˈkaʊnt] — Sparkonto
mortgage [ˈmɔːɡɪdʒ] — Hypothek
to enhance [ɪnˈhɑːns] — verbessern
preferential [ˌprefərˈenʃl] — bevorzugt
consequently [ˈkɒnsɪkwəntli] — folglich
to prioritise [praɪˈɒrɪtaɪz] — den Vorrang geben
to extend [ɪkˈstend] — verlängern, vergrößern
Exercise 4
ATM (automatic teller machine) [ˌeɪtiːˈem] [ˌɔːtəmætɪk ˈtelə məˌʃiːn] — Geldautomat

B Tasks and services of retail banks
to transfer [trænsˈfɜː] — transferieren, überweisen
to debit [ˈdebɪt] — belasten
safe custody account [ˌseɪf ˈkʌstədɪ əˌkaʊnt] — Depotkonto
direct debit [daɪˌrekt ˈdebɪt] — Lastschrift
credit transfer [ˈkredɪt ˌtrænsfɜː] — Überweisung

standing order [ˌstændɪŋ ˈɔːdə]	Dauerauftrag
corporate financing [ˌkɔːpərət ˈfaɪnænsɪŋ]	Unternehmensfinanzierung
intermediary [ˌɪntəˈmiːdɪərɪ]	Zwischenhändler/-in, Mittelsmann
stock market [ˈstɒk ˌmɑːkɪt]	Aktienmarkt
Exercise 3	
probation period [prəʊˈbeɪʃn ˌpɪərɪəd]	Probezeit
savings scheme [ˈseɪvɪŋz ˌskiːm]	Sparplan

Exercise 4
Tapescript Track 17

tight [taɪt]	knapp (zeitlich)
standing order [ˌstændɪŋ ˈɔːdə]	Dauerauftrag

C Banking theory – financial intermediation

crucial [ˈkruːʃl]	entscheidend
demand [dɪˈmɑːnd]	Nachfrage
influx of funds [ˌɪnflʌks əv ˈfʌndz]	Mittelzufluss
financial intermediation [faɪˌnænʃl ˌɪntəmiːdɪˈeɪʃn]	Finanzintermediation
Exercise 2	
flow of money [ˌfləʊ əv ˈmʌnɪ]	Geldbewegung
deposit [dɪˈpɒzɪt]	Einlage
lot size transformation [ˈlɒt ˌsaɪz trænsfəˌmeɪʃn]	Losgrößentransformation
to bundle [ˈbʌndl]	bündeln
period transformation [ˈpɪərɪəd ˌtrænsfəˌmeɪʃn]	Fristentransformation
risk transformation [ˈrɪsk trænsfəˌmeɪʃn]	Risikotransformation

D Tasks of the European Central Bank

Exercise

purchasing power [ˈpɜːtʃəsɪŋ ˌpaʊə]	Kaufkraft
to balance [ˈbæləns]	ausgleichen
currency [ˈkʌrənsɪ]	Währung
to protect [prəˈtekt]	schützen
to conduct [kənˈdʌkt]	durchführen
monetary policy [ˌmʌnətrɪ ˈpɒlɪsɪ]	Geldpolitik
to issue [ˈɪʃuː]	herausgeben
to deem [diːm]	erachten
payment system [ˈpeɪmənt ˌsɪstəmz]	Zahlungssystem
shareholder [ˈʃeəˌhəʊldə]	Aktionär/-in
GDP (gross domestic product) [ˌdʒiːdiːˈpiː] [ˌgrəʊs dəˌmestɪk ˈprɒdʌkt]	Bruttoinlandsprodukt

treaty [ˈtriːtɪ]	Vertrag

E Alternative models of banking

microcredit [ˈmaɪkrəʊˌkredɪt]	Mikrokredit
vicious circle [ˌvɪʃəs ˈsɜːkl]	Teufelskreis
poverty [ˈpɒvətɪ]	Armut
viable [ˈvaɪəbl]	realisierbar
collateral [kəˈlætərəl]	Sicherheit
mutual [ˈmjuːtʃʊəl]	gegenseitig
peer pressure [ˈpɪə ˌpreʃə]	Gruppendruck
eligible [ˈelɪdʒəbl]	berechtigt, geeignet
to supervise [ˈsuːpəvaɪz]	überwachen
nutritional standard [njuːˌtrɪʃənl ˈstændəd]	Ernährungsstandard

Unit 8
Insurance

seafaring [ˈsiːˌfeərɪŋ]	Seefahrer-
trader [ˈtreɪdə]	Händler/-in
initially [ɪˈnɪʃəlɪ]	anfänglich, ursprünglich
to destroy [dɪˈstrɔɪ]	zerstören
essential [ɪˈsenʃl]	unverzichtbar
home entertainment system [ˌhəʊm entəˈteɪnmənt ˌsɪstəm]	Heimunterhaltungssystem
dependants [dɪˈpendənts]	Angehörige
liability insurance [laɪəˌbɪlətɪ ɪnˈfɔːrəns]	Haftpflichtversicherung
coverage [ˈkʌvərɪdʒ]	Versicherungsdeckung

A Managing risk
Exercise 1

to expose [ɪkˈspəʊz]	aussetzen (einer Gefahr, einem Risiko)
electrical surge [ɪˌlektrɪkl ˈsɜːdʒ]	Überspannung
premium [ˈpriːmɪəm]	Versicherungsprämie
loss [lɒs]	Verlust
to make a claim (made, made) [ˌmeɪk ə ˈkleɪm]	Schadenersatz beanspruchen
compensation [ˌkɒmpenˈseɪʃn]	Schadenersatz
worst case scenarios [ˌwɜːst ˌkeɪs sɪˈnɑːrɪəʊz]	Schlimmstfall-Szenarios
invalid [ɪnˈvælɪd]	ungültig
valuable [ˈvæljuəbl]	wertvoll
property [ˈprɒpətɪ]	Grundbesitz, Eigentum
Exercise 4	
devastation [ˌdevəˈsteɪʃn]	Zerstörung, Verwüstung

B The insurance industry

peril [ˈperəl]	Gefahr, Versicherungsrisiko
knock-on effect [ˌnɒkˈɒn ɪˌfekt]	Dominoeffekt, Kettenreaktion
significant [sɪgˈnɪfɪkənt]	signifikant, bedeutend

159

Exercise 1

current [ˈkʌrənt]	aktuell, gegenwärtig
at a glance [ət ə ˈglɑːns]	auf einen Blick
staff [stɑːf]	Personal

Exercise

setting [ˈsetɪŋ]	Rahmen, Umfeld
affected [əˈfektɪd]	betroffen
policyholder [ˈpɒləsɪ ˌhəʊldə]	Versicherungsnehmer/-in

C Insurance fraud

fraud [frɔːd]	Betrug, Schwindel
fraudulent [ˈfrɔːdjʊlənt]	betrügerisch
exaggerated [ɪgˌzædʒəreɪtɪd]	übertrieben
deception [dɪˈsepʃn]	Täuschung
collision [kəˈlɪʒn]	Kollision
pre-existing [ˌpriːɪgˈzɪstɪŋ]	vorher vorhanden
to fake [feɪk]	fälschen
law-abiding [ˈlɔːəˌbaɪdɪŋ]	gesetzestreu
alike [əˈlaɪk]	gleichermaßen

Exercise 2

evidence [ˈevɪdəns]	Beweis
to pretend [prɪˈtend]	vorgeben, vortäuschen
to drown [draʊn]	ertrinken

D Quote choice claim

quote [kwəʊt]	Angebot
choice [tʃɔɪs]	Auswahl
claim [kleɪm]	Schaden(sfall)

1 Quote

practice [ˈpræktɪs]	Arztpraxis
contents insurance [ˈkɒntents ɪnˌʃʊ.rəns]	Hausratversicherung

---

Exercise 1
Tapescript Track 19

GP (General Practitioner) [ˌdʒiːˈpiː] [ˌdʒenrəl prækˈtɪʃənə]	Allgemeinarzt,-ärztin
proposal form [prəˈpəʊzl ˌfɔːm]	Versicherungsantrag
to attach [əˈtætʃ]	anhängen (Anlage bei E-Mail)
assumptions checklist [əˈsʌmpʃnz ˌtʃeklɪst]	Checkliste zur Prüfung der Versicherungsberechtigung

---

Exercise 2

to incorporate [ɪnˈkɔːpəreɪt]	einbeziehen, aufnehmen

Exercise 3

panel [ˈpænl]	Ausschuss
to tailor [ˈteɪlə]	zuschneiden

Exercise 5
Tapescript Track 20

mix-up [ˈmɪksʌp]	Durcheinander
vital [ˈvaɪtl]	unbedingt notwendig
to invalidate [ɪnˈvælɪdeɪt]	unwirksam machen

Exercise 6

to shop around [ˌʃɒp əˈraʊnd]	Preise vergleichen
provider [prəˈvaɪdə]	Anbieter/-in
reluctantly [rɪˈlʌktəntlɪ]	ungern, widerwillig
commission [kəˈmɪʃn]	Provision
comparison site [kəmˌpærɪsən ˈsaɪt]	Preissuchmaschine

Exercise 7

no claims bonus [ˌnəʊ ˌkleɪmz ˈbəʊnəs]	Schadenfreiheitsrabatt
all risks cover [ˌɔːl ˌrɪsks ˈkʌvə]	Allgefahrendeckung
lump sum [ˌlʌmp ˈsʌm]	Pauschalbetrag
accidental damage [ˌæksɪdentl ˈdæmɪdʒ]	Unfallschaden
to recap [ˈriːkæp]	(kurz) zusammenfassen
to spin [spɪn]	sich drehen
joking aside [ˌdʒəʊkɪŋ əˈsaɪd]	Spaß beiseite

2 Choice

Exercise 1

outbuilding [ˈaʊtˌbɪldɪŋ]	Außengebäude

Exercise 3

to apply [əˈplaɪ]	gelten

Exercise 4

renewal [rɪˈnjuːəl]	Erneuerung
tacit (renewal) [ˌtæsɪt rɪˈnjuːəl]	stillschweigend(e Verlängerung)
to expire [ɪkˈspaɪə]	ablaufen

E Complaining

Communicating across cultures

to take offence (took, taken) [ˌteɪk əˈfens]	sich angegriffen fühlen
conciliatory [kənˈsɪliətrɪ]	versöhnlich
to antagonize [ænˈtægənaɪz]	gegen sich aufbringen, verärgern

Exercise

annoyance [əˈnɔɪəns]	Ärgernis

Unit 9
Job application

destination [ˌdestɪˈneɪʃn]	Ziel
vacancy [ˈveɪkənsɪ]	freie Stelle
recruitment centres [rɪˈkruːtmənt ˌsentəz]	Einstellungsfirmen
unsolicited [ˌʌnsəˈlɪsɪtɪd]	unverlangt (eingesandt)
application [ˌæplɪˈkeɪʃn]	Bewerbung
initial selection [ɪˌnɪʃl səˈlekʃn]	Vorauswahl

A Looking for a job

Exercise 2

grade [greɪd]	Note
mark [mɑːk]	Note (in der Schule)
degree [dɪˈgriː]	Abschluss

Exercise 3

command [kə'mɑ:nd]	Beherrschung	
reputation [ˌrepjʊ'teɪʃn]	Ruf	
property ['prɒpəti]	Haus, Gebäude	
liability [ˌlaɪə'bɪləti]	Haftpflicht	
motor ['məʊtə]	Kraftfahrzeug-	
predominant [prɪ'dɒmɪnənt]	überwiegend, hauptsächlich	
accurate ['ækjərət]	genau	
approach [ə'prəʊtʃ]	Herangehensweise, Ansatz	
draft [drɑ:ft]	Wechsel	
teller ['telə]	Kassierer/-in	
benefit ['benəfɪt]	Leistung	
legal assistance [ˌli:gl ə'sɪstəns]	Rechtsbeistand	
disability [ˌdɪsə'bɪləti]	Berufsunfähigkeit	

B CV / Résumé

tabular ['tæbjələ]	tabellarisch
achievement [ə'tʃi:vmənt]	Leistung

Exercise 2

record ['rekɔ:d]	Unterlage, Dokument

Exercise 4

to process ['prəʊses]	bearbeiten
to distribute [dɪ'strɪbju:t]	vertreiben
to maintain [meɪn'teɪn]	verwalten

C Writing a letter of application

to mention ['menʃn]	erwähnen
to demonstrate ['demənstreɪt]	beweisen

Info:

to be noticed [bɪ 'nəʊtɪst]	zur Kenntnis genommen werden

Exercise 2

expense [ɪk'spens]	Kosten

D Preparing for a job interview

prospective [prə'spektɪv]	in Aussicht stehend
prior [praɪə]	vorherig

Exercise 1

inevitable [ɪ'nevɪtəbl]	unvermeidlich

Exercise 3
Tapescript Track 21

up to par [ʌp tə 'pɑ:]	den Anforderungen entsprechend
run-of-the-mill [ˌrʌnəvðə'mɪl]	gewöhnlich, nullachtfünfzehn

Unit 10
Globalisation and global markets
A Defining globalisation
Exercise

challenge ['tʃælɪndʒ]	Herausforderung

to propel [prə'pel]	antreiben
borderless ['bɔ:dələs]	grenzenlos
domestic [də'mestɪk]	inländisch
to restrict [rɪ'strɪkt]	einschränken
issue ['ɪʃu:]	Problem
to perceive [pə'si:v]	wahrnehmen
to excite [ɪk'saɪt]	erregen

Exercise 3

fierce competition [ˌfɪəs kɒmpə'tɪʃn]	harter Wettbewerb

Communicating across cultures

insurgency [ɪn'sɜ:dʒənsi]	Aufruhr
to appease [ə'pi:z]	besänftigen

Exercise 4

blunder ['blʌndə]	grober Fehler, Patzer

B How do companies globalise

competitor [kəm'petɪtə]	Wettbewerber

Exercise 1

acquisition [ˌækwɪ'zɪʃn]	Firmenübernahme
takeover ['teɪkˌəʊvə]	Firmenübernahme
core competence [ˌkɔ: 'kɒmpɪtəns]	Kernkompetenz
foreign direct investment (FDI) [ˌfɒrən daɪˌrekt ɪn'vestmənt] [ˌefdi:'aɪ]	Auslandsdirektinvestition
joint venture [ˌdʒɔɪnt 'ventʃə]	Joint Venture, Beteiligungsunternehmen
incentive [ɪn'sentɪv]	Anreiz
affiliate [ə'fɪlɪət]	Tochtergesellschaft
merger ['mɜ:dʒə]	Fusion
offshoring [ˌɒf'ʃɔ:rɪŋ]	Standortverlagerung
outsourcing ['aʊtˌsɔ:sɪŋ]	Auslagerung
consent [kən'sent]	Einverständnis
hostile ['hɒstaɪl]	feindlich

Exercise 2

capitalisation [ˌkæpɪtəlaɪ'zeɪʃn]	Kapitalisierung
to launch [lɔ:ntʃ]	starten
bid [bɪd]	Gebot
subsidiary [səb'sɪdɪəri]	Tochterunternehmen
expertise [ˌekspɜ:'ti:z]	Expertise
renowned [rɪ'naʊnd]	renommiert
to embrace [ɪm'breɪs]	umarmen
to issue ['ɪʃu:]	herausgeben
to unveil [ʌn'veɪl]	bekanntmachen
to streamline ['stri:mlaɪn]	rationalisieren
automotive production [ɔ:təˌməʊtɪv prə'dʌkʃn]	Fahrzeugproduktion
return on assets [rɪˌtɜ:n ɒn 'æsets]	Gesamtkapitalrentabilität

C Global financial markets

to hedge [hedʒ] absichern

Exercise 1

bond [bɒnd] Anleihe

commodity [kə'mɒdətɪ] Rohstoff

creditor ['kredɪtə] Gläubiger

currency ['kʌrənsɪ] Währung

foreign exchange Devisen
[ˌfɒrən ɪks'tʃeɪndʒ]

tangible ['tændʒɪbl] greifbar, materiell

Exercise 2

quotation [kwəʊ'təɪʃn] Börsenpreis

to correlate ['kɒrəleɪt] korrelieren

D Financial markets and their risks: The subprime crisis

Exercise 2
Tapescript Track 22

crunch [krʌntʃ] Krise

Federal Reserve Bank US-Notenbank
[ˌfedərəl rɪˌzɜːv 'bæŋk]

credit rating ['kredɪt ˌreɪtɪŋ] Einstufung der Kreditwürdigkeit

value ['væljuː] Wert

commission [kə'mɪʃn] Kommission

to securitise [sɪ'kjʊərɪtaɪz] verbriefen

rating agencies Rating-Agenturen
['reɪtɪŋ ˌeɪdʒənsɪz]

to repossess [ˌriːpə'zes] pfänden

Exercise 3

subprime loans Darlehen, die in Hinsicht auf
[ˌsʌbˌpraɪm 'ləʊnz] Kundenbonität nicht dem
  Standard ‚Prime' entsprechen.

property ['prɒpətɪ] Immobilien, Eigentum

to default on a loan in Zahlungsrückstand
[dɪˌfɒlt ɒn ə 'ləʊn] geraten

E A perspective on globalisation

check ['tʃek] Hindernis

abuse [ə'bjuːs] Missbrauch

to push [pʊʃ] forcieren

inequality [ˌɪnɪ'kwɒlətɪ] Ungleichheit

to be prone to do sth. geneigt sein, etwas zu tun
[bɪ ˌprəʊn tə 'duː ˌsʌmθɪŋ]

counterproductive kontraproduktiv
[ˌkaʊntəprə'dʌktɪv]

to be inclined [bɪ ˌɪn'klaɪnd] geneigt sein

to trickle down [ˌtrɪkl 'daʊn] heruntertröpfeln

alienation [ˌeɪlɪə'neɪʃn] Entfremdung

inevitable [ɪ'nevɪtəbl] unabwendbar

to compromise ['kɒmprəmaɪz] beeinträchtigen

to circumscribe beschränken
[ˌsɜːkəm'skraɪb]

(T) = Tapescript

A

ability [əˈbɪləti] Fähigkeit 38
abuse [əˈbjuːs] Missbrauch 147
access [ˈækses] Zugang 22
accidental damage [ˌæksɪdentl ˈdæmɪdʒ] Unfallschaden 117
accommodation [əˌkɒməˈdeɪʃn] Unterbringung, Unterkunft 32
account [əˈkaʊnt] Konto 10
accounts [əˈkaʊnts] Buchhaltung 26
account balance [əˈkaʊnt ˌbæləns] Kontostand 81
to accumulate [əˈkjuːmjəleɪt] ansammeln 98
accurate [ˈækjərət] genau 60
achievement [əˈtʃiːvmənt] Leistung 128
to acquire [əˈkwaɪə] erwerben 11
acquisition [ˌækwɪˈzɪʃn] hier: Firmenübernahme 87
to address [əˈdres] anreden 65
administrative offices [ədˈmɪnɪstrətiv ˌɒfɪsiz] Verwaltungsbüros 11 (T)
affected [əˈfektɪd] betroffen 112
affiliate [əˈfɪliət] Tochtergesellschaft 141
agenda [əˈdʒendə] Tagesordnung 32
aid [eɪd] Hilfsmittel 43
aim [eɪm] Ziel 39
alienation [ˌeɪliəˈneɪʃn] Entfremdung 147
alike [əˈlaɪk] gleichermaßen 113
all risks cover [ˌɔːl ˌrɪsks ˈkʌvə] Allgefahrendeckung 117
amazing [əˈmeɪzɪŋ] unglaublich 97
annoyance [əˈnɔɪəns] Ärgernis 121
annual [ˈænjʊəl] jährlich 33
to antagonize [ænˈtægənaɪz] gegen sich aufbringen, verärgern 121
to appeal [əˈpiːl] ansprechen 85
to appease [əˈpiːz] besänftigen 140
application [ˌæplɪˈkeɪʃn] Bewerbung 124
application form [ˌæplɪˈkeɪʃn ˌfɔːm] Antrag 10
to apply [əˈplaɪ] gelten 72
to appoint [əˈpɔɪnt] ernennen 57
appointment [əˈpɔɪntmənt] Termin, Verabredung 24
to appreciate [əˈpriːʃieɪt] schätzen 40
apprenticeship [əˈprentɪʃɪp] Ausbildung, Lehre 7
approach [əˈprəʊtʃ] Ansatz, Herangehensweise 65
appropriate [əˈprəʊpriət] geeignet, angemessen 50
approval [əˈpruːvl] Billigung, Einverständnis 59
area code [ˈeəriə ˌkəʊd] Ortsvorwahl 24
to arouse (interest) [əˈraʊz] (Interesse) wecken 43
to assess [əˈses] beurteilen, bewerten 10
asset [ˈæset] Vermögenswert 33

asset management [ˈæset ˌmænɪdʒmənt] Vermögensberatung 12
to assume [əˈsjuːm, əˈsuːm] annehmen 25
assumptions checklist [əˈsʌmpʃnz ˌtʃeklɪst] Checkliste zur Prüfung der Versicherungsberechtigung 114
to assure [əˈʃʊə] versichern 30 (T)
at a glance [ət ə ˈglɑːns] auf einen Blick 111
ATM (automatic teller machine) [ˌeɪtiːˈem] [ˌɔːtəmætɪk ˈtelə məˌʃiːn] Geldautomat 14
to attach [əˈtætʃ] anhängen (Anlage bei E-Mail) 78
at the latest [ət ðə ˈleɪtɪst] spätestens 30 (T)
at your fingertips [ət jɔː ˈfɪŋgətɪps] parat, verfügbar 24
audience [ˈɔːdiəns] Publikum 16
automotive production [ɔːtəˌməʊtɪv prəˈdʌkʃn] Fahrzeugproduktion 143
to award [əˈwɔːd] vergeben, verleihen 50
axis [ˈæksɪs] Achse 47 (T)

B

backslash [ˈbækslæʃ] umgekehrter Schrägstrich 29
bank clerk [ˈbæŋk ˌklɑːk] Bankkaufmann/-frau 7
to balance [ˈbæləns] ausgleichen 104
bank transfer [ˈbæŋk ˌtrænsfɜː] Banküberweisung 11 (T)
bar chart [ˈbɑː ˌtʃɑːt] Balkendiagramm 43
to bear in mind, bore, borne [ˌbeə ɪn ˈmaɪnd] bedenken, beachten 49
to be inclined (to) [bɪ ɪnˈklaɪnd] geneigt sein (zu) 147
beneficiary [ˌbenəˈfɪʃəri] Begünstigte(r) 33
benefit [ˈbenəfɪt] Leistung 127
to be noticed [bɪ ˈnəʊtɪst] zur Kenntnis genommen werden 132
to be prone to do sth. [bɪ ˌprəʊn tə ˈduː ˌsʌmθɪŋ] geneigt sein, etwas zu tun 147
beverage [ˈbevərɪdʒ] Getränk 60
bid [bɪd] Gebot 142
bill [bɪl] Rechnung 14
blunder [ˈblʌndə] grober Fehler, Patzer 140
body of the letter [ˌbɒdɪ əv ðə ˈletə] Textteil des Briefes 73
bold [bəʊld] fett gedruckt 73
bond [bɒnd] Anleihe 144
borderless [ˈbɔːdələs] grenzenlos 139
to bore [bɔː] langweilen 39
bottom line [ˌbɒtəm ˈlaɪn] Untergrenze 62
to bottom out [ˌbɒtəm ˈaʊt] den Tiefstand erreichen 46
bridging-loan [ˈbrɪdʒɪŋ ˌləʊn] Überbrückungskredit 76 (T)
to brief [briːf] kurz informieren 42

brief [briːf] kurz 38
broadly [ˈbrɔːdli] weitgehend 86
to bundle [ˈbʌndl] bündeln 103
buoyant [ˈbɔɪənt] lebhaft, steigend 49 (T)

C

capitalisation [ˌkæpɪtəlaɪˈzeɪʃn] Kapitalisierung 142
to capitalise [ˈkæpɪtəlaɪz] groß schreiben 73
cash benefit [ˌkæʃ ˈbenəfɪt] Barleistung 45
cash dispenser [ˈkæʃ dɪˌspensə] Geldautomat 14
cashier [kæˈʃɪə] Kassierer(in) 12
to catch (caught, caught) [kætʃ] mitbekommen, verstehen 24
to catch out (caught, caught) [kætʃ ˈaʊt] erwischen 51
to cater for [ˈkeɪtə fɔː] sich kümmern um 95
to cater to [ˈkeɪtə tuː] abzielen auf, sich kümmern um 85
CEO (Chief Executive Officer) [ˌsiːiːˈəʊ] [ˌtʃiːf ɪgˌzekjʊtɪv ˈɒfɪsə] Vorstandsvorsitzende(r), Firmenchef(in) 55
to chair [tʃeə] den Vorsitz haben 26
chairman, pl. chairmen [ˈtʃeəmən] Vorsitzender, Plur. Vorsitzende 32
challenge [ˈtʃælɪndʒ] Herausforderung 139
charge [tʃɑːdʒ] Gebühr 56
check [tʃek] hier: Hindernis 147
choice [tʃɔɪs] Auswahl 114
to circumscribe [ˌsɜːkəmˈskraɪb] beschränken 147
claim [kleɪm] Schaden(sfall) 114
classmate [ˈklɑːsmeɪt] Klassenkamerad(in) 7
coherently [kəʊˈhɪərəntli] zusammenhängend 51
collateral [kəˈlætərəl] Sicherheit 105
collision [kəˈlɪʒn] Kollision 113
colon [ˈkəʊlən] Doppelpunkt 29
comeback [ˈkʌmbæk] Reaktion 23
command [kəˈmɑːnd] Beherrschung 126
commission [kəˈmɪʃn] Kommission 135
commodity [kəˈmɒdəti] Rohstoff 145
common [ˈkɒmən] üblich 72
comparison site [kəmˌpærɪsən ˈsaɪt] Preissuchmaschine 116
compensation [ˌkɒmpenˈseɪʃn] Schadenersatz 109
to compete [kəmˈpiːt] wetteifern 93
competitor [kəmˈpetɪtə] Wettbewerber 141
complimentary close [ˌkɒmplɪmentrɪ ˈkləʊz] Schlussformel im Brief 73
to compromise [ˈkɒmprəmaɪz] beeinträchtigen 147
to concede [kənˈsiːd] einräumen, gewähren 62

forecast ['fɔːkɑːst] Vorhersage 45
foreign direct investment (FDI)
[ˌfɒrən daɪˌrekt ɪn'vestmənt] [ˌefdiː'aɪ]
Auslandsdirektinvestition 141
foreign exchange [ˌfɒrən ɪks'tʃeɪndʒ]
Devisen 144
fragmented [fræg'mentɪd]
unzusammenhängend 71
fraud [frɔːd] Betrug, Schwindel 113
fraudulent ['frɔːdjʊlənt] betrügerisch 113
funding ['fʌndɪŋ] Finanzierung,
Förderung 35 (T)
furthermore [ˌfɜːðə'mɔː] überdies,
außerdem 53

G

to gather ['gæðə] sammeln 40
GDP (gross domestic product)
[ˌdʒiː.diː'piː] [ˌgrəʊs də'mestɪk 'prɒdʌkt]
Bruttoinlandsprodukt 104
GP (General Practitioner) [ˌdʒiː'piː]
[ˌdʒenrəl præk'tɪʃənə] Allgemeinarzt,-
ärztin 114 (T)
gesture ['dʒestʃə] Geste 6
to get back (to) (got, got) [get 'bæk tə]
zurückrufen 24
gist [dʒɪst] das Wesentliche 52
to go down well (went, gone)
[ˌgəʊ daʊn 'wel] gut ankommen 65
grade [greɪd] Note 125
graduate ['grædʒʊət]
Hochschulabsolvent(in) 98
grid [grɪd] Tabelle, Raster 30

H

to handle ['hændl] bearbeiten,
erledigen 12
handout ['hændaʊt] Informations-
blatt 43
to hedge [hedʒ] absichern 144
to hesitate ['hezɪteɪt] zögern 79
hesitation [ˌhezɪ'teɪʃn] Zögern,
Verzögerung 51
holding company ['həʊldɪŋ ˌkʌmpəni]
Kapitalbeteiligungsgesellschaft,
Dachgesellschaft 84
home entertainment system [ˌhəʊm
entə'teɪnmənt ˌsɪstəm] Heimunter-
haltungssystem 108
hostile ['hɒstaɪl] feindlich 141
household contents (insurance)
[ˌhaʊshəʊld 'kɒntents] Hausrat(versicherung) 48
HR (Human Resources) [ˌeɪtʃ'ɑː]
[ˌhjuːmən 'riːsɔːsɪz] Personalwesen 98
hub [hʌb] Mittelpunkt, Zentrum,
Basis 87
hug [hʌg] Umarmung 65
human resources department
[ˌhjuːmən 'riːsɔːsɪz dɪˌpɑːtmənt]
Personalabteilung 11 (T)
hyphen ['haɪfən] Bindestrich 29

I

If all else fails [ɪf ˌɔːl els 'feɪlz] wenn
alle Stricke reißen 25
imposing [ɪm'pəʊzɪŋ] beeindruckend
49 (T)
in advance [ɪn əd'vɑːns] im Voraus 39
incentive [ɪn'sentɪv] Anreiz 141
in conclusion [ɪn kən'kluːʒn]
schließlich, zum Schluss 42
to incorporate [ɪn'kɔːpəreɪt]
einbeziehen, aufnehmen 114
to increase [ɪn'kriːs] zunehmen 46
to induce [ɪn'djuːs] herbeiführen 98
inequality [ˌɪnɪ'kwɒlɪti] Ungleichheit 147
inevitable [ɪ'nevɪtəbl] unabwendbar 147
influx of funds [ˌɪnflʌks əv 'fʌndz]
Mittelzufluss 102
in-house training [ˌɪnhaʊs 'treɪnɪŋ]
firmeninterne Weiterbildung 11 (T)
initially [ɪ'nɪʃəli] anfänglich,
ursprünglich 108
initial selection [ɪˌnɪʃl sə'lekʃn]
Vorauswahl 124
instalment [ɪn'stɔːlmənt]
Ratenzahlung 97
in stock [ɪn 'stɒk] vorrätig 31
insurance [ɪn'ʃɔːrəns] Versicherung 33
insurance agent [ɪn'ʃɔːrəns ˌeɪdʒənt]
Versicherungsvertreter(in) 9
insurance broker [ɪn'ʃɔːrəns ˌbrəʊkə]
Versicherungsmakler(in) 42 (T)
insurance clerk [ɪn'ʃɔːrəns ˌklɑːk]
Versicherungskaufmann/-frau
insurance cover [ɪn'ʃɔːrəns ˌkʌvə]
Versicherungsdeckung 33
insurgency [ɪn'sɜːdʒənsi] Aufruhr 140
interference [ˌɪntə'fɪərəns] Störung 26
intermediary [ˌɪntə'miːdɪəri]
Zwischenhändler(in), Mittelsmann 99
invalid [ɪn'vælɪd] ungültig 109
to invalidate [ɪn'vælɪdeɪt] unwirksam
machen 116 (T)
invasion of privacy [ɪnˌveɪʒn əv 'prɪvəsi]
Verletzung der Privatsphäre 40
investigative [ɪn'vestɪgətɪv]
erforschend 65
investment banking [ɪn'vestmənt
ˌbæŋkɪŋ] Kapitalanlagenberatung 8
investment consultant [ɪn'vestmənt
kən'sʌltənt] Anlagenberater(in) 9
in working order [ɪn ˌwɜːkɪŋ 'ɔːdə] in
betriebsfähigem Zustand 60
IPO (Initial Public Offering) [ˌaɪpiː'əʊ]
Börsengang 85
issue ['ɪʃuː] Problem 139
to issue ['ɪʃuː] herausgeben 142

J

jerky ['dʒɜːki] ruckartig 51
joint [dʒɔɪnt] gemeinsam 35
joint venture [ˌdʒɔɪnt 'ventʃə] Joint
Venture, Beteiligungsunternehmen 141

joking aside [ˌdʒəʊkɪŋ ə'saɪd] Spaß
beiseite 118
justified ['dʒʌstɪfaɪd] gerechtfertigt 23

K

keen (competition) [kiːn] heftig, heiß 94
to keep doing sth., kept, kept [kiːp]
ständig etwas tun 39
to keep an account (kept, kept) [ˌkiːp
ən ə'kaʊnt] Buch führen 61
key skill [ˌkiː 'skɪl] Schlüsselqualifikation, -fertigkeit 38
knock-on effect [ˌnɒk'ɒn ɪˌfekt]
Dominoeffekt, Kettenreaktion 111

L

landline ['lændlaɪn] Festnetzanschluss 22
lasting ['lɑːstɪŋ] dauerhaft 70
to launch [lɔːntʃ] starten 142
law-abiding ['lɔːəˌbaɪdɪŋ] gesetzestreu 113
to leave a message (left, left) [ˌliːv ə
'mesɪdʒ] eine Nachricht hinterlassen 24
legal (insurance) ['liːgl]
Rechtschutz(versicherung) 48
legal assistance [ˌliːgl ə'sɪstəns]
Rechtsbeistand 127
legal department ['liːgl dɪˌpɑːtmənt]
Rechtsabteilung 11 (T)
letterhead ['letəhed] Briefkopf 70
to level off [ˌlevl 'ɒf] sich einpendeln,
sich stabilisieren 46
liability [ˌlaɪə'bɪləti] Haftpflicht 126
liability insurance [laɪəˌbɪləti ɪn'ʃɔːrəns]
Haftpflichtversicherung 108
life assurance [ˌlaɪf ə'ʃɔːrəns]
Lebensversicherung 48
limb [lɪm] Glied, Gliedmaße 45
line graph ['laɪn ˌgrɑːf]
Liniendiagramm 43
lively ['laɪvli] lebendig, spritzig 50
loan [ləʊn] Darlehen 30 (T)
loan advisor ['ləʊn ədˌvaɪzə]
Darlehensberater(in) 9
loan agreement ['ləʊn əˌgriːmənt]
Darlehensvereinbarung 76
local ['ləʊkl] lokal, örtlich 7
loss [lɒs] Verlust 109
lot size transformation ['lɒt ˌsaɪz
trænsfəˌmeɪʃn] Losgrößentransforma-
tion 103
luggage ['lʌgɪdʒ] Gepäck 18
lump sum [ˌlʌmp 'sʌm] Pauschal-
betrag 117
to lure [ljʊə] ködern 92

M

to maintain [meɪn'teɪn]
aufrechterhalten 131
major ['meɪdʒə] Haupt-, bedeutend 40
to make a claim (made, made)
[ˌmeɪk ə 'kleɪm] Schadenersatz bean-
spruchen 109

to make up (made, made) [meɪk ˈʌp] erfinden, ausmachen 28
manner [ˈmænə] Art und Weise 39
marital status [ˌmærɪtl ˈsteɪtəs] Familienstand 72
mark [mɑːk] Note (in der Schule) 125
to mention [ˈmenʃn] erwähnen 132
to merge [mɜːdʒ] fusionieren 89
merger [ˈmɜːdʒə] Fusion 141
microcredit [ˈmaɪkrəʊˌkredɪt] Mikrokredit 105
mix-up [ˈmɪksʌp] Durcheinander 116 (T)
to modify [ˈmɒdɪfaɪ] ändern, verändern 46
monetary policy [ˌmʌnətri ˈpɒləsi] Geldpolitik 104
mortgage [ˈmɔːgɪdʒ] Hypothek 98
motor [ˈməʊtə] Kraftfahrzeug- 126
mutual [ˈmjuːtʃʊəl] gegenseitig 105

N

need [niːd] Bedürfnis 11 (T)
negotiation [nɪˌgəʊʃiˈeɪʃn] Verhandlung 54
net worth [ˌnet ˈwɜːθ] Reinvermögen, Gesellschaftskapital 85
no claims bonus [ˌnəʊ ˌkleɪmz ˈbəʊnəs] Schadenfreiheitsrabatt 117
Nobel Peace Prize [ˌnəʊbel piːs ˈpraɪz] Friedensnobelpreis 97
nutritional standard [njuːˌtrɪʃnəl ˈstændəd] Ernährungsstandard 106

O

objective [əbˈdʒektɪv] Ziel 54
obtrusive [əbˈtruːsɪv] aufdringlich 65
occupation [ˌɒkjʊˈpeɪʃn] Beruf 9
offshore [ˌɒfˈʃɔː] im Ausland 93
offshoring [ˌɒfˈʃɔːrɪŋ] Standortverlagerung 141
to omit [əˈmɪt] weglassen 24
on behalf of [ɒn bɪˈhɑːf əv] im Auftrag von 26
to operate [ˈɒpəreɪt] abwickeln 22
oral [ˈɔːrəl] mündlich 38
organigram [ɔːˈgænɪgræm] Organigramm 43
originally [əˈrɪdʒɪnəli] ursprünglich 7
outbuilding [ˈaʊtˌbɪldɪŋ] Außengebäude 118
outcome [ˈaʊtkʌm] Ergebnis 65
outsourcing [ˈaʊtˌsɔːsɪŋ] Auslagerung 141
overdraft [ˈəʊvədrɑːft] Kontoüberziehung 98
overdraft facility [ˈəʊvədrɑːft fəˌsɪləti] Überziehungskredit 74
owner occupied flat [ˌəʊnə ˌɒkjʊpaɪd ˈflæt] Eigentumswohnung 11 (T)

P

PA (Personal Assistant) [ˌpiːˈeɪ] [ˌpɜːsnl əˈsɪstənt] Chefsekretär(in) 55

panel [ˈpænl] Ausschuss 114
payment system [ˈpeɪmənt ˌsɪstəmz] Zahlungssystem 104
to peak [piːk] den Höchststand erreichen 46
peer pressure [ˈpɪə ˌpreʃə] Gruppendruck 105
pension scheme [ˈpenʃn ˌskiːm] Versorgungsplan 75
to perceive [pəˈsiːv] wahrnehmen 139
percentage [pəˈsentɪdʒ] Prozentsatz 48
performance [pəˈfɔːməns] Aufführung 39
peril [ˈperəl] Gefahr, Versicherungsrisiko 110
period transformation [ˈpɪəriəd ˌtrænsfəˌmeɪʃn] Fristentransformation 103
personal liability [ˌpɜːsnl ˌlaɪəˈbɪləti] Privathaftpflicht 48
pie chart [ˈpaɪ ˌtʃɑːt] Tortendiagramm 43
to place [pleɪs] investieren 96
to plummet [ˈplʌmɪt] stürzen, absacken 46
to poach [pəʊtʃ] abwerben 92
policy [ˈpɒləsi] (Versicherungs-)Police 75
policyholder [ˈpɒləsi ˌhəʊldə] Versicherungsnehmer(in) 47
polite [pəˈlaɪt] höflich 6
post code [ˈpəʊst ˌkəʊd] Postleitzahl 9
to postpone [pəsˈpəʊn] verschieben 26
poverty [ˈpɒvəti] Armut 105
practice [ˈpræktɪs] Arztpraxis 114
to praise [preɪz] anpreisen 93
predominantly [prɪˈdɒmɪnəntli] überwiegend, hauptsächlich 127
pre-existing [ˌpriːɪgˈzɪstɪŋ] vorher vorhanden 113
preferential [ˌprefəˈrenʃl] bevorzugt 98
premature [ˈpremətʃə] vorzeitig 33
premises [ˈpremɪsɪz] Geschäftsräume, Firmengelände 32
premium [ˈpriːmiəm] Versicherungsprämie 109
preparation [ˌprepəˈreɪʃn] Vorbereitung 38
presence [ˈprezns] Präsenz 87
pressure [ˈpreʃə] Druck 22
prestigious [presˈtɪdʒəs] angesehen, renommiert 85
pre-tax profits [ˌpriːtæks ˈprɒfɪts] Vorsteuergewinn 45
to pretend [prɪˈtend] vorgeben, vortäuschen 113
previous [ˈpriːviəs] vorherig 71
prior [praɪə] vorherig 134
to prioritise [praɪˈɒrɪtaɪz] den Vorrang geben 98
probation period [prəʊˈbeɪʃn ˌpɪəriəd] Probezeit 100
proceedings [prəˈsiːdɪŋz] Handlungsverlauf 60
to process [ˈprəʊses] bearbeiten 131
profoundly [prəˈfaʊndli] tief, hochgradig 65
to propel [prəˈpel] antreiben 139
property [ˈprɒpəti] Immobilien, Eigentum 146
proposal form [prəˈpəʊzl ˌfɔːm] Versicherungsantrag 114 (T)
prospective [prəˈspektɪv] in Aussicht stehend 134
to protect [prəˈtekt] schützen 104
provider [prəˈvaɪdə] Anbieter(in) 116
provisional [prəˈvɪʒənl] vorläufig 32
to purchase [ˈpɜːtʃəs] kaufen 86
purchasing power [ˈpɜːtʃəsɪŋ ˌpaʊə] Kaufkraft 104
to push [pʊʃ] forcieren 147
to put (s.o.) through (put, put) [pʊt ˈθruː] (jmdn.) durchstellen, verbinden 24

Q

quite a lot [ˌkwaɪt ə ˈlɒt] ziemlich viel 7
quotation [kwəʊˈteɪʃn] Preisangebot, Börsenpreis 145
quote [kwəʊt] Angebot 114

R

to range from … to … [reɪndʒ] reichen von … bis … 38
rate of interest [ˌreɪt əv ˈɪntrest] Zins, Zinssatz 22
rating agencies [ˈreɪtɪŋ ˌeɪdʒənsiz] Rating-Agenturen 146
real estate [ˈrɪəl ɪˌsteɪt] Immobilien 96
real estate assistant [ˈriːlˌsteɪt əˌsɪstənt] Immobilienverkäufer(in) 12
real estate department [ˈriːlˌsteɪt dɪˌpɑːtmənt] Immobilienabteilung 11 (T)
to recap [ˈriːkæp] (kurz) zusammenfassen 117
recipient [rɪˈsɪpiənt] Empfänger(in) 70
record [ˈrekɔːd] Unterlage, Dokument 130
recruitment centres [rɪˈkruːtmənt ˌsentəz] Einstellungsfirmen 124
to refer (to) [rɪˈfɜː] sich beziehen auf 39
to refocus [ˌriːˈfəʊkəs] sich neu konzentrieren 42
regional branch office [ˌriːdʒənl ˈbrɑːntʃ ˌɒfɪs] regionale Zweigstelle 11
to rehearse [rɪˈhɜːs] proben 39
relationship [rɪˈleɪʃnʃɪp] Beziehung 6
reluctance [rɪˈlʌktəns] Widerwille 65
reluctantly [rɪˈlʌktəntli] ungern, widerwillig 116
to remain stable [rɪˌmeɪn ˈsteɪbl] sich (stabil) halten 46
renewable [rɪˈnjuːəbl] erneuerbar 45
renewal [rɪˈnjuːəl] Erneuerung 119
renowned [rɪˈnaʊnd] renommiert 142
repetition [ˌrepəˈtɪʃn] Wiederholung 51
repetitive [rɪˈpetətɪv] monoton, sich wiederholend 50

to repossess [ˌriːpəˈzes] pfänden 146 (T)
reputation [ˌrepjʊˈteɪʃn] Ruf 126
to request [rɪˈkwest] bitten 71
to require [rɪˈkwaɪə] benötigen 79
requirement [rɪˈkwaɪəmənt] Bedarf 32
respondent [rɪˈspɒndənt] Befragte(r) 51
to restrict [rɪˈstrɪkt] einschränken 139
retail bank [ˌriːteɪl ˈbæŋk] Privatkundenbank 96
retirement plan [rɪˈtaɪəmənt ˌplæn] Altersvorsorgeplan 75
to retrieve [rɪˈtriːv] abrufen 12 (T)
return on assets [rɪˌtɜːn ɒn ˈæsets] Gesamtkapitalrentabilität 143
revenue [ˈrevənjuː] Erlös, Einnahmen, Einkünfte 87
to revise downwards [rɪˌvaɪz ˈdaʊnwədz] nach unten korrigieren 45
revision [rɪˈvɪʒn] Korrektur 45
to rise, rose, risen [raɪz] steigen 46
risk transformation [ˈrɪsk trænsfəˌmeɪʃn] Risikotransformation 103
to rocket [ˈrɒkɪt] in die Höhe schießen 46
rude [ruːd] unhöflich 6
run-of-the-mill [ˌrʌnəvðəˈmɪl] gewöhnlich, nullachtfünfzehn 135 (T)
rural [ˈrʊərəl] ländlich 64 (T)

S

safe custody account [ˌseɪf ˈkʌstədɪ əˌkaʊnt] Depotkonto 99
salary [ˈsælərɪ] Gehalt 15
salutation [ˌsæljʊˈteɪʃn] Anrede 72
savings account [ˈseɪvɪŋz əˌkaʊnt] Sparkonto 22
savings scheme [ˈseɪvɪŋz ˌskiːm] Sparplan 100
to scare [skeə] erschrecken 38
scope [skəʊp] Raum, Umfang 63
seafaring [ˈsiːˌfeərɪŋ] Seefahrer- 108
section [ˈsekʃn] Teil, Abschnitt 72
to secure a loan [sɪˌkjʊərə ˈləʊn] ein Darlehen absichern 33
securities [sɪˈkjʊərətɪz] Wertpapiere, Effekten 46
to securitise [sɪˈkjʊərɪtaɪz] verbriefen 146 (T)
security [sɪˈkjʊərətɪ] Sicherheit 76 (T)
self-employed [ˌselfɪmˈplɔɪd] selbstständig 45
senior staff [ˌsiːnɪə ˈstɑːf] leitende Angestellte, Führungskräfte 49
services provider [ˈsɜːvɪsɪz prəˌvaɪdə] Dienstleister 90
setting [ˈsetɪŋ] Rahmen, Umfeld 112
share [ʃeə] Anteil 48
shareholder [ˈʃeəˌhəʊldə] Aktionär(in) 144
share issues [ˈʃeə ˌɪʃuːz] Aktien-emission 85
sharply [ˈʃɑːplɪ] hier: steil (ansteigen) 46
to shed [ʃed] abwerfen 92

to shop around [ˌʃɒp əˈraʊnd] Preise vergleichen 116
signature block [ˈsɪgnətʃə ˌblɒk] Name und Unterschrift 73
significant [sɪgˈnɪfɪkənt] signifikant, bedeutend 111
to signpost [ˈsaɪnpəʊst] ausschildern 19 (T)
sincerity [sɪnˈserətɪ] Aufrichtigkeit 40
to skip [skɪp] überspringen, auslassen 64 (T)
slap [slæp] Klaps, Schlag 65
slash [slæʃ] Schrägstrich 29
solidity [səˈlɪdɪtɪ] Zuverlässigkeit, Solidität 85
solution [səˈluːʃn] Lösung 11 (T)
to spin [spɪn] sich drehen 118
staff [stɑːf] Personal 111
stage [steɪdʒ] Stufe 39
stake [steɪk] Aktienanteil 49 (T)
stand-alone [ˌstændəˈləʊn] eigenständig 98
standing order [ˌstændɪŋ ˈɔːdə] Dauerauftrag 99
to state [steɪt] angeben 49
statement [ˈsteɪtmənt] Kontoauszug 14
statement printer [ˈsteɪtmənt ˌprɪntə] Kontoauszugsdrucker 14
to stipulate [ˈstɪpjəleɪt] vereinbaren, festlegen 33
stock market [ˈstɒk ˌmɑːkɪt] Aktienmarkt 99
to streamline [ˈstriːmlaɪn] rationalisieren 143
stroke [strəʊk] Schrägstrich 29
subject line [ˈsʌbdʒekt ˌlaɪn] Betreffzeile 73
subprime loans [ˌsʌbˌpraɪm ˈləʊnz] Darlehen, die in Hinsicht auf Kundenbonität nicht dem Standard (Prime) entsprechen 146
subsequent [ˈsʌbsəkwənt] darauf folgend 72
subsidiary [səbˈsɪdɪərɪ] Tochterunternehmen 142
substantial [səbˈstænʃl] beträchtlich 47 (T)
to substantiate [səbˈstænʃɪeɪt] begründen 50
succinctly [səkˈsɪŋktlɪ] kurz und bündig, prägnant 54
suitable [ˈsuːtəbl] geeignet 25
superfluous [suːˈpɜːfluəs] überflüssig 76
superior [suːˈpɪərɪə] der/die Vorgesetzte 6
supervise [ˈsuːpəvaɪz] überwachen 106
supplementary [ˌsʌplɪˈmentərɪ] zusätzlich 56
supportive [səˈpɔːtɪv] unterstützend 51
to swap [swɒp] tauschen 48
to switch off [ˌswɪtʃˈɒf] ausschalten 25

T

tabular [ˈtæbjələ] tabellarisch 128
tacit (renewal) [ˌtæsɪt rɪˈnjuːəl] stillschweigend(e Verlängerung) 119
to tailor [ˈteɪlə] zuschneiden (auf) 114
tailor-made [ˌteɪləˈmeɪd] maßge-schneidert 11 (T)
to take down (took, taken) [teɪk ˈdaʊn] notieren 28
to take offence (took, taken) [ˌteɪk əˈfens] sich angegriffen fühlen 121
to take out insurance (took, taken) [ˌteɪk aʊt ɪnˈʃɔːrəns] eine Versicherung abschließen 33
takeover [ˈteɪkˌəʊvə] Firmenübernahme 141
tangible [ˈtændʒɪbl] materiell, berührbar 144
teller [ˈtelə] Kassierer(in) 127
term (life) assurance [ˈtɜːm (ˈlaɪf) əˌʃɔːrəns] Risikolebensversicherung 33
to terrify [ˈterɪfaɪ] in Schrecken versetzen 51
third-party assets [ˌθɜːdpɑːtɪ ˈæsets] Fremdvermögen 90
tight [taɪt] knapp 49 (T)
trader [ˈtreɪdə] Händler(in) 108
to transfer [trænsˈfɜː] transferieren, überweisen 99
to transmit [trænzˈmɪt] übertragen 70
treaty [ˈtriːtɪ] Vertrag 104
to trickle down [ˌtrɪkl ˈdaʊn] heruntertröpfeln 147
trusting relationship [ˌtrʌstɪŋ rɪˈleɪʃnʃɪp] Vertrauensverhältnis 65
turnover [ˈtɜːnˌəʊvə] Umsatz 64 (T)
twitch [twɪtʃ] Zucken 51

U

unavoidable [ˌʌnəˈvɔɪdəbl] unvermeidbar 23
unaware [ˌʌnəˈweə] nichtsahnend 40
to underestimate [ˌʌndərˈestɪmeɪt] unterschätzen 65
understroke [ˈʌndəstrəʊk] Unterstrich 29
unit trust [ˌjuːnɪt ˈtrʌst] offener Investmentfond 86
unsolicited [ˌʌnsəˈlɪsɪt] unverlangt, unaufgefordert (z. B. Briefsendung) 124
to unveil [ʌnˈveɪl] bekanntmachen 143
upper and lower case letters [ˌʌpər ˌn ˌləʊəkeɪs ˈletəz] Groß- und Kleinbuchstaben 43
up to par [ˌʌp tə ˈpɑː] den Anwforderungen entsprechend 135
urgently [ˈɜːdʒəntlɪ] dringend 24

V

vacancy [ˈveɪkənsɪ] freie Stelle 124
valuable [ˈvæljuəbl] wertvoll 109
value [ˈvæljuː] Wert 147
to value [ˈvæljuː] schätzen 93

value judgment [ˈvælju: ˌdʒʌdʒmənt]
Werturteil 65
vehicle [ˈvɪəkl] (Hilfs)mittel 71
viable [ˈvaɪəbl] realisierbar 106
vicious circle [ˌvɪʃəs ˈsɜːkl] Teufelskreis 105
visual [ˈvɪʒʊəl] visuell 43
visual aids [ˌvɪʒʊəl ˈeɪdz] visuelle
Hilfsmittel 39
vital [ˈvaɪtl] entscheidend, wesentlich 41

Bildquellennachweis

Textquellennachweis